SPIRITUAL

Direction in Context

EDITED BY
Nick Wagner

MOREHOUSE PUBLISHING

Morehouse Publishing, P.O. Box 1321, Harrisburg, PA 17105

Morehouse Publishing, 445 Fifth Avenue, New York, NY 10016

Morehouse Publishing is an imprint of Church Publishing Incorporated.

Cover design by Brenda Klinger

Library of Congress Cataloging-in-Publication Data

Spiritual direction in context / edited by Nick Wagner.
    p. cm.
  ISBN-13: 978-0-8192-2209-1 (pbk.)
  1. Spiritual direction.   2. Spiritual directors.   3. Love—Religious aspects—Christianity. I.
Wagner, Nick, 1957-
BV5053.S69 2006
253.5'3—dc22
2005034717

Printed in the United States of America

06 07 08 09 10 9 8 7 6 5 4 3 2 1

Contents

Introduction

Spiritual Directors International lists more than twenty definitions and descriptions of "spiritual direction" on its Web site (www.sdiworld.com), representing various faith traditions, formation practices, and spiritualities. What is common to each of the entries is a sense that, as humans, we are seeking. *What* we are seeking seems to be the core question that drives the ministry of spiritual direction. The "what" (or, perhaps, "who") is most often called "God" but is also called the Holy One, the Divine, the Other, Allah, the Sacred, a Higher Power, and the Blessed One.

For the authors of the essays collected here from various issues of *Presence: An International Journal of Spiritual Direction*, naming the "what" or "who" we seek is not so important. What is more important is the seeking itself.

The ministry of the spiritual director is, at its core, one of service to the seeker. Depending on the context in which the "director" and the "directee" find themselves, a director might also be called a companion, a guide, a teacher, a spiritual friend, a father or mother, a master, or a midwife. Shaun McCarty, ST, in "Spiritual Directors: Teachers and Guardians of Mystery," suggests we add to that list the role of "mystagogue." He points out that pedagogues teach children, and androgogues teach adults. A mystagogue (from the Greek *mystes* or "one initiated in the mysteries" and *agogos* or "leader") teaches or forms or leads one in the mysteries.

The mystery that we long to explore is not some complicated jigsaw puzzle, missing a central piece that can only be supplied by a distant and unapproachable deity. It is the Mystery of the Incarnation, the intimate relationship of the Divine made manifest in the human. It is the mystery of relationship. It is the mystery of love.

Because spiritual direction is an exploration of a love relationship, it is not to be confused with counseling, which has overtones of healing an illness or recovering something that has gone missing. In "Pastoral Counseling or Spiritual Direction: What's the Difference?" Thomas Hart points out that God is already active in our lives, and the goal of the director is to help the directee notice and respond to God's initiative. Hart, a trained psychotherapist who does therapy "in a spiritual context," notes that at one end of the spectrum are clinical helping professionals who have no use for the "mystery" of a relationship with God. Their interest is focused purely on fixing the problems an individual may be experiencing. At the other end are those who are focused only on the spiritual aspects of a person's life, dealing with prayer, discernment, and spiritual practices. In the broad middle are those who attend to both the spiritual and temporal concerns of the individual in order to serve him or her in the best possible way. For those engaged in the ministry of spiritual direction, Hart suggests that the most important single ingredient is the quality of the relationship itself—with ourselves, with each other, and with God. It is in these relationships that we experience the Mystery. It is that level of deep relationship that all humans seek.

It would seem, then, that spiritual direction is a ministry that would be beneficial for any human being who is on a journey to discover the depths of mystery. While that may be true, all true mystagogues know that every journey happens within a particular context. This collection of essays is about those contexts. Whom is spiritual direction for? How is spiritual direction practiced in different communities and cultural situations? How do particular groups with particular needs benefit from spiritual direction? As we grow and change, how does the process of direction change for us? What practices or disciplines can directors use to navigate these varying contexts? And what is the ultimate goal of spiritual direction in any context?

Whom Is Spiritual Direction For?

While this collection is not a sociological study of the practice of spiritual direction, it will come as no surprise to even the most casual observer that most people engaged in spiritual direction in Europe and North America are women. Clearly, the ministry of spiritual direction meets a need for a great number of women who are exploring their sacred journey. Patricia D. Brown ("Circle of Hearts: Women's Spirituality Groups") suggests male readers consider the feminine aspect of spirituality. Women, she notes, encourage a balance of relationships that is manifested in women's "circles" from as far back as biblical times. Like Hart, she points out that recovery or therapy groups we might belong to are different from a women's circle or spirituality group in that the former is focused on problems and the latter on exploring relationships with each other and with God. She also notes that a common characteristic of women in spirituality groups is that many have denied the truth about themselves, living conflicted and even frantic lives. By engaging in the exploration of mystery with sisters on a like journey, many women experience a deep inner reorientation and reconciliation.

Men come to spiritual direction for similar reasons, but in a different context, according to Donald Bisson, FMS. In "Melting the Iceberg: Spiritual Direction for Men," he contrasts the frantic repression described by Brown with a frozen, stoic attitude that leaves the root of their denial of self buried under emotional ice caps and snowdrifts. He asks both women and men to reexamine the unspoken assumption that men find meaning in traditional patriarchal structures; nor, says Bisson, should we assume that men find meaning in the feminine models such as those described by Brown as being so helpful for women. Men are initially less focused on the emotions raised by their exploration and more energized by the insights that come to them through reflection and probing of thoughts.

A common critique of men, which Bisson would prefer be seen as a gift or natural characteristic, is that they are too focused on the "head" or intellectual aspects of the spiritual journey. While reveling in the intellect may be the path for many men, it seems to be a hindrance for those in training to be religious leaders—seminarians. In what she admits to be more of a collection of anecdotes than a scientific study, Jane E. Vennard found that many seminarians suffer from a lack of balance when the academic rigor of spiritual study is emphasized and there is little time for discovering and naming the emotions raised in the intensity of the seminary system. In "Spiritual Direction with Seminary Students," an interview of twelve Protestant seminarians, Vennard notes that seminarians are seeking what all directees seek: presence, compassion, acceptance, connection. These are the fundamental elements of every relationship that all humans seek on their journey into the Mystery.

Although trained to be spiritual leaders, it can be difficult for the clergy to maintain their own spiritual growth. The ordained, says Peter Ball in "Spiritual Direction with the Clergy: A View from the Church of England," have accepted a daunting mission. They have committed their lives to being fully open to both God and the people of God—something that is humanly impossible to ever fully accomplish. The resulting frustration can seriously impede the spiritual life of the minister if he or she cannot find adequate support. Unfortunately, says Ball, institutionalized support systems are often lacking or nonexistent. He sees spiritual direction with clergy as an important and necessary component in the life of the ordained.

In most Western traditions, the ministry of spiritual direction is open to both women and men. However, in the Christian East, spiritual direction has for centuries been seen as a male, clerical preserve, according to John Chryssavgis in "The Spiritual Elder: The Early Desert Tradition and the Eastern Orthodox Way." The practice of spiritual direction in the Eastern Christian tradition can seem odd and even extreme to westerners. Drawing heavily on the tradition of the fourth-century desert fathers, the expectation is that even if the spiritual elder gives directions that seem absurd, his will is to be followed without question. This emphasis on absolute obedience to one's spiritual guide eventually leads to ultimate freedom that can only be found in relationship with the community of faith. The guide is likened to Moses, who led the Hebrews out of captivity and into the freedom of the Promised Land.

Where Spiritual Direction Happens

The Promised Land, of course, is wherever we encounter the Mystery of God. The Mystery is not an ethereal, abstract concept. It is an incarnate, historical reality, in this time and place. The sense of place, *where* we are, can have a powerful influence on us and our relationship with God, according to Loretta Ross in "Rural Spiritual Direction." Those in rural areas are more accustomed to a slower pace that allows them to interact more easily with creation. Rural settings also foster a simplicity and even a sense of poverty that assist us in responding to the initiative of God in our lives. The more removed we are from the conveniences of the city, the more we must adapt to the environment and accept the place in which we find ourselves on its own terms. For this reason, the place of encounter with the Holy, says Ross, ought to be a place that is difficult to reach, a wilderness.

Ross knows, of course, that the wild place of encounter may also be found in the city. River Sims makes that explicit in his graphic portrayal of spiritual direction with the homeless in "Riding the Monsters: Spiritual Direction with People Who Live on the Street." In contrast to the bucolic images of spiritual direction in Ross's essay, Sims says his experiences of direction sessions include dealing with people who are sleeping in alleys, taking drugs, and waiting at street corners to prostitute themselves. All spiritual directors speak of the dark side, and Sims' experiences are darker than most. But all spiritual directors also speak of the hope that intimacy with the Mystery can bring, and Sims' stories are equally hopeful.

Another place spiritual direction happens is in hospitals. It seems natural that when people are facing physical crises, they would also be facing spiritual questions. Gordon Self, who has worked as a chaplain in health-care settings, notes that while this is the case, many pastoral visits with patients are too brief to be considered traditional spiritual direction. In "A Little Soul Work Does a Hospital Well: Spiritual Direction in Health Care," he wonders if the institution itself might be a subject for spiritual direction. If an organization, particularly a service organization, such as a hospital, can be said to have a "soul," then that soul is capable of direction and deepening its relationship to the Mystery. Like individuals, a corporate body can mimic the prevailing values of society, or it can stand apart, proclaiming a prophetic difference and having a spiritual impact on the community it serves.

Spiritual Communities

A corporation is, after all, simply a collection of people with a common mission. Spiritual directors spend a lot of time helping people recognize the action of the Holy in their lives, and it becomes increasingly evident that Mystery is most profoundly experienced in relationship with others who share the journey of faith. This recognition has led to a growing interest in group spiritual direction. Ann Kline, in "Widening the Lens: The Gift of Group Spiritual Direction," likens this shift in focus to a photographer's perspective. While a photographer might focus her lens on an individual daisy or a whole field of flowers, the subject is still the same. The process of spiritual direction, whether through the lens of an individual or that of a group, still has the journey into Mystery as its goal. While the goal is the same, the sense of interconnectedness that group spiritual direction provides reminds us that the Mystery we seek is found primarily in relationship with others and with the world.

In "Spiritual Companioning within Small Christian Communities," Helen Marie Raycraft, OP, sees spiritual groups as a way to combat the extreme individualism of modern society. She describes how Christian small faith communities can benefit those most harmed by the negative effects of individualism—the extreme poor. Like Sims' experiences with the marginalized people of the streets, Raycraft's experiences do not fit into conventional images of spiritual direction. In the midst of innovative methods of leading a group to more profound experiences of God, Raycraft says small faith communities develop a communal spirituality and salvation history.

Another often marginalized group of people are those who are "non-heterosexual," a term used by Peg Thompson to describe gay, lesbian, and bisexual people in "The Coming Out Process in Spiritual Direction." Those who are just starting to grapple with their sexual identity are entering a time of discernment. Gay, lesbian, or bisexual seekers may have a particularly difficult time finding support in their religious communities. Thompson says coming out almost always involves religious issues, challenging our assumptions about religion: doctrine, scripture, community, clergy, and ultimately our relationship with the Mystery of God. Spiritual directors can be very important companions to those exploring their relationship to God and the community of faith in the process of coming out.

Stages of Life

In some ways, all of life is a coming out process, for non-heterosexuals and heterosexuals alike. Not necessarily a process of coming to understand our sexuality, it is certainly a journey of coming to understand the mystery of our relationships with ourselves and others more deeply. At some point, we begin a new journey, what Susan P. Sihler calls the "second journey" in "Hallowing Our Diminishments: Spiritual Guidance in Later Life." Society doesn't necessarily give us a lot of positive models for the second half of life, but Sihler believes our elder years can be "reframed" into a time of great growth and opportunity for spiritual development. She sees this as a time of death to our youth and a rebirth into a simpler, more focused spiritual life. It is a paradox that as our bodies begin to diminish, our spiritual selves have the potential of much greater strength. The spiritual guide who accompanies second life journeyers has the opportunity to serve as a companion to those who are detaching themselves from material goods and entering into the vastness of the unknown Mystery.

That "unknown" is profoundly evident in those whose journey may mean slipping into dementia. In "Companioning People with Dementia" by Rita Hansen,

John R. Mabry, and Robert B. Williams, we learn that for those who are newly diagnosed, there will be grieving over the impending loss of a known and predictable identity. The skills of spiritual companions will be challenged in this context perhaps
more than any other since no one can really serve as an adequate guide through the
entire journey that those with dementia must travel. Spiritual support is often taken
up not by pastors and trained spiritual directors but rather by caregivers and atten-
dants. Caregiving personnel have the opportunity of offering respect and dignity to
the still-spirit-filled individuals in their care. If they can continue to be a source of
comfort for their patients, how much more will a God of infinite love comfort those
who, essentially, must travel this journey alone?

Methods

Though we may not be able to fully comprehend the journey of dementia, all of
us can, perhaps, gaze through a small window onto that world of disconnected and
random patterns. All of us experience brief journeys like that every time we dream. In
"Dreams and Spiritual Direction," Craig M. Mueller tells us that each night we let go
of ourselves and, in a way, die to all that exists in our conscious, rational lives. Once
asleep, we do not exist in a black nothingness but rather in a rich inner world of symbols and complex meanings. By exploring the possible meanings of our dreams, we can
see more clearly the Mystery we seek to know more fully. Mueller finds wisdom in
dreams and suggests that with the help of a spiritual guide, we can too.

Dreams are ambiguous, however, and for those of us with a tendency to doubt
our own goodness, we can too easily let our (false) perceptions of the Mystery send us
spiraling into guilt and self-doubt. In "Discernment of Spirits as an Act of Faith,"
William A. Barry, SJ, cautions us that we must bring our faith to bear when discerning where the Spirit is leading us. Do we believe the God of Mystery is a loving God,
filled with delight at our every breath, or a judging God, scowling down upon us at
every false step and fearful hesitation? Barry suggests we make a choice as to which God
we are going to believe in and then live out the consequences of our choice. He says
our fundamental task is to discern how God wants us to live our lives and struggle to
understand how to best do that in tune with God's Spirit.

A spiritual director assists seekers in that discernment process through a very simple practice: focus. Lucy Abbott-Tucker, in "Live Nearby, Visit Often: Focusing and
the Spiritual Direction Process," recounts the story of the first time a spiritual director asked her to focus on her feelings. That was more than twenty years ago, and
Abbott-Tucker has come to understand the process of spiritual direction as a process
of focusing on the gracious action of the God of Mystery in the ordinary, everyday
activities of our lives. By focusing on those experiences, noticing one's inner reaction
to them, individuals make a loving response to the loving gift of God. In being with
the seeker, assisting him or her in a focused response to God, the spiritual director is,
as McCarty said, serving as a teacher and guardian of the mysteries—a mystagogue.

Bringing It All Together

The mystagogue leads us deeper into the mystery of God's love, and the deeper we go, the more we are drawn into love for God's people. It is from that stance of love that our hearts are rent because we recognize the desolate condition of the vast majority of people on the earth. In his essay "To Bring All Things Together: Spiritual Direction as Action for Justice," James M. Keegan, SJ, examines the role of the spiritual director in the face of the crushing oppression most of the population experiences. He notes that many ministers who are involved in spirituality work feel desolate themselves because they do not believe they are contributing significantly to the work of justice and the restoration of right order in the world. He notes that some directors have attempted to deal with this by moving their centers into neighborhoods where the poor live or perhaps limiting their direction practice to those who do "direct" justice ministry.

However, Keegan sees this as a misunderstanding of what it means to take action on behalf of justice. He says that at its core, action for justice is showing respect for others—honoring the mystery of each individual. He notes that while social ministries are praiseworthy, there is nothing deficient about or missing from the ministry of spiritual direction.

In the end, all action for justice is ultimately about a profound, intimate relationship with the God of Mystery. God created us to be lovers. When we love, we are in right relationship. We are acting for justice. The ministry of every spiritual director, in any context, is to serve as a guide into the depths of that love relationship.

Spiritual Directors:
Teachers and Guardians of Mystery
Shaun McCarty, ST

In ancient times there was a king who decided to find and honor the greatest person in his realm. A man of wealth and property was singled out. Another was praised for her healing powers; another for his wisdom and knowledge of the law. Still another was lauded for his business acumen. Many other successful people were brought to the palace, but it became evident that the task of choosing the greatest would be difficult.

Finally the last candidate stood before the king. She was a woman. Her hair was white. Her eyes shone with the light of knowledge, understanding, and love.

"Who is this?" asked the king. "What has she done?"

"You have seen and heard all the others," said the king's aide. "This is their teacher!"

The people applauded and the king came down from his throne to honor her.

The role of those who accompany others on journeys of faith has been seen in a variety of ways: spiritual directors, masters, fathers, mothers, midwives, guides, counselors, mentors, companions, friends, and so on. For some, a given designation for the ministry of spiritual direction may say too much; for others, too little. Rather than restrict terminology to a single role or set of words, I prefer to employ a variety. This enables me to explore more creatively the richness of this multifaceted gem of pastoral care.

For some time, I've thought it would be enriching to explore the role of "mystagogue," a special kind of teacher whom the king honors. Pedagogues teach children. Androgogues teach adults. As mystagogues, spiritual directors are teachers of mysteries. This particular term has helped me focus on what I would call one of the "sacral" (in contrast with some of the more "secular" or "professional") facets of this ministry. It has been my experience that the heart of what we do in companioning people on their journeys is concerned with keeping the mystery of it all in focus, and I hope this exploration of the role of a "mystagogue" will promote this way of looking at spiritual direction.

At a time when there is a veritable smorgasbord of spiritual entrées and desserts for practicing and prospective spiritual directors, a caution may be in order. It may be easy to succumb to the subtle illusion that it is primarily learned skills that will make us better "hunting guides" for those in search of God. Perhaps we need reminders now and then that God is not necessarily where or how we expect to find God, that God's presence is often about elusive mystery. Nor is God's kingdom manageable primarily by dint of acquired human proficiency. I would suggest that mystery is at the heart of what we do and not do as spiritual directors. Indeed, I would suggest that it is at the heart of who we are as spiritual directors.

The Role of Mystagogue

The term "mystagogue" is rooted in two Greek words: *mystes*, which means "one initiated in mysteries," and *agogos*, which means "leader." Thus "mystagogue" conveys the notion of leading into, building up, supporting, revealing more clearly how awesome and impressive mystery is. Or, to put it another way, mystagogues find ways of helping people see everything in God. "Mystagogue" is a term often used to refer to those who lead people in sacramental preparation and follow-up; it is also an appropriate way to describe those who help people celebrate the holy in the midst of everyday life.

This role of mystagogue has a long tradition within many faith communities and contexts. With Paul, Cephas, and Apollos, mystagogues are "stewards of God's mysteries" (1 Cor 4:1). Previously, Priscilla and Aquila, partners in ministry with Paul, had performed a mystagogic service for Apollo by explaining "the Way of God to him more accurately" (Acts 18:2, 26; Rom 16:3).

According to Celtic spiritual tradition (inherited from the time of the Druids), the soul is thought to shine around the body as a luminous cloud. When a person is very open, appreciative, and trusting with another, that person has found an *anam cara* or "soul friend" who beholds the other's light and beauty and accepts that person for who she or he truly is. This friendship awakens the fullness and mystery of that person's life. The two are joined in an ancient union with humanity that transcends barriers of time, convention, theology, and ethnic background. When one is blessed with an *anam cara*, the Irish believe one has arrived at that most sacred place—home. Likewise, mystagogues awaken the fullness and mystery of peoples' lives and guide them on their journeys home.

In the Roman Catholic Rite of Christian Initiation for Adults, the term "mystagogue" is associated with newly baptized adults in the last stage of their formation process, called the *mystagogia* (post-baptismal catechesis). Ideally, it is meant to be a lifelong process of deepening faith. Candidates for *mystagogia* are those deemed ready for the "solid food" of which the author of Hebrews speaks: "Everyone who lives on milk, being still an infant, is unskilled in the word of righteousness. But solid food is for the mature, for those whose faculties have been trained by practice to distinguish good from evil" (Heb 5:13–14).

Characteristics of the Mystagogue

As bearers of the mystery of God, mystagogues are not primarily functionaries. Yet they do have a role in facilitating others' attentiveness to mystery. They do this first by knowing (that is, experiencing) and allowing themselves to be caught up in mystery receptively, patiently, reverently, and with abandon. They learn best by being led themselves into mystery, enthused by it, directed by it, possessed by it. Those candidates they help learn more by way of contagion than infusion.

Effective mystagogues pique interest in mystery by helping others to discover the enlightening dimensions of mystery hidden in the plain sight of everyday human experience. To help this happen, mystagogues foster a contemplative attitude toward those who seek their help. They communicate a sense of wonder, awe, and reverence more by letting their words emerge from fertile silence. They are of more help to others by raising questions rather than by supplying premature answers. They support others in living the questions and finding their own answers at their own pace.

Entrusted with stewardship for the mysteries of faith, mystagogues are, indeed, a special, perhaps somewhat unconventional, kind of teacher. Mystagogues teach by helping people name and claim their own religious experience. They evoke truth more than they impart it. They lead people to see everything in God. They teach spiritual things spiritually by being witnesses to the truth in proclaiming, celebrating, and living the paschal and pentecostal mysteries.

Spiritual Directors as Mystagogues

Spiritual directors serve as mystagogues of faith and personal piety. We lead our directees more deeply into these mysteries in such a way that they become revelatory for life, and we help them develop language to talk about it. In our mystagogical role, we are people who traffic in mystery and possess some fluency in this "second language."

As responsible stewards like Paul, Cephas, and Apollos, our task is not to dispel mysteries by making them more reasonable or comfortable; rather, our task is to help our directees learn to live with the ambiguity of the weeds and the wheat in their lives. In this role, spiritual directors are "midwives" of the soul, evocateurs of transformation and growth.

Spiritual directors as mystagogues minister to others especially by being guardians of the mysteries of God's elusive presence and unlikely kingdom. We promote mystery by refusing to become accessories in domesticating it. At times we become "loving iconoclasts" for those we companion, lest mind or imagination substitute dead idols for the living God. We cherish the unpredictability of God's ways and timing. In short, as mystagogues we exercise charisms of spiritual leadership by leading disciples (Jesus', not ours!) ever more deeply into a "devotional knowledge" of the mysteries of faith.

Each of these words—"devotion," "knowledge," and "mystery"—has a common meaning with which most of us are familiar. Set into the context of our faith journeys, their meanings change and take on certain nuances that might be helpful to explore. Let's look first at "devotional knowledge" and then at "mystery."

Devotional Knowledge

In this context, "knowledge" is more than a conceptual understanding of some-one or something. It is the fruit of intimate and personal experience of the Other rather than the result of study, a quest guided by love rather than intellectual curiosity, received more by the heart than the head. Scripture tells us that this kind of knowl-edge is hidden from the learned and the clever and revealed to little ones (Matt 11:27) and disciples (Matt 13:11).

Knowledge becomes "devotional" when it leads one to the service of God and is tested by the expression of other acts of love. It represents a desire to make a total gift of self to God. It manifests itself especially in prayer, fidelity, and unselfish love. As with all grace, God is the initiator of devotion and the one who invites our response. True devotion brings holiness of life, which is to say, a life of love. St. Francis de Sales describes devotion in metaphor: "Charity and devotion differ no more . . . than the flame from the fire. . . . Charity, when it works out into flame, is called devotion."[1]

Mystery: The Heart of Spiritual Direction

"Mystery" is about personal experience of God and the inexhaustible riches of ever-unfolding meaning available through God's self-revelation. Used in the context of Christian faith, "mystery" refers to "truth hidden which has been revealed; something unapproachable which invites entry, something unknowable which offers true under-standing."[2] Devotional knowledge of the mysteries of faith is more than knowing about them as spectator or observer; it is knowing oneself as drawn into them as participant.

Mysteries of faith are elusive. The God of biblical experience invites our reach but eludes our grasp. Mysteries defy domestication. They aren't subjects for analysis, control, or other forms of manipulation. What we say about God is always by way of analogy. This means that what we say about or how we image God is more unlike than like God. God is like a shepherd. God is like a mother hen. But God is not confined by or limited to these names or images or any others. Mysteries demand, on the one hand, that we not make them inaccessible, but, on the other, that we dare not tame them by trying to make them more reasonable or more comfortable. In this sense, might we not say that mystagogues are "guardians" of mystery?

The Language of Mystery

There is a story told of a mother cat out for a stroll with her three kittens when confronted by a ferocious-looking dog headed in their direction. Under siege, she quickly ushers her kittens under a nearby porch. She then proceeds to move directly toward the dog. When she comes up eyeball-to-eyeball with him, she barks as loudly as she can, "Ruff, ruff, ruff!" Startled by this unexpected turn of events, the dog turns abruptly and, with its tail between its legs, runs in the opposite direction. With that, the mother cat retrieves her kittens and, shaking a paw at them, says, "Now do you see why I want you to learn a second language?"

As Daniel Matthews, rector of Trinity Church in New York, has pointed out, many of us in ministry today are faced with the challenge of learning a "second language." Not just Spanish or English, but the language of mystery. Many religiously and spiritually educated people are quite adept at speaking the language of rationality; fewer, the language of mystery. In Western culture in particular, we tend, perhaps, to idolize reason. We've been taught to theorize, analyze, synthesize, criticize, categorize, and, consequently, suffer the illusion that everything can be understood or explained. This, unfortunately, leaves little space for mystery, which is at the core of religious belief and experience. Faith is built on truths (not to the exclusion of goodness and beauty) that transcend reason.

We struggle with the ineffability of the experience of the presence of a God who is unpredictable (save for an unwavering fidelity). We stumble, fumble, and stutter as we try to learn this "second language" of mystery, to find expression for things we can't see but somehow know; can't explain but somehow understand; moments that are real but resist articulation. The language of mystery includes paradox, metaphor, the language of passion, parable, ritual, and, ultimately, silence.

Paradox

Paradox is language about truth that seems contradictory, unbelievable, or absurd. The Gospels are replete with paradoxical expressions; for example, "Those who want to save their life will lose it, and those who lose their life for my sake will save it" (Luke 9:24). Cousin to paradox is a figure of speech known as "oxymoron," which jolts convention and stymies expectation by combining opposite or contradictory terms; for example, God dwells in "bright darkness." We approach mysteries with "learned ignorance."

How often do we hear our directees (and catch ourselves, too) not knowing how to be with that which seems contradictory, often choosing to focus on part of the experience while dismissing another equally valid part? A spiritual director may encounter a directee who talks about how relieved she is that her mother has finally died after a long illness. As the director listens, he or she may sense conflicting emotions that coexist with the directee's sense of relief—perhaps anger that her mother has abandoned her, not uncommon when someone dies. A director might invite her directee to be with both the

relief and the anger, to hold these emotions that, while both real and valid, feel contradictory on the inside. In so doing, the director has invited her directee to dwell in the
realm of the seemingly impossible—to embrace paradox.

Metaphor

Metaphors are implied comparisons in which a word or a phrase ordinarily and
primarily used of one thing is applied to another; for example, "All the world's a stage."
Lively metaphors appeal to the imagination as well as to the mind. They conjure up
images that reveal new aspects of reality. Metaphors abound in mystical literature, for
example, St. Teresa's "dart of love"; St. John of the Cross's "dark night of the soul."

The Language of Passion

The language of passion seems especially apt for communicating the experience
of mystery that propels desire and fires love. The passionate verses of John Donne
enable him to address his living, concerned, dynamic God of human experience with
the ardor of a lover:

> Batter my heart, three person'd God; for you
> As yet but knock, breathe, shine and seek to mend;
> That I may rise and stand, o'erthrow me, and bend
> Your force, to breake, blow, burn and make me new.[3]

During times when our directees are experiencing God in a particularly passionate way, we can help them feel more comfortable with their passion by offering
such examples or encouraging them to write their own. The Song of Songs articu-
lates well such experience; the poetry of John of the Cross ("Living Flame of
Love") provides other examples. Directees who have not felt this way before need
reassurance, space to explore, and encouragement to express their passions and their
underlying mystery.

Parable

Parables are thought-provoking, unfinished short stories drawn from familiar,
everyday experiences of those who hear them. They might be said to carry the aura
of "dark sayings," suggesting mystery. Jesus used them to allow for a gradual unfolding of God's mysterious ways. They are invitations for his hearers to get involved in
the stories and to be questioned by them. They are meant to lead to choice, either to
reject or to accept, which latter choice brings a new vision and a changed life. Parables
are ways of imparting the "folly" of God's wisdom and ways. Human wisdom, for
instance, would find "folly" in leaving the ninety-nine to find the one lost sheep.

Ritual

Rituals are symbolic actions that enable people to celebrate and to commemorate significant events. Because rituals operate at deeper levels of consciousness than ordinary discourse, they can connect the people who share in them. Rituals have the potential for condensing, communicating, and transforming a variety of meanings, and they reveal mystery to us as little else can. As mystagogues, we can help people celebrate special moments of grace through appropriate rituals. As directees tell their stories, we can listen for times when rituals might be appropriate—times of closure, such as a change in job, retirement, or the loss of a close friend who has died or moved away; or times of celebration, such as the completion of a task or even a small achievement that a person has finally realized. Because these moments often pass without much recognition, we can serve our directees by noticing these times and asking them if some small ritual, perhaps one that is carried out within the context of a direction session, might help them process the event.

Silence

Few things allow us to live into mystery more than shared silence before the Lord. It was St. John of the Cross who said that "the language that God hears best is the silent language of love." This silence is not the mere absence of noise; rather, it is the presence of the unspoken. Some feelings are too deep for words; some thoughts, too lofty for expression. In the role of mystagogue, we can inculcate a sense of awe more by keeping silent than by speaking. In so doing, both director and directee are enabled to look inward to hidden resources of their own beings where the Spirit dwells, speaks, and leads. As directors, we can cultivate within ourselves a deeper comfort with silence so that when silence enters a session, we are able to welcome and support it rather than rush to fill it with words.

Dispositions for Living into Mystery

I would suggest that the primary disposition for living into mystery is a childlike spirit. This disposition has roots in the tradition of the *anawim* (the poor of Yahweh). It finds biblical expression in various places: "Enough for me to keep my soul tranquil and quiet like a child in its mother's arms. As content as a child that has been weaned, Israel, rely on Yahweh" (Ps 131:2).

This disposition is epitomized in the first of the beatitudes: "How blessed are the poor in spirit; the reign of God is theirs" (Matt 5:3). It can be said that each of the subsequent beatitudes is a ramification of the first.

Jesus describes this disposition in the same fashion when he says: "'If anyone wishes to rank first, he must remain the last one of all and the servant of all.' Then he took a little child, stood him in their midst, and putting his arms around him, said to them, 'Whoever welcomes a child such as this for my sake welcomes me. And whoever welcomes me welcomes not me, but him who sent me'" (Mark 9:35–37).

Why are children singled out by Jesus as models for his disciples? In their innocence, they are icons of trust in and dependence upon God. They possess a capacity for wonder, awe, and surprise. In their simplicity, they are uncomplicated and uncluttered. Theirs is an attitude marked by the absence of self-preoccupation. Children tend to let go of hurts more easily and readily than "grown-ups."

In her *Story of a Soul*, St. Therese of the Child Jesus writes of her "little way" of spiritual childhood as a childlike disposition of heart. What made her pleasing to God, she says, was the way she loved her littleness and poverty coupled with her trust in the mercy of the good God.

Conclusion

Unlike the king in our opening tale who honored the greatness in his realm, our Shepherd-King honors littleness in those who "teach" mysteries.

As mystagogues—as teachers and guardians of precious mystery—we help our directees name, claim, and celebrate surprises by the Spirit. We are called to realize that experience of God can't be programmed in church, in liturgy, in yoga, in centering prayer, in retreat, or in any of the other spiritual disciplines. We are invited to know that God may come "outside the camp"—in a chance meeting, in a dream, in an unexpected request, in a phone call or letter. God seems often to act like that. God revels in surprise. It's the way of mystery.

In her poem "The Rowing Endeth," Anne Sexton projects an image of a poker-playing God. "At the dock of the island called God," she is dealt a royal flush; but God wins because God holds five aces. A wild card had been announced, but she did not hear it. God starts to laugh, and everything and everyone around (including Anne) joins in the laughter. She ends with these verses:

> . . . Dearest dealer,
> I with my royal straight flush,
> love you so for your wild card,
> that untamable, eternal, gut-driven ha-ha
> and lucky love.[4]

As mystagogues courting and guarding mystery, we realize that God simply doesn't play poker according to Hoyle. May we embody the humor, delight, and intimacy so well expressed by Anne Sexton as we walk with others.

Recommended Reading

Combes, Abbe, ed. *Collected Letters of Therese of Lisieux*. New York: Frank. J. Sheed, 1949.
Gratton, Carolyn. *The Art of Spiritual Direction*. New York: Crossroads, 1992.

Kelly, Thomas R. *A Testament of Devotion*. New York: Harper & Row, 1941.
Norris, Gunilla. *Sharing Silence*. New York: Bell Tower, 1992.
Otto, Rudoloph. *The Idea of the Holy*. New York: Oxford University Press, 1923.
Ulanov, Ann and Barry. *Primary Speech*. Atlanta: John Knox Press, 1982.

SHAUN MCCARTY, ST, is an ordained member of a religious community (Missionary Servants of the Most Holy Trinity), presently serving as spiritual director for the Blessed Trinity Missionary Institute (a lay branch of his religious family whose members live vowed or consecrated lives). He has been assigned to be available to the wider church for retreat, renewal, and other spiritual ministries and is currently on the faculty of the Spiritual Directors Training Program of the Episcopal Diocese of South Carolina.

Notes

1. Francis de Sales, *Introduction to a Devout Life* (Garden City, N.Y.: Image Books, 1972), 41.

2. Philip Gleason, *The New Dictionary of Theology* (Collegeville, Minn.: Liturgical Press, 1993), 688–89.

3. John Donne, "Holy Sonnet 14," *Poems of John Donne* (ed. E. K. Chambers; London: Lawrence & Bullen, 1896), 165.

4. Anne Sexton, "The Rowing Endeth," *The Awful Rowing Toward God* (Boston: Houghton Mifflin, 1975).

Pastoral Counseling or Spiritual Direction: What's the Difference?

Thomas Hart

Sometimes my spiritual direction clients tell me I am not spiritual enough. That is true. But that is not what they mean. What they mean is that I have not mentioned God very much for a while. This catches me by surprise. My values, perspectives, and understandings are all Christian and constitute the framework within which I listen and respond. What they are remarking is that I take my spirituality so much for granted that I sometimes neglect to name it.

My clients in psychotherapy, by contrast, sometimes chide me for being too spiritual. "Let's leave religion out of this, Tom. That's up in the air somewhere. Let's talk about my problems. How do you really see me?" This is curious too. I am listening and responding to these people from within that very same Christian framework. So sometimes I speak from there explicitly. These folks are less attuned to spiritual considerations, so even a single remark from a spiritual perspective really stands out for them. But my point is, with everyone who comes, I am always doing the same thing.

I have been asked to write here of the difference between pastoral counseling and spiritual direction. I come at the question as a person who has long done both spiritual direction and psychotherapy. I did spiritual direction for many years first, then got a degree in psychotherapy and have operated under the label of "psychotherapist" for twenty-five years now, but always doing psychotherapy, too, within a spiritual framework. I want to answer the question by broadening it so that it takes in all the main kinds of helping professionals: spiritual director, church pastor, pastoral counselor with a degree in that field, and psychotherapist. How shall we compare and contrast what these four kinds of helpers do?

Each comes into view most clearly when I place them on a continuum, and I will do that in the first section of this essay. Then I will reflect on what most distinguishes the spiritual director from the other kinds of helpers. Next, I will zero in on the crucial ingredient in all four kinds of helping relationships, the factor that really helps. Finally, I will suggest cultivating two specific habits from the field of psychotherapy to enhance your work as a spiritual director.

Helping Professionals Provide a Spectrum of Services

At the left end of the spectrum of helping professionals are practitioners who have no use for religion or spirituality and want to leave them out of the discussion.

They may focus on the client's personal development and seek insight into patterns of behavior and their roots in childhood. Or they may focus on some particular problem in the present, seeking a solution rather than insight into causes and patterns. In either case, their interest is feelings, behaviors, problems, past experiences, interpretations, and practical solutions, not spirituality.

At the right end of the spectrum are practitioners whose entire concern is the spiritual life and spiritual growth. The conversation centers on methods of prayer, the discernment of God's will in important choices, temptations, spiritual practices, ministries to others, and so on.

Those are the ends of the continuum, but there is a very broad space between them. Spiritual people have many other concerns besides prayer and discernment and usually appreciate all the feedback they can get from any perspective, if it is helpful. And many people concerned with other life problems are open to, and sometimes quite eager to hear, a spiritual perspective on those concerns if it makes sense to them. Always the person seeking help is a human being, a unity with many dimensions, and we relate to the person and his or her life as a whole. The largest number of clients and practitioners fall somewhere between the two poles and value some blend of psychological and spiritual perspectives.

Between the pure types of psychotherapist at the left end and spiritual director at the right, I would place pastoral counselors and ordinary pastors. By *pastoral counselors* I mean people who have, in addition to theological training, a master's degree or doctorate in the field of pastoral counseling, and so have gained a good grasp of psychology and counseling techniques. These people often do counseling full-time, typically at counseling centers rather than churches, and are qualified to collect insurance payments as psychotherapists. They are sought out precisely for that blend of psychological and spiritual sophistication. *Ordinary pastors* are kindred spirits, usually richer in theology and poorer in psychology. But they have had a couple of seminary courses in basic counseling skills and personal development and are often the people of first recourse when churchgoers have a problem. Parishioners already know and trust their pastors and expect that the counsel offered, whatever might be in it, will come from within a shared faith perspective.

If the psychotherapist is at the far left end of the continuum, the pastoral counselor belongs just right of that. Then comes the ordinary pastor, then the spiritual director.

But rarely are these four kinds of helpers pure types. "Secular" psychotherapists often know something about spirituality, especially in today's climate of greater open-mindedness, and respectfully allow it to come into the discussion even if they are not particularly versed in it. Pastoral counselors are certainly a mixed type. Ordinary pastors might have some psychological skill. And spiritual directors find spiritual relevance in many more aspects of life than prayer and temptations and might bring some knowledge of psychology to the conversation as well.

Though a spiritual approach to human life is paramount for both the ordinary pastor and the spiritual director, there are some basic differences in what these two practitioners do, and perhaps those differences most directly answer the question of this article. The principal difference is that the pastor typically sees the client just once, maybe twice, the discussion centering on a crisis or problem that brings the person in. When someone asks for spiritual direction, by contrast, she or he is usually looking for something less problem-focused and of longer duration—regular meetings, usually monthly, over a year or even several years, aiming toward open-ended growth in the spiritual life.

Interestingly, many pastors do not feel comfortable in the role of spiritual director. It may be that they simply do not have the time for this ongoing relationship with individuals. Some also feel that they do not know enough about the spiritual life. In this respect, they sometimes underestimate themselves. I am currently seeing a pastor who has done pastoral counseling in the ordinary sense comfortably for years. Having just completed a training program to be a spiritual director, she tells me of the trepidation she feels as she approaches sessions with her first clients. She is trying to figure out how she should be different. I tell her she should not be different at all, except perhaps to sit back more and let the clients' stories unfold over time, as the stories range into more and more areas of the clients' lives.

To be true to our four varieties of helpers, we must also recognize that there is immense diversity in the way individual helpers, even in the same profession, approach their task. In 1985 I attended the Evolution of Psychotherapy Conference. Here were gathered many of the founders of the major schools of psychotherapy in use today—psychoanalysts, humanistic psychologists, behaviorists, logotherapists, Gestalt and transactional analysis experts, systems and strategic therapists, Jungians, hypnotherapists—and we could watch them actually work with clients, live onstage or through videotape. What most struck me was the tremendous variety of approaches they took to clients and their concerns, all in the name of psychotherapy. In one session, Salvador Minuchin, a family systems therapist, was supposed to offer a response after watching a prominent behaviorist work with a depressed man in his fifties. Minuchin said, "I don't have any response. I simply do not think in the same terms you do and don't have the slightest idea how to respond intelligently to what we just saw. So if you don't mind, I am going to use my time to talk briefly about something else." This refusal to engage at all seemed to me a bit extreme, but it does suggest how widely approaches can vary within the same field of endeavor.

The same degree of variation occurs among spiritual directors. I have been to quite a few myself and have seen how widely they differ in how they envision the focus of concern, what they listen for, and how they respond to the same issues. Their theologies differ, as do the ways they conceive the helping relationship and conduct themselves in it. They have distinctive personalities, too, introducing another huge factor into the experience.

The essential point here, as the continuum and discussion have tried to show, is that although there are four distinguishable types of helping professionals, there is considerable overlap among them. Psychology and spirituality are easily blended, in various proportions and various ways, across the spectrum.

What Makes Spiritual Direction Unique?

What most distinguishes spiritual direction, I would say, is its goal, which is to achieve growth in the spiritual life. I doubt that any other helping relationship would say it has the same purpose.

This goal can be broken into two parts: to help directees become more aware of the presence and activity of God in their lives, and to help them respond to that presence appropriately.

We used to say that God created the world once and for all. Now we know that God is still creating it, day and night. We used to talk as if God dwelt above us or in outer space. Now we recognize more clearly that God is our very ambience, like the air we breathe: "In God we live and move and have our being" (Acts 17:28). So God is always where we are and is ever at work. The trick is to become aware of God's presence and activity and to cooperate with it. If we do, our lives are gradually changed. As our alignment with the Divine grows, our lives are increasingly marked by recognizable virtues. Paul names several of them: "love, joy, peace, patience, kindness, generosity, faithfulness, gentleness, and self-control" (Gal 5:22–23). Every spiritual tradition tries to foster such virtues and recognizes them as manifestations of spiritual vitality.

It is good to alert the client from the beginning of a spiritual direction relationship that the field of concern is the whole of his or her life, not just prayer, theology, and religious practice. One way I state the principle is this:

Where the action in your life is, that is where God is present and active with you. So let us focus on the action. Why? Because right there is where your becoming is most at stake, and that is what God is interested in. If you are battling depression, that is the place. If you are trying to heal from sexual abuse, that is the place. If you are struggling in a difficult relationship with parent, child, spouse, or friend, that is where the action is. If you are a new mother, both stirred by the ecstasy of this amazing new life given to you and overwhelmed by its relentless demands, that is where God is most engaged with you. If you are battling sexual or chemical addiction, that is the locus of the encounter. God is where the action is in your life.

If the client is at a loss as to what to talk about or how to get out of the rut of a too narrowly focused conversation, we can lead the way into these broader plains by asking some questions: What do you enjoy in life? What do you struggle with? What do you most want out of life? How do you feel about yourself? How do you spend your days? What do you do with your evenings and weekends? The answers to these questions will tell you where the client really lives. And that is where God is at work with him or her. We are trying to make the client aware of that and help him or her respond.

A couple came for marriage counseling. It was clear as they described their life together that their marriage was on the verge of falling apart. They were not seeking spiritual direction. But after listening awhile, I felt moved to say,

> This may surprise you, but at bottom all your issues are spiritual. By that I mean that they have to do with the kinds of persons you are making of yourselves. The core issue in our becoming persons is learning how to love. Marriage is a school for that. And all the grist for growth comes up in the marital dialogue. As I listen to you complaining to me about one another, I hear you calling each other to growth. And inside those voices of yours, I hear God calling you to growth. If you heed what God is calling you to in your partner's words, you will grow. You will become better at the highest and most difficult of all the arts, the art of loving, and so realize God's purpose for you. Your marriage will change from a situation of prevailing unpleasantness to one of deep pleasantness. You have a choice, and the consequences are huge. If you do not both dedicate yourselves to learning how to love, your marriage will soon come to an end.

It is the same in everyone's life. The voice of God keeps speaking in our daily ambience, calling us to growth, offering us abundant challenges and opportunities. It is then up to us. The goal of spiritual direction is to help us become more aware of the presence and activity of God in our lives and respond appropriately. It is this synergy of God's leading and our responding that produces growth.

If our whole life is the locus of our engagement with the Divine, where do prayer and religious practice fit in? They are indispensable supports to that total life of faith. In prayer, we focus all our attention on our ground and innermost core. We tune in completely, in solitary silence or in prayerful rituals with others. This fixed concentration heightens our awareness, expresses and celebrates our faith. Without some of this focus, the spiritual easily slips further and further toward the margins of awareness or beyond them. But prayer is more than support. It is also the enjoyment of our hearts' desires. It is peace in, and a relishing of, the gracious Presence. So prayer (meditation, ritual) and religious practice play a vital role in the spiritual life. But they are by no means the whole of it, as this story from the ancient wisdom tradition shows:

> So passionate was Krishna's love for truth that he traveled to distant places in search of *sannyasis* to teach him, and he felt no inhibitions about drawing

infidels at the bazaar into discussions about the truths of his faith. One day his wife told him how unfairly he was treating her—and discovered that her husband had no interest whatsoever in that kind of truth.

Whatever You Call What You Do, the Relationship Is the Thing

Carl Rogers once remarked that therapists are born, not made. "So we should spend our resources not on training, but on recruitment," he told an audience of therapists at the Evolution of Psychotherapy Conference in Anaheim, California, 1985. The same is true of spiritual directors. If the gift is not there, you can train and train and never get the product you desire. If the gift is there, training will refine it.

For twenty-one years I lived in various Jesuit communities, where we all had spiritual directors by rule. After the first few years, we could choose our own. Typically, several individuals were available, well qualified at least on paper. All I had to do was hear them preach or teach, and eat a meal or two with them, and I quickly narrowed the field. It came down to a feeling about certain ones: I like who you are, and I feel certain you have something for me.

How do you know whether *you* have the gift to be a spiritual director? The indicator is this—that long before you had or sought a credential, people were already telling you their personal stories and seeking your input. Some of them may even have told you that you were a born counselor and should counsel for a living.

There has long been interest in knowing what kind of psychotherapy is most effective. Much research has been done on the question, especially in recent years. And the same answer keeps coming back: no school of therapy can be shown to be more fruitful than any other. Effectiveness all comes down to the quality of the relationship between the client and the therapist. The therapist (and a spiritual director is a kind of therapist) manages to create a certain kind of relationship, which proves to be therapeutic. The client usually describes that relationship like this: "I feel safe with you. I know you care for me. I can talk freely about anything. You listen respectfully and carefully. You are wise and gentle yet honest with me. I know you believe in me and have hope for me. And the perspectives, suggestions, and support you give are usually very helpful." When these are the ingredients of the relationship, no matter what the therapist's school or program, the client heals and grows.

Years ago a friend and mentor of mine, a Jesuit priest and clinical psychologist, summarized his long years of helping people: "When I was a priest in a parish, they called me a pastoral counselor. When I got my degree in psychology, I worked in a counseling center on a university campus and they called me a psychologist. Then my superior asked me to be director of novices for our province, and they called me a spiritual director. So I have been called by many names, but I have always done exactly the same thing! I listen to people with care, and I give them my honest responses. I suppose you could say it comes down to this: What I do is me." He was a gifted counselor because, whatever his particular assignment, he always managed to create the kind of relationship that supported, healed, and freed people.

I hope it is clear from what I have been saying that spiritual direction is therapeutic. If the direction relationship is what it should be, it will produce healing and growth, personal and spiritual.

Two Habits Worth Cultivating

Two aspects of effective relating in the counseling situation that are usually inculcated in psychotherapy training are equally applicable to spiritual direction.

The first is to be genuine. Be genuine because sincerity is refreshing: "To tell you the truth, I've never read Saint John of the Cross." Be genuine because honesty is the only thing that works: "I've studied so-called Ignatian spirituality, but I don't think I've ever understood it. Maybe it is just not for me." Be genuine because authenticity will invite your client to be genuine. Don't pretend to be more than you are, another plodding pilgrim. Don't put on a hat. The one thing I ask of every client I begin a relationship with is honesty. I ask clients to be honest with me particularly when it is hardest, for example, when they are unhappy with me. I also make a practice of asking them from time to time how they are feeling about our work together, to elicit honest feedback. And I promise to be just as honest with them. My aforementioned friend and mentor gave me another bit of advice, which fits right in here: "Learn everything you can from your courses, keep reading, and get good supervision. But when you are with someone in the counseling room, set all that aside and just be yourself with this person."

My second suggestion is to pay attention to your feelings. They are an elaborate information system, with a great deal to tell you. Let me give you an example. A young woman came to me for counseling. I do not remember what her concern was, but I do remember this: We had just begun a session, and I got in touch with something. And I took a risk. I said to her, "You know, this is our sixth meeting. And I am noticing something. I don't feel any closer to you today than I did the first time you came in. That is really unusual for me. Usually by this time I am feeling a strong connection." She took this in without moving, was silent a few moments, and then said, "That is the story of my life! I don't seem to be able to connect with anyone. I never feel any closer either." I had scored a bingo with this gamble based on what I was feeling. So together we began to explore what she was doing that created all these superficial, unsatisfying relationships. I always work on the principle that what the directee is doing with me is probably what the directee is doing with other people, too, and if it isn't working, we have a great opportunity right here to take a close look at it and figure out what is wrong.

In a first session with a man many years ago, it occurred to me ten minutes before we stopped that I would never see him again. He wasn't saying that. In fact, when I asked if he wanted to make another appointment, he said yes, and we made it. But he never came back. Now when I get a feeling like that, I do something with it. I say something like, "Let me tell you what's in my mind. This could be entirely wrong, but I have the feeling I will never see you again. Is there anything to that?" or "Are we connecting?" This flushes out whatever may be going on between us. The client may assure me he or she feels joined and comfortable, and with that I may be satisfied. The client also has the opportunity to tell me he or she is somehow dissatisfied, which confirms my hunch.

Of course, I am not always going to share baldly the feelings I am experiencing in encounters with clients: "I am bored." "I don't like you." "You turn me on." "You scare me." But those feelings are all honest human feelings. In counseling, my question to myself is, how can I use this emotion somehow for the benefit of this person, or perhaps my own benefit? My anxiety may be telling me that I am out of my element, which is salutary information. I should refer this person to someone else with more expertise on an important issue, or I should at least consult another professional. But I remember a supervisor's using her feeling of anxiety once in a quite different way. In our getting-acquainted session with her, when my colleagues and I were trying to answer her question about what we wanted, she said to one colleague, "I'm feeling anxious right now. I wonder if I am picking up on your anxiety." That prompted some self-examination in my colleague, who acknowledged that she was indeed anxious, and told why, which gave the supervisor a lot to work with.

What do you do with, "I feel bored with this person?" What I do first is try to remember a time when I felt more engaged with her or him and refer back to it, saying, "I remember when we were discussing such and so, and I felt very engaged and very connected with you. Somehow today I am feeling less engaged. Are you feeling that? Do you have any idea why that is?" If there has never been a time of real engagement, you might ask something like this: "Let me share a question that is kicking around in my mind. Are we getting to what is really important for you?"

What do you do with, "Somehow I don't like you?" I would not just bear with it, because again it is important information. I would reflect and pray on it and perhaps also consult another professional, trying to understand what it is about. Then, if it seems to be mostly about the client, I would try to find its root. What makes it unpleasant to be with this person? Too-high expectations? A bottomless pit of neediness? Something sexual? An edge of anger? Nothing but "Poor me" and "Yes, but" every time I make a suggestion? Once I figure out what is behind my reaction, I try to determine how I can call attention to it in a constructive way. I take a look at myself too. Might I have some bias or some clear limitation? Might I, for instance, need to do some work to become more comfortable with sexuality, such a significant dimension of every person's life? Both of us ought to be growing through this work of counseling.

What if I am attracted to my client? I do not share that information with her or him, because I do not see how it can be helpful to the client. I just let it be, regarding it as a part of nature. I am aware of it, but I am not going to do anything with it. My focus is on the person's concerns.

Well, what if the client tells me she or he is in love with me? I just receive that, thanking her or him both for the love and for being honest about it. It need not be a problem in our work. I am the one responsible for the boundaries. I keep the focus on what we are here to do. But I circle back to ask about these feelings from time to time, because they are part of the client's life and our relationship, and I want to know how she or he is doing with them.

Are all these concerns really spiritual? you might wonder. I say yes. If God pervades all aspects of our existence, and if all our loves, concerns, and struggles are therefore spiritual in their deepest dimension, then attending to our relationships is germane to spiritual growth. For Jesus, in fact, nothing is more central to the spiritual life than relationships. So anything I can do to help someone better the quality of a relationship, not just with me, will enhance their life immeasurably, and that enhancement is surely of God. Truth is another core value, and it lies at the heart of all spirituality. To be in the truth is to be in God, even if one is only dimly aware that truth has much to do with God. The Letter to the Ephesians frames this well, deftly describing the Christian ideal as "speaking the truth in love" (Eph 4:15). Honesty between us moves us more deeply into the truth.

I make a practice of praying in the morning for all the people I will be seeing that day. And I usually ask myself, what does each person need? Sometimes something crystallizes in my mind, and I bring it to the session. On those occasions, instead of assuming my usual posture, which is that of respondent, I take the initiative. Just the other day, for example, in talking with a woman trying to rebuild her marriage, I said, "As I was praying this morning, I thought I might share with you what I see God doing in your life and in your husband's since the devastation of his affair." She was, of course, eager to hear it, and when she did, she said she could see it, too, though not clearly enough to have put it into words herself. And it was a comfort to her in her efforts to heal.

Conclusion

The various kinds of professional helpers, and their clients, can be placed on a continuum in which psychology and spirituality are blended in varying degrees. The real question for any given helper in a particular situation is, what does this person want or need now, and how can I best assist him or her?

In the relationship of spiritual direction, the spiritual director's goal is to help the client become more aware of the presence and activity of God in her or his life so that the client can make a fuller and more apt response to that presence and activity. The most important single ingredient in any fruitful counseling is the quality of the relationship itself, and to that the counselor should always be attending. Finally, I suggest cultivating two habits that are especially fruitful: being genuine and paying attention to one's feelings.

Recommended Reading

Hart, Thomas. *The Art of Christian Listening*. New York: Paulist Press, 1980.

————. *Hidden Spring: The Spiritual Dimension of Therapy*. New York: Paulist Press, 1994. Reissued in 2002 by Fortress, Minneapolis, Minnesota.

————. *Spiritual Quest: A Guide to the Changing Landscape*. New York: Paulist Press, 1999.

————. *What Does It Mean to Be a Man?* New York: Paulist Press, 2004.

THOMAS HART, PHD, is a psychotherapist and spiritual director in Seattle, Washington.

Circle of Hearts:
Women's Spirituality Groups

Patricia D. Brown

Anytime you are in the same room with a group of powerful women and God's Spirit, look out! I know firsthand that women's spirituality groups are risky business. A group is a living organism. It takes patience, compassion, and at times the willingness to risk and "run naked," being vulnerable and exposing imperfections. So, kicking and screaming, I joined my first such group with women participants. I thought it would mean digging into topics and issues that I was personally struggling with. I was right. As a group member, I was forced to clarify many of my own thoughts and assumptions, and I discovered within myself feelings about women and spirituality that are deeper and more complex than I ever imagined. I had to sort out my own herstory—the good, the bad, and the ugly—face my failings, and celebrate my victories.

Here is some of what I have learned about group spiritual direction with and for women, both as a participant and as a director. This is about the theory and practice of being sisters and friends in discernment. If you are a woman who resonates with what is here, I encourage you to think about becoming involved in a group. If you are a man, please thoughtfully consider what spirituality looks like through women's eyes, how freedom and balance are encouraged, and how women organize themselves in the absence of conscious or unconscious "giving over" to male authority.

Women's spirituality groups help change how we get together as women. It is about what women can do when they gather specifically for the purpose of spiritual growth. Many women seek a deeper spirituality, perhaps denying and repressing for years what they have known to be true about themselves, living in contradiction, inviting internal conflict, and feeling frantic. But as they join other women and turn their hearts toward God, they experience deep inner reorientation. Through the process of a spirituality group, women can clarify their values, claim their own giftedness, and return these new strengths to their closest relationships and to the larger community. With a gentle touch, women meeting together can discover how the Spirit is working uniquely in their own lives—that is, how God is working through them to be a channel of light and love to the world. Groups that I have facilitated have a dual purpose: to help those gathered develop their relationships with God and at the same time discover new ways to inspire, encourage, and affirm one another.

Spirit-Directed Women

The word "spirit" comes from the Latin *spirare*, which means "to breathe." In Hebrew, the word for "spirit" is *ruah*, which also means "breath." In essence, our spirit is what gives us life and breath. When we speak of spirituality, we are talking about that which connects us as humans to the life of God who is the breath of life that sustains the world.

Sacred scripture tells about this connection with women in an ancient story (Matt 25:1–13). Seven bridesmaids, thinking ahead, bring enough oil for their lamps to last the entire evening of the wedding celebration. Seven other bridesmaids do not. When the wedding is delayed, the foolish women ask those who were wise to share their lamp oil. But the wise women say no to this request. They realize that if they share their oil, they, too, will not have enough to last the night. Then the entire wedding party will sit in darkness. The foolish bridesmaids decide to return to their homes for more oil. But when they return, they realize they have missed the wedding entirely. The rabbi is quick to point out the moral of the story to those who are walking numbly through life: "Keep awake!"

Spiritual direction is about waking up and staying awake—alive and aware of our relationship with ourselves, with others, and with God. It is about an intentional, awakened state that reminds us again and again that God has a deeper design on our lives than what may appear on the surface. On this spiritual quest, we embark on a journey to make sense out of what might appear to be random or chaotic.

What, then, is this "group spiritual direction with women" thing? Something New Age? A millennium craze? The latest congregational growth gimmick? Women's spiritual direction groups may seem like a new idea to some, but the truth is that they are not.

Women's Groups Past and Present

Throughout history, women around the globe have come together in groups, usually circles, to seek direction and wisdom, to pray and worship, to explore their relationships with God, and to celebrate the important passages of their lives. In her book *Group Spiritual Direction: Community for Discernment*, Rose Mary Dougherty, SSND, defines it this way: "Ideally in spiritual direction, two people (or more in group spiritual direction) experience God drawing them together precisely to pay attention to love, the prayer of God unfolding in the heart of the person seeking spiritual direction."[1]

Since biblical times, women have gathered together to worship, pray, and sing. Women's circles are a longtime tradition of congregational life. Remnants of our Judeo-Christian grandmothers' Sarah Circle, Esther Circle, Martha Circle, or Mary Circle remain today. These circles create a haven—a place for us to be who we are, to explore our relationships to God and one another, and to celebrate God's work in the everyday happenings of our lives. Rural and urban women gather in circles to quilt, work on mission projects, and study the Bible. In the midst of it all is the mutual seeking of guidance and discernment. Together we come to understand our connection as sisters and then reach out in service and mission. In essence, we are reclaiming our herstory. Old ways to form women of spirit are being rediscovered—for greater service to the world in our time.

Yet times have changed since our grandmothers' day—even our mothers' day. The majority of us hold part- or full-time jobs. Women are in the home caring for children, the elderly, and households, having more demands than ever. Most of us no longer live in communities where children can walk to school and extracurricular activities. The volunteer work required to chaperone children's school field trips, help at the community bazaar, and work in the congregation's office, once spread out over a large number of women, has been loaded on the few available during the day. This gives even more reason to take time from our busy lives to gather and connect with other women.

"Life with three children and a preacher husband is pretty crazy most days. So I look forward to my weekly discernment circle," explains Amy, a thirty-year-old who juggles family, church, and her work as a registered nurse. "That one hour helps me to reconnect with myself, other women, and God. It's my chance to step away so I can return to my daily life with deeper clarity that lets me savor the moment. And my family knows that when I return home I am a nicer person to live with." Amy finishes her explanation with a laugh: "Some weeks the kids practically push me out the door!"

It may seem antifeminist to be advocating women-only groups when women finally are working alongside men in secular occupations as well as ministry. Even though I work in partnership with men in other avenues of my life, I yearn for a feminine oasis—a place where being a woman is the norm, embraced and not just accommodated. I need a place to know myself within a supportive circle of women.

Today, like women throughout the ages, we can feel confident in our own abilities to create sacred times and invite others to join us, while living and respecting our own faith traditions. Together we can conceive a safe place for the Spirit to find form in our lives.

How Spirituality Groups Differ

What is the difference between a women's spirituality group and others you may belong to—such as support, encounter, therapy, and recovery groups? Although all of these offer important vehicles for growth, subtle yet profound differences exist between them.

First, both recovery and therapy groups are problem-oriented. People come to work on specific difficulties or even addictions. Their primary focus is on the pain of the past and obstacles to be overcome in the present. What's more, their work can get centered around the personalities in the group. Perhaps you have also attended self-improvement or self-help groups that meet to help participants lose pounds, gain parenting skills, or learn better marriage communication techniques. Meetings are an important source of teaching, information, and mutual support.

Women's spirituality groups are both informative and intensely personal but are not focused on personalities. Instead, they are community-centered, allowing women to explore, express, and develop their experiences and understandings of God and how God is at work in their lives. Just as praying, reflecting on scripture and sacred stories, taking a walk in the outdoors, singing, and reading inspirational books are tools for spiritual growth and nourishment, so also are spirituality groups an avenue for remembering who we are as daughters of God. In these groups, women most often want to deepen and celebrate God's presence in their everyday lives. Spirituality is not something separate from life but a new, deeper, and intentional way to live day by day.

If you are directing a women's spirituality group, you will need to be clear about the kind of group you are facilitating and monitor it to remain faithful to your core purpose: to nourish the participants' spiritual development. Group spirituality needs to take care not to turn spiritual work into another form of self-improvement. Self-improvement groups, articles, and books usually have the premise that there is something terribly wrong with the participants, having women dwell on their "warts" instead of their "beauty marks." They propagate the belief that people can save themselves. In the work of the Spirit, God tells people to give up trying to save themselves. Saved-ness comes freely as they live in God's grace and love. God does not ask women to live up to magazine and movie images. They can be fine just as they are, knowing that God is working within and through their lives.

Basic Components and Core Characteristics

For women's spirituality group facilitators, I offer four basic components:

1. Sacred stories and holy readings teach the texts in new ways to move and change lives.

2. Personal storytelling encourages women to share their lives, identify their concerns, and see more clearly who they are and where they are going.

3. Down-to-earth practices teach women to use the time they have for themselves and God—to slow down and include in their daily lives

activities such as relaxation exercises, deep breathing, journaling, reflection, and quiet times.

4.   Prayer rituals help women find identity as individuals and in community.

My experiences show that women's groups also have six core characteristics in common: prayer, sacred stories, storytelling, rituals and celebrations, shared leadership, and "the feminine within." Because of the shortness of space, I will speak about only two—prayer and the feminine.

Prayer

As my group members begin their journey, I encourage them to make a commitment to prayer, centering on a constant awareness of the holy within themselves and every other woman. I ask them to pray that as we gather, the Spirit will be at work, bringing clarity and deepened spirituality.

When we pray, we experience the truth that God lives both with us and within us. The breakdown comes when there is so much noise in our heads and confusion in our hearts that we cannot be present to God. Prayer is a matter of becoming aware of God's sacred presence in every dimension of life. Simply put, prayer is being in the presence of God.

In your group, some prayers may be determined and planned (written or selected ahead of time). At other times, prayers may be spontaneous. For example, the group may come to a point of awe with the arrival of a new baby, or experience wonderment when a member makes a life-changing decision. Intuitively, somewhere from deep within, we turn to prayer to give thanks or to make sense out of what appears to be the randomness that life brings.

At any time during your group gathering, it is appropriate to stop, take time out with God, and pray. Prayer may be either spoken or held in a time of quiet. Here is a sample prayer that could be said after a woman has shared: "Dear God, we know that you have heard what Peggy shared with us. We thank you for her story. Continue to surround her with your steadfast love. Amen." The group, having demonstrated compassion and care for Peggy, may decide whether to move on or not.

The Feminine Within

The "feminine within" is what puts us women in touch with the earth. We feel our bodily connections to it and try to live accordingly. As women, we understand that we do not have dominion over the earth—the mistaken notion that the earth exists for human exploitation. Instead, we hold a reverence for our interdependence with the earth and God's creation.

For example, many of us view gardening as a spiritual practice and share an interest in herbs and flowers. Women's prayer rituals tend to be "earthbound," in close touch with nature. Your group may want to meet in a garden, park, or someone's yard.

Women are also generally at ease with body prayer. We understand it to be good to use our bodies and bring our whole person to God. Our bodies are a constant reminder of our earthiness. Women's prayer rituals may recognize with respect the bodily processes created by God—reproductive and nurturing powers, menstruation and monthly cycles, pregnancy and birth, and menopause are seen as blessings and part of the Creator's plan. Our bodies are worth caring for.

Adele Wilcox sums it up well:

Self-care of the body directly impacts self-care of the self and soul. . . . When you finally get to the point where you love your body and treat it appropriately, you will no longer obsess about it. In fact, it will be so much a part of you that you will forget about it. It will be your body—your healthy, loving body, the temple that it is.[2]

Group Leadership

As the spiritual director for a group, I take on the responsibility of shaping the membership. That is, I extend invitations to specific women with an understanding that having them decline will not hurt my feelings. I do not invite "crazymakers," or women with overwhelming needs. A few group members may also be in individual spiritual direction with me. Making (or not making) this fact known to the group is their choice.

Generally speaking, smaller groups offer more intimacy; larger circles, chosen with care, yield greater diversity—bringing together women of varying ages and cultural backgrounds, both rich and poor, as well as women with divergent outlooks. Ultimately I leave the outcome up to God, trusting that the women who finally appear are the ones God chooses to be there. I remember that when the circle becomes a reality, I am not forming it in my image but in God's.

I advocate spirituality groups that are, for the most part, nonhierarchical. In some ways, hierarchy—when there are up/down relationships—is a familiar and therefore comfortable way to operate. But this arrangement has not always been nurturing for women.

My task in a beginning group is usually to be general facilitator and contact person. In groups where there are many mature women of faith (perhaps other spiritual directors), they can take over leadership tasks at different intervals. Leadership is not seen as a position but as a cluster of different roles needed in caring for group process. Roles might include proposing direction, offering information, harmonizing for unity, encouraging, or offering alternative solutions.

In a safe women-only group environment, we become teachers and mentors, offering advice and wisdom to one another instead of turning to a leader. We may speak not only of our experience as women but also of our feelings, needs, and yearnings. As we talk about motherhood, seek to redress women's suffering, recall our ancestors, and share concerns about our relationships, we teach each other. Because women take delight in one another's company, we come together as we are, with all our frailties and strengths. We leave the gathering different, more ready to cope with the demands on our lives. Lesley A. Northrup summarizes the result this way: "This strategy is effective in helping women to redefine their religious selves positively, to present themselves as strong and outspoken religious leaders, and to understand themselves as crucial actors in the larger story of their faith."[3]

Be-Attitudes

The following Be-Attitudes are not a set of rules for living or a ladder to moral success in spiritual direction. Instead, they have served in my groups as guidelines and a description of what it is like to live within the commonwealth of God, seeing life from that perspective. Encourage group members to take their time reading through each one, adding their own reflections and stories.

- **Begin and end on time.** Sixty-minute gatherings should end in sixty minutes. Ninety-minute meetings should end in ninety minutes. Many women have childcare or eldercare responsibilities and will sandwich this time for themselves in between a child's ball game and a dentist appointment. If they can count on beginning and ending times, they will plan accordingly. Be respectful and value your own and others' precious time.

- **Be trustworthy.** Respect each woman's thoughts, feelings, and beliefs based on her life experiences and knowledge. Trust that others will respect you. This means you do not talk about each other outside the group, even among yourselves. If you have something to say about someone, say it to her face or not at all. This rule applies to the rest of your life as well. If you find the need to discuss another, make it a hard-and-fast rule to pray for the person before and especially after the discussion.

- **Be committed to creating a community of the Spirit.** Intentionally remain focused on your core purpose of spiritual growth. Continually ask the hard questions that will keep your group centered on relationship with God. Members will miss group meetings occasionally. Have grace for one another in these times, trusting that each woman is where she needs to be. However, also be conscious of your commitment. Put the date on your calendar and keep it for your own spiritual nourishment.

- **Be accepting of each person.** Live in nonjudgment. Know that we seek God in different ways. Some of us do this intellectually; as we gain more knowledge, we come to know God. Others have a more intuitive approach to relationship with God, taking into account subjective experiences. God's Spirit works individually with each one of us. Your way of knowing God may be different from that of the woman sitting next to you. Respect different ways of knowing.

- **Be a keeper of confidences.** With privacy issues I recommend a hard-and-fast rule: never say hurtful things behind others' backs. Keep confidences or keep quiet. As trust grows, each of you will be open to experience the discomfort of both giving and receiving honest, constructive feedback. If any of you are keeping prayer journals, share with the circle only as you choose. Otherwise, your writings are private and confidential.

- **Be a supportive and affirming presence.** Do not preach, give advice, problem-solve, make interpretations, or try to rescue others. Someone may disagree with this approach, saying that she feels odd not responding to the speaker immediately in a verbal way. Nevertheless, commit to giving one another the space to be your true selves. As each of you gains clarity, you will learn to solve your own problems.

- **Be gentle-hearted with yourself and others.** Give yourself permission to talk or to pass. Share in the role of leadership as the opportunity comes to you and as you are able. Many of us don't have compassion for ourselves or acceptance of our true selves. It is an illusion to think we have compassion for others when we don't have it for ourselves. Don't be fooled. We cannot care for others when we have little, if any, forgiveness for our own humanness.

- **Be a consensus-builder.** Circle decisions are made collectively. Problems are solved primarily though consensus. How are decisions made? The answer is by alignment. You decide together by talking through the matter at hand. There is no vote. As you talk things over, the circle eventually pulls together.

- **Be open to share from your true self.** Use first-person language (I, me, my, myself) when speaking. Habit often leads us to use a general "we" when talking. Although it is not the norm in mixed groups, stating your experience as yours is important. Don't generalize about how "they" feel or what "everyone" thinks. This important "I" leads to accountability for the choices made in life.

- **Be honest.** Personal authenticity and genuine community are essential. When we stop using our energy to look good and acceptable to others, to be right, or to appear perfect, we can wholeheartedly put our vitality into being real and whole.

- **Be comfortable with silence.** One community of monks lives in the understanding that silence is the rule unless speaking will improve the silence. What a refreshing notion to the usual chatter we experience in women's groups. Some believe, "If I'm not speaking, then nothing is happening." Silence is truly golden because it is so rare.

- **Be responsible for your own needs.** Don't blame others for your feelings of anger or hurt. No one is responsible for your feelings but you. Ask for what you need. Don't expect people to read your mind and respond appropriately.

There may be intuitive individuals in your circle, but chances are good that they are not psychics. It is perfectly acceptable to choose to decline to participate in a discussion or prayer ritual when you feel the need to be quiet—or for any other reason. The rest of the group does not have to change to accommodate you. You are not the center of the universe.

Asking the Hard Questions

Assessing the "health" of short-term groups can be informal and as-we-go. But I recommend that ongoing circles intentionally set aside times, even intense times (like a retreat), to take stock. Are we growing in our relationship to God and one another? Are we open to the movement of God's Spirit? Do our original intention and commitment remain clear? Are we keeping our Be-Attitudes? Are we having fun yet? Remember that your focus is to foster faith-centered spiritual formation for all but that signs of change look vastly different with each woman. Barbara has returned to school by taking classes at the local community college. Arlene is making a concerted effort not to repeat the past by being drawn into unhealthy relationships. Sue left a position that had become more of a burden than a challenge. Each has become freer, more hopeful, prayerful, and empowered.

A Final Word

I've had a variety of experiences with women's spiritual direction groups through the years—the vast majority good; a few not so hot. So it has been with some trepidation that I've shared my knowledge of how to facilitate spirituality groups for women. This isn't meant to scare you off. My hope is that this overview has encouraged you to begin the journey, as a participant or a leader. Keep in mind that there are no right or wrong ways to do it, that you can be a participant in the groups that you lead, and that everything doesn't depend on you.

Sara directs a large church-based childcare facility and is a member of a group I presently facilitate. She is in the group so she can slow down, be in a quieter space, and listen to herself and others. The circle is a place for her to examine her life. She relates, "When I first began I hesitantly shared my feelings. Now I look forward to unpacking my weekly escapades. And I get to hear where other women are coming from. I've discovered that I'm not alone."

With other women may you find a place that will sustain you in your tears, make you laugh, and heal you, and a place where your heart will be centered on God's love. I make only one guarantee about this journey—it will be full of surprises.

PATRICIA D. BROWN, PHD, is associate professor of Christian Formation and Educational Ministries at Seattle Pacific University, Washington. She is the author of

Heart to Heart: A Spiritual Journey for Women and *From the Heart: A Personal Prayer Journal* (both from Abingdon Press, 1999) and *Paths to Prayer: Finding Your Own Way to the Presence of God* (Jossey-Bass, 2003).

Notes

1. Rose Mary Dougherty, SSND. *Group Spiritual Direction, Community for Discernment* (New York: Paulist Press, 1995), 15.

2. Adele Wilcox, *Self and Soul: A Woman's Guide to Enhancing Self-Esteem through Spirituality* (New York: Daybreak, 1997), 64, 71.

3. Lesley A. Northup, *Ritualizing Women: Patterns of Spirituality* (Cleveland, Ohio: Pilgrim Press, 1997), 101.

Melting the Iceberg:
Spiritual Direction for Men

Donald Bisson, FMS

Frozen ice caps, rivers covered with ice, snow in Los Angeles, snowdrifts to the roof, frozen landscapes surrounded by springs—these are all images men have shared with me from their dreams when they began spiritual direction. Most men begin with layers of frozen emotions, deeply longing for springtime to emerge. They seek God in order to be reconnected to life, body, relationships, and authentic passion; in other words, they yearn for a meaningful and heartfelt life. God has stirred up this hunger, sometimes causing men to reach out for spiritual direction. Unfortunately, after a period of time, many men drop out of direction, feeling failure or abandonment in the process. As a man, a spiritual director, a trainer of directors, a supervisor, and a consultant, I am concerned about the lack of understanding, by both women and men, of men's spiritual journeys. The vast majority of trainers and directors are women. This ministry has been enthusiastically embraced by women and has been renewed and given new life through a feminist model. This has obvious meaning and power for the rejuvenation of an old model based on structures. There is a growing body of literature on women's experience and language for articulating religious experience. There is an unspoken assumption that men find more meaning in and relationship to the traditional patriarchal structures. From my experience, this is not true. Robert Moore and Douglas Gillette illustrate in their now-classic work, *King, Warrior, Magician, Lover,* that the roots of oppressive patriarchy is boy psychology and not man psychology. They state:

We focused as these men sought their own structures through meditation, prayer, and active imagination, that as they got more and more in touch with the inner archetypes of mature masculinity, they were increasingly able to let go of their patriarchal self—and other wounding thought, feeling, and behavior patterns and become more genuinely strong centered and generative towards themselves and others—both women and men.[1]

When a seeking man seeks this transformative space, he must let go of both the patriarchal system and a feminine model, which may not speak to his experience. This is God asking him to go more deeply into his masculine self to find his truth. The soul work of spiritual direction may be one way to assist a man to face himself before God with a truth and honesty that can be transformative.

There is a growing consciousness that men and women enter into experiences with differing agendas, histories, expectations, and prejudices. This insight needs to be more developed by spiritual directors. The masculine modality for spiritual direction looks and feels different than the feminine model. This came to me more clearly as I worked with two directees on a monthly basis at Mercy Center in Burlingame, California. He had a two o'clock and she a three o'clock appointment on Sunday afternoon. He would begin the session sharing with me the many new *insights* he had read and journaled about during the month. He would be enthused and desired conversation on these topics with me. I would hear his insights, probing with questions and asking why these insights had such heart and meaning. I would ask him to personalize the insights into his present life struggles, fears, relationships, causing him to move slowly to the center of his passion. At some point the conversation would slow down and he would have an "aha" experience with a parallel release of emotion. He reconnected his insight into an emotional stance where he felt more whole. He would apologize for his emotional release, which is very common for men, and saw with time that God had been with him through both the insights that had heart and meaning and the vulnerability with me as it came together in emotional release.

The following hour was spent with an educated professional woman with a PhD. Within minutes she would be in tears. She would be frustrated because she felt very unclear as to the undifferentiated *emotions* that would be immediately released in the safe container of the direction room. I would remain with her, probing the levels of emotions that she presented, going more deeply into what had heart and meaning in her experience. In time she would gather her composure with an insight, then experience an "aha" moment, linking her emotional vulnerability with that place in her life which God was touching. She would leave with a sense of empowerment resulting from the process.

These two mature people were visible models of differing methods leading to the same holistic end. I then recognized that undifferentiated feeling is no closer to God than undifferentiated thinking. I have heard too often from men and women that "he's stuck in his head" because he does not have a presenting emotion. It is violating to a woman to move her out of her emotional state because of the director's discomfort or imposed insight. It is also violating to dismiss a man's insight, because he is presenting the keys to interior life—those elements that lead to the inner quest. It is also violating to place too much pressure on him by asking him to melt the frozen landscape prematurely. Spring thaw takes time and patience; otherwise there is a destructive flood. Men know quickly when they are "not doing it right" by sensing the subtle frustration of the director, which serves to prevent them from entering the emotional level prematurely. The directee may not return if he has felt invisible, nonengaged, and frightened by the prospects of releasing too much emotion at one time. A truly holistic approach, combining both masculine and feminine models, needs to be open, leading to the revelation of how God is working in our lives. I have also noticed a percentage of women doing the masculine process with similar frustrations. A percentage of men also may feel more comfortable in a feminine methodology. The director must be adaptable, nonjudgmental, and flexible with either process in order to truly show up for the directee.

Men's Issues in Spiritual Direction

As discussed, many men enter the direction conversation in their own masculine style. This way of entering religious experience needs to be respected and transformed into a holistic conclusion of both insight and emotional integration.

There are many issues that impact a man's approach to God, others, and his own life. I will introduce a number of the most common issues I have noticed in doing spiritual direction with men.

Grieving as Spiritual Practice

I have never encountered a man who began the inner journey without coming face-to-face with forgotten or repressed grief. Men are rarely given permission to appropriately let go of bottled-up emotions and sorrow from their earliest losses. They have been trained and told to move on, bottle up, do it alone, don't embarrass yourself, be in control. To be human is to experience loss, both in tragic and in ordinary ways. Parents die, children move out of the house, divorces occur, jobs are lost, and men either freeze or explode. In Columbine, we witnessed the tragic violence done by young men. Boys who were dumped, shamed, or abused then exploded in murder or suicide. Simone Weil once said, "The false God changes suffering into violence. The True God changes violence into suffering."[2] This is particularly apt for men who must suffer their grieving consciously to end cycles of rage and violence toward self or others. The True God calls men to this suffering.

Robert Miller suggests the importance of grief work during the entire inner journey. To grieve as men allows for the acceptance of an inner emotional world, the need for relationships, God, and spiritual journey with personal honesty and integrity. Without an appropriate connection to the grief process, men are nearly condemned to expand the frozen tundra.[3]

Detoxifying Shame

In spiritual direction, men need to tell their stories slowly, with all of their ambivalence and incompleteness intact. There is no perfect way to become whole, only authentic risk-taking, struggle, and discernment. Patriarchy imposes a powerful dose of shame on men (and women). Shame means I must cover who I am because I will never be adequate. Men are shamed through homophobic fear of seeming or feeling feminine. Most fear ambivalence toward relatedness and any expression of neediness. Weakness is abhorred. The end result is a coldness, which creates the environment for frozen emotions. When men begin to be present to themselves and to another, they will go through a period of intense vulnerability. They must face the lies of a false self, which attacks the very fragile beauty of the human soul.

Philip Culbertson suggests that there is a terrible price men pay for their held shame. He suggests four main costs keeping up a false front. They are as follows:

1. Being on guard.

2. A falling silence except for external areas of success.

3. Protecting one's turf to protect oneself.

4. Feeling stressed and unavailable.[4]

The direction relationship invites the man to be present as he really is before God, a freeing yet terrifying invitation.

Recovering from Trauma and Abuse

Women have done a great deal in this area to develop support systems and wrestle with the spiritual issues. Men are gradually emerging and sharing their stories. There is a large percentage of men who also have been sexually abused. These are the last great taboos of the culture. I have journeyed with many men who were sexually abused by alcoholic mothers, single mothers, both parents, neighbors, clergy, older women, and friends of the family. The secrets are deep. Like women, they must confront the reality of evil, the silent God, and the dark side of their images of family, parents, and church. These are the places that overwhelm. Spiritual directors need to work with a good therapist to help men renegotiate their images of God in the face of abuse and neglect.

Robert Grant, in his book *Healing the Soul of the Church*, looks at the impact on the churches due to unresolved trauma held on to by clergy. So much rigidity and fear theologically and spiritually a result of unresolved trauma.[5]

As a result of war, millions of men still carry the scars of trauma only a memory away. When a man comes to spiritual direction, he brings his entire history, which may still haunt his dreams and feelings.

Seasons of Life

There are particular seasons when men seem to need spiritual direction. Levinson's classic book, *The Seasons of a Man's Life*, may be of help to deal with the developmental aspects of a man's life.[6] I notice three main times when men seek spiritual assistance. They usually occur during the thirties transition, midlife, and retirement. During the thirties transition, the young adult needs to acquire a committed outer and inner reality. This is where, in our culture, the young man seems to have a sense of urgency in bringing adolescence to a close, thus creating a structure for outer life that also renews and deepens relationships. Men come to spiritual direction in an atmosphere of discernment.

During midlife, the man renegotiates his life structure in order to find greater meaning and depth. This is an invitation to interiority and intimacy. Jung stated that he never knew a patient in the second half of life who did not need a new religious outlook. This outlook implies a connection to inner life.

The older man who retires and leaves the workforce will need to wrestle with limits, aging, and death of spouse or friends. His relationship with God needs a final reevaluation and commitment.

Renewing Images of God

Men have unique issues with God imagery. They also have difficulty with father imagery if their own father has been absent, abusive, or emotionally numb. I find many men relate to God as they related to their father. For example, don't expect much, there is nothing to say, do what you need to do and keep out of trouble. I have worked with many priests and ministers who say the party line but simply don't expect much from God. God is there but really doesn't make a difference. If spiritual direction is going to assist a man to grow, he needs to reflect on his images and let go of those that are cold and distancing, in which God dwells in heaven, cut off from creation. I believe men spend time reading about prayer but do not give enough time to prayer. They enjoy the map but don't really believe they are allowed on the journey.

Martin Pable in *A Man and His God* dedicates a chapter to a man's quest for love as care for his spirituality.[7] I believe this comparison is useful, but I believe a man must allow himself the actual experience of love somewhere; a love that is gratuitous and freely given by a man or woman, young or old, related or not; a love that his being witnesses and reverences as holy. He needs to learn to trust in a loving God who nudges and loves tenderly.

Discovery of an Inner Reality

After many years of giving spirituality seminars, I have seen many groups composed of a majority of women given the invitation to close their eyes and to go within. There are always some men in the group, especially if they are new to these experiences, who look at me in absolute terror. What are you asking me to do? I've never gone there; what will I see? Will there be anything of value there? Then what? Unless they have a natural disposition in their typology to develop an interiority, the vast majority of men avoid inner things. This is also tragically true for men in training for the ministry of most denominations; theology and academics are encouraged, but the focus is not primarily religious experience.

I find working with dreams very helpful to men in discovering a rich inner landscape of dream symbols and a nonlinear language of meaning and revelation. Through dreams they are revealing their deepest desires and God's deepest desires for them. Robert Hopke, in *Men's Dreams, Men's Healing*, explores the unique way in which the unconscious speaks to men's experience of feelings, fatherhood, sexuality, and love.[8] Unless a man acquires a sense of interiority, the spiritual direction process will remain too much on the surface of his reality and not go to the deeper human questions.

Relational Issues

Men can be lulled into an overdependency on their spouses for their emotional and spiritual development. They look to the feminine in their lives for assurance and safety. When a marriage begins to fall apart, often to the surprise of the husband, his denial begins to break, not only about the relationship, but about himself, his needs, and what life issues are emerging. I have noticed that divorce has become a major spiritual initiation for midlife men. There are critical dangers during this time, especially for a man not prepared for intense grief and loss. The director needs to be present to the whole spectrum of a man's losses and allow God's presence to emerge. The pain can create whole new responses to life. The man may escape to another relationship, lose himself in work, or choose an addiction. The director needs to listen to the deepest desires of the directee and not just stop with resolution of pain. Stuart Miller, in *Men and Friendship*, reflects the near-tragic environment in which men create and sustain friendships in our culture.[9] This becomes clear during periods of crisis, when a man does not have a friend to share with or be supported by. The supporting role in the direction relationship is intensified because of the lack of emotional networking, which men usually have not created earlier. The director needs good supervision during these times in order to maintain appropriate boundaries.

Ambivalence toward Organized Religion

Though women have suffered considerably at the hands of organized religion, they paradoxically remain the most faithful participants in most communities. Men vote with their feet and have withdrawn from active membership at a higher rate than women. Many men do not actively engage in religion until some event causes them to reconsider their position, for example, the religious education of their children and the handing on of a tradition. Men desire clarity and are more at risk of various forms of fundamentalism. I have had several men in spiritual direction who are in recovery from abusive and manipulative religious systems. In their enthusiasm and innocence, they were hurt by simplistic views of evil and negative views of human development. They surrendered their total personal authority to church leadership.

Men, like women, desire to participate in communities of faith where they can receive as well as give support. Unfortunately, men are not treated as adults in some religious communities, and this presents a difficulty. This tension can become a point of discussion within the direction experience, an ongoing discernment of continued participation in traditional religious practices.

Conclusion

More men can be invited to spiritual direction in order to process their lives with God and to become more sensitized to the internal issues that impact them. Men simply do a lot of things differently than women. It is not better or worse, less mature, more defended, more difficult, and so on. All of these judgments get in the way of simply being with a person where he is at—without blame, judgment, or criticism. Men or women can be effective spiritual directors for men. Yet the men before them must become more visible and real.

I began with dream imagery of frozen landscapes. With time, prayer, and self-disclosure, those images of my directees were transformed into flowing streams, planted seeds, budding fruit trees, and rainbows. God's power can be reflected in the souls of loving men. There are unique challenges for men to become whole and spiritual, but with proper guidance to help facilitate the transformation, it can be accomplished.

DONALD BISSON, FMS, is a Marist Brother who serves on his community's leadership team and does spiritual direction, retreat work, and workshops throughout the country. He has an MA in Christian spirituality from Creighton, an MA in liturgy from Notre Dame, an MA in psychology from the Institute of Transpersonal Psychology, a CPM in spiritual direction from the University of San Francisco, and a DMin from the Pacific School of Religion in the area of spiritual direction and Jungian psychology.

Notes

1. Robert Moore and Gillette Douglas, *King, Warrior, Magician, Lover: Rediscovering the Archetypes of the Mature Masculine* (San Francisco: HarperCollins, 1990), xvii.

2. Simone Weil, *Gravity and Grace* (London: Routledge, 1987), 65.

3. Robert Miller, *Grief Quest* (Winona, Minn.: St. Mary's Press, 1996), 76.

4. Philip Culbertson, *Counseling Men* (Minneapolis: Fortress Press, 1994), 28–29.

5. Robert Grant, *Healing the Soul of the Church: Ministers Facing Their Own Childhood Abuse and Trauma*, (San Francisco: self-published, 1994).

6. Daniel J. Levinson, *The Seasons of a Man's Life* (New York: Ballantine Books, 1986 [reissue]).

7. Martin Pable, *A Man and His God* (Notre Dame, Ind.: Ave Maria Press, 1988), 73.

8. Robert Hopke, *Men's Dreams, Men's Healing* (Boston: Shambala, 1990), 7.

9. Stuart Miller, *Men and Friendship* (Los Angeles: Jeremy P. Tarcher, Inc., 1992).

Spiritual Direction with Seminary Students

Jane E. Vennard

More and more students in Protestant seminaries are seeking spiritual directors. These students recognize their need to integrate their academic studies with their spiritual journeys and realize that without intentional spiritual practices they could forget the call from God that brought them to seminary in the first place. They long to discover their wholeness so that they can serve God and others from the depths of who they are and who they are becoming. Because seminary is a time of transition and intense transformation, students bring special issues to spiritual direction. To explore these issues I interviewed twelve students at the Iliff School of Theology in Denver, Colorado, about their experience in spiritual direction. Other than asking for some factual information (provided at the end of this essay), I had no set questions. I simply invited them to share their experiences with me. Their stories, as well as my own experience of being in spiritual direction during my seminary years, are the basis of this discussion.

Discovering Spiritual Direction

I first heard of spiritual direction twenty years ago in a class called "The History of Christian Spirituality" at the Jesuit School of Theology in Berkeley, California. The priest teaching this particular course traced spiritual direction through the history of the church and talked about how the ministry was continuing today, not only for ordinands and those entering convents and monasteries, but for laypeople as well.

After class I rushed to speak with him, wondering if I had to be Catholic to receive spiritual direction. He assured me that this ministry was available to anyone who wanted it. He gave me the name of a woman near the campus, who met with me. That began a relationship that sustained me through my six years of study. I often wonder how I would have graduated without her encouragement and support as well as her probing questions and listening heart.

The students I spoke with had similar experiences. Many of them first heard of spiritual direction in a seminary class or from another student. Others heard of it before seminary from priests or pastors or retreat leaders. One student had read about it in spiritual books he had been studying before seminary, and another found it discussed on the Internet. Some began looking for a director as soon as they learned of the ministry, but more waited until the time felt right. Whether they began direction before or during seminary, all of them said that being in spiritual direction while in seminary was a gift they had not expected. The experience became an integral and important part of their preparation for ministry.

A Safe and Sacred Space

Spiritual direction provides seminary students a safe and sacred place where they are free from evaluative judgments and able to focus on God's presence in their lives. "I love my monthly meeting with my director," one student told me. "I drive forty-five minutes to see her, and I know she is waiting and that our time together is just for me. I can tell her anything—my doubts and anger and confusion as well as my excitement and joy. I cannot do that in my church or in many places at school. I need a place to share from my heart."

"Spiritual direction is a place where I can be seen and heard and accepted for who I am. It's a place to honestly grapple with questions of faith and doctrine and personal integrity," another student said. "I don't feel able to do that in the structure of the church where I am being judged whether I am fit for ministry."

In an educational system designed to train people for ministry, students are continually evaluated. Evaluation is necessary if the seminary is going to say to the church at large that its graduating students are prepared to meet the demands of ministry—whether it be in congregations, hospitals, nonprofit organizations, or the academy. Papers are graded, sermons are critiqued, exams are passed or failed, counseling and guidance requirements are fulfilled. The students do not disparage or dismiss the rigor of the training, but they do recognize the lack of safety in the system. They can find that safety in the companionship of a spiritual director.

The sacred dimension of spiritual direction is as important as the safety of that relationship. "Counseling is safe," one student said, "but it does not feel holy. The silence, the prayers, the religious and spiritual symbols in [my spiritual director's] office are all important to me. I am reminded of why I went to seminary in the first place."

"It is easy to overlook the holy moments," another student told me. "My director keeps my focus on God and my feet on the spiritual path. She is always asking me where I find God in my daily life, and after two years I find I am asking myself that question over and over in the midst of internships, classes, and seminary activities. Her gentle voice has lodged itself in my heart."

In this sacred place a number of students found their directors helpful in discovering a prayer practice, establishing new spiritual disciplines, or creating a rule of life. One was encouraged to return to journaling, another learned to pray with scripture, and still another discovered a ritual way to begin her day with God. In addition, all of them mentioned learning something about the gift of silence, whether it was through the silence shared in direction, the encouragement to find silence at home, or the exploration of different forms of silent prayer. One student could be speaking for all when he said, "In an environment that pulls me every which way, spiritual direction has helped me stay grounded in God."

Discernment

Being grounded in God is at the heart of discernment, and many students looked to their directors for help with this process. The students who had been in direction before seminary said that they had explored their call to seminary and ministry with their director. "I don't think I would be here if I had not had the opportunity to sort and sift through all my conflicting feelings about being called to the ministry," one student shared. "My director confirmed my call to ministry," another said.

When these students entered seminary, their need for discernment continued. Some began to doubt their call after they had been in school for a while and new worlds had been opened to them through their study and field education work. One student told me that he did not doubt his call to ministry but was very confused about what form that ministry should take. "My director kept asking where my passion was, where I felt the fire. Over time my call to parish ministry became clear."

Many of the students I spoke with struggled with their call to bear witness in places of oppression and violence and war. "I had to decide whether to go to the Holy Land when I had the opportunity, and many family and friends advised against it. I struggled with this for months. Spiritual direction helped me get clear," a student said. Another shared that much of her spiritual direction time was spent on discovering how best to serve. "One session, my director asked me not what my gifts were but how I am a gift to others. This question opened a new way to explore who I am and what I am supposed to be doing," she said.

The students brought personal issues as well as vocational issues to spiritual direction for discernment. Many faced major life decisions before and during seminary, such as divorce and marriage, uprooting children for the sake of their call, or living apart from a spouse while they completed their studies. "One of the most important parts of spiritual direction for me was not making the decisions, although I did a lot of that," a student said. "Most of my spiritual work of discernment was accepting the decisions I had made and living with them with the assurance that, right or wrong, the meaning of my choices would become clear." Many students discovered that seminary called them to examine and often rearrange their priorities regarding their use of time.

How many projects could they commit to? How much time do their families need? What about their own self-care? Could they afford to take Sabbath time? And whatever happened to relaxation and fun? They brought these issues to spiritual direction knowing not only that they were of concern while they were in school but that these issues would follow them into ministry. They were looking for a balance in their lives between work and play, between the intellectual and the spiritual, between their heads and their hearts.

Integrating Head and Heart

The academic work of seminary is challenging to all students, especially those who return to school after many years spent earning money, raising families, and pursuing secular careers. In addition to discovering or rediscovering the disciplines of graduate school, such as critical thinking, analysis, memorization, and writing, the content of many seminary classes forces students to rethink what they thought they already knew. Courses on the Bible, theology, Christian history, ethics, and other world religions can shake a student's faith to its foundation. As one student described it: "When faith and intellect clash, there is a crisis."

"I depend on my spiritual director to serve as an anchor in the midst of chaos as I am questioning everything," one student said. Another told me how important it was to share some of what she was learning in seminary with her director. "I'm glad she is seminary trained, for she is able to ask probing intellectual questions and offer me further readings and resources to deepen my learning experience. To continue my academic explorations in a sacred place helps me to use my head and my heart together."

"I need my director to challenge me as to why I am so attached to my 'A' average," a student confessed. "I could make my studies the center of my life, not only the learning but the earning of good grades. He helps me to find a balance between the academic and the spiritual and warns me when he sees the academic taking over my life."

For many students spiritual direction serves as a balancing force to their academic work. Most of them enjoy the discipline of study and are excited to be thinking in new ways about things that matter deeply to them. They like to dialogue with other students and faculty who come from different experiences of faith and hold different beliefs. They are not against the demands of the intellectual life; in fact, many of them welcome it. But they know they could get lost in it, allow it to consume them, and not find ways to integrate it into their spiritual lives and their ministries. "Seminary education is more about the head than the heart," a student told me. "What I am receiving here is out of balance, and that imbalance is not what I want to bring to the world."

Discovering Wholeness

The students all expressed in some way their desire to bring themselves as fully as possible into the world of ministry to which they were called. They all believed that spiritual direction was integral to their search for wholeness and authenticity. "My spiritual director lifts me up so I can be authentic to myself," one student said. Another said that her director helped her see where her ego gets caught and blocks the flow of the spirit. "He counters my tendency toward arrogance and strips me of my drama," she said.

Other interventions that students said were helpful in their search for wholeness were the offerings of images, new vocabulary, and connections. "When I was so hard on myself for 'backsliding,' a term that comes from my early religious training, my director suggested that I might think of my experiences as the growth rings of a tree. This image helped me understand that what I was going through was not endless repetition of old issues but in fact was leading to new growth."

Another student said, "I've always had trouble with the idea of and the word 'call.' I resisted even looking at the possibility that I might be 'called' to anything. When my director started talking about my inclination toward ministry, I was able to let go of my resistance and explore what form of ministry I was being pulled toward."

"My spiritual director seems able to hold my many pieces and my diverse experiences in her head and her heart," a student shared in wonder. "She will make connections between childhood experiences I have mentioned, a theology paper I wrote and shared with her, an image from a dream, a piece of scripture. The patterns she sheds light on help me see that I am more congruent with myself than I thought."

A number of students shared that they did important grief work in spiritual direction and that the healing was part of their movement toward wholeness. "I have worked in therapy on the many losses in my life, but I had not experienced the solace of taking my hurt and my anger to God in prayer. I reached a new level of healing and a new appreciation for my wounds," one student said. Another put it this way: "My director meets me in my deepest hurt places and holds my wounds in a place of love. Being held in her compassionate heart allows me to heal in ways I could not imagine."

The Way of Compassion

The students found healing and new growth when they were listened to with compassion. They also were willing to see their directors with compassion. "I was surprised one time when I was struggling with a relationship issue, and my director told me what I should do," one woman said. "She had never done that before, and her advice confused me. I told her that, and after being silent for a few moments, she said that her caring for me had gotten in her way of truly compassionate listening. In thinking about this later, I realized that her willingness to see what she had done deepened my trust in her."

Another student told me this story: "My director responded negatively when I told him I was considering going to seminary. He even said, 'That place will ruin you!' At our next session he apologized, saying that he had been speaking from his own experience and woundedness and that now he would step back and help me make my own decision."

Discovering that their directors were not perfect, that they had their own blind spots and their own wounds, allowed the students to know the goodness of traveling with another soul who was also pursuing his or her own path. "I know my director is in a life transition and in his own process of discernment," a student said. "Although I know no details, it is helpful to me to witness him doing his own work."

"My director shared with me that she had experienced a similar loss to the one I was grieving," another student said. "She told me her wound was still tender. I was glad she told me, for now I can hold her with the same compassion that she holds me."

Parting Words of Wisdom

Calling on the compassion and wisdom that I saw in all the students I spoke with, I ended most of our interviews by telling them that this article would be read by spiritual directors who are seeing seminary students in their direction practice or who may be called on to direct seminary students in the future. I then asked them what they would like to say to these spiritual directors. Their responses touch the core of the ministry of spiritual direction.

"You need to remember how vulnerable seminary students can be. So much is happening at once. We are often making changes in all aspects of our life."

"Serve as a model of one who is grounded in God and continuing to grow and change."

"Please appreciate the depths of the experience we are undergoing. It is very intense."

"Intervene, interact, challenge us. Do not be too careful and cautious. Your taking risks is affirming to us."

"Try to keep current and open to new ideas so that we can dialogue about our studies. Your knowledge and wisdom are important to us."

"Be careful not to identify your own experiences of seminary with ours. Help us find our own way through and name the journey for ourselves."

"What we truly need is someone who will follow our experience and witness what we are going through. Otherwise we feel so alone."

"Create a space for us, physically, intellectually, emotionally, and spiritually, where we can breathe deeply of the goodness of God."

"Most of us are being taught to figure things out and think things through. Help us to see and honor the mystery of our journeys. Help us to remember and live with the mystery of God."

Conclusion

In many ways seminary students are seeking in spiritual direction what most directees from all areas of life want from their directors: presence, compassion, acceptance, connection. The difference is the unique situation in which they find themselves. Seminary students are on a path not only for their own spiritual formation but for the spiritual formation of others through their ministry. They will be called to nurture and guide the spiritual journeys of those they serve, and they feel the awesome responsibility of this calling. Students who seek out spiritual direction realize that seminary education alone will not prepare them for ministry. They recognize their need to share their spiritual journeys in safe and sacred spaces, to develop the habit of self-care, and to practice the spiritual discipline of receiving regular spiritual direction. When I asked these students if they would continue with spiritual direction after graduation, they all told me that they would not consider doing ministry without it.

Factual Information

The twelve students I interviewed were in their late twenties to their early fifties. Their experience in spiritual direction ranged from two months to seven years. Of the two men and ten women, three were United Methodists, two were Episcopalians, and the rest were Presbyterian, Mennonite, Catholic, Unitarian Universalist, Lutheran, United Church of Christ, and one student with no particular faith tradition. Their directors included people from those traditions as well as one Sufi. Five of the directors were ordained clergy, and the rest were laypersons. Five students chose directors from the same faith tradition or denomination, while the others intentionally looked for someone of a different tradition.

Of the two men interviewed, one was in direction with another man, the other with a woman. Eight of the women were with other women, and two were directed by men. Six of the students were working for their Master of Divinity degree that would qualify them for ordination. Six were studying for their Master of Theological Studies in preparation for lay ministries in churches, organizations, and the wider community. Two expressed interest in possibly pursuing doctoral-level work.

Although I teach in the spiritual formation program at the Iliff School of Theology, and all those interviewed had been in at least one of my classes, none of them were my directees. They volunteered to be interviewed in response to a request I placed in the seminary newsletter. They all gave me written permission to share their experience, knowing that their privacy and the privacy of their directors would be maintained. I am grateful for their time and wisdom, and I have come to realize that directing seminary students is a challenge and a gift. May you, the reader, be among those who are called to receive this special grace.

JANE E. VENNARD is ordained to a special ministry of teaching and spiritual direction in the United Church of Christ. She is senior adjunct faculty of prayer and spirituality at the Iliff School of Theology and is a spiritual director in private practice. She teaches classes in a variety of ecumenical settings and leads retreats nationally. She is the author of numerous articles and four books, *Praying for Friends and Enemies* (Augsburg Fortress 1995), *Praying with Body and Soul* (Augsburg Fortress 1998), *Be Still: Designing and Leading Contemplative Retreats* (Alban Institute 2000), *Embracing the World: Praying for Justice and Peace* (Jossey-Bass 2003), and *A Praying Congregation: The Art of Teaching Spiritual Practice* (Alban Institute 2005).

Spiritual Direction with the Clergy: A View from the Church of England

Peter Ball

For all its growth in popularity over the past twenty years, spiritual direction is still something of a minority interest in Britain. There is no way of collecting national statistics to find out how many people seek direction or what kinds of people do. However, my own experience and that of friends who offer direction suggests that a large proportion of Anglicans who work with a spiritual director are ordained men and women. This article looks at areas of special interest and need for those who are deacons and priests in the church. It draws on my own experience and that of a number of others who share this ministry.

Roots

Contemporary spiritual direction in the Church of England has a long and varied tradition. Two roots are significant. The first is the importance of pastoral care as a prime responsibility of a parish priest, as instanced both in the ordination liturgy of the Book of Common Prayer and in the words used by the bishop when instituting a rector or vicar: "Receive the cure of souls in this place. . . ." The second is the Anglican use of the sacrament of confession and absolution, with its emphasis on "ghostly counsel."

For our purpose, it is enough to note the reappearance of what we can now recognize as spiritual direction with the catholic revival in the nineteenth-century Oxford Movement. This revival saw the reintroduction of private confession and such outstanding confessors and counselors as E. B. Pusey and Bishop Edward King. In the first

45

half of the twentieth century, the writings and retreat work of Evelyn Underhill and the extensive ministry of Reginald Somerset Ward and others greatly expanded the use of spiritual direction. In the last half of the twentieth century, Kenneth Leech's *Soul Friend* brought before a far wider public spiritual direction as a ministry that could help all sorts of people. In the South London diocese of Southwark, the SPIDIR course of training and support led by Gordon Jeff brought many laypeople into the work as trained directors. What had been largely limited to priests began to be recognized as a ministry fully open to and appropriate for laypeople, mostly women. Most Anglican dioceses now offer training in spiritual direction, including that coordinated by the new Centre for Spirituality at Saint Edmund the King, Lombard Street, London, England.

Directing Priests

In one sense, the work of accompanying priests is no different from that of directing others; after all, priests are men and women both before and after ordination. The same principles apply as the director accompanies anyone on his or her journey: the director must maintain the same respect for the individual, the same confidentiality, and the same shared discernment of God's will in the events and choices of life. And yet certain factors make directing priests special. Those factors include the double vocation that most priests are called to as members of a family and as leaders in a parish, and the unique dynamics of priests accompanying priests and of laypeople accompanying priests. There are also the considerations of parish life, of the priest's life of prayer, of women in the priesthood, of churchmanship, and of spiritual direction under pressure from authority.

The Two Vocations of Priests

Vocation is ideally part of every Christian's view of her or his life, but it lies at the center of a priest's view of life. Priests see themselves as having accepted the invitation to spend their lives consciously open to God and to the needs of other people. This immediately presents a problem: the model is unattainable, but the priest often feels pressure to achieve it, either from people around or from internal urging.

Add to this a commitment to marriage, which most Anglican clergy have also made, and there arises the second pressure of double and often conflicting vocations. On the practical level, this raises an almost insoluble difficulty with time. Management of time is a vital skill for any priest in pastoral ministry, with the need to sort a vast range of demands and interests. For married clergy, there is the clear and often conflicting double demand from ministry and people in the parish on the one hand, and marriage and family on the other. Real problems occur when a priest is unable to recognize the validity of this vocational responsibility to family. Consider the case of Desmond, who was the secretary of our parish church council. When I asked him if he would accept a second term of office, he declined. He told me that as the son of a parson, he had hardly known his father because his father was so totally occupied with church business. He did not want his own children not knowing him for the same reason. Family pressures affect priests who are mothers with perhaps even greater urgency.

Both the parish priest and the priest's family are open to the public, and this results in stress of different kinds. Most clergy in the Church of England work from home. Their study-office is in the vicarage. Parish calls arrive at the family's front door. Our second daughter spent her gap year between high school and university working at the local library. At her interview for that job, the librarian said that strange people often came into the library, and asked how she felt she would cope with them. Mary answered that, living in a rectory, she was quite used to meeting strange people at the door. Priests and their families may need some guidance to handle the influx of parish members who cross their threshold.

Apart from the strains caused by pressure on time and availability, there is the deeper strain on clergy marriages arising from the need for the priest to express different sorts of love. The pastor is called to care for the flock as a whole as well as the individuals in it, which can present all sorts of challenges to the relationship between husband and wife. The possibilities for this strain are always there, but they can be more obvious when people are ordained later in life. Jane spent the first part of her marriage committed to raising a family, then went back to her original profession as a schoolteacher. In her early fifties, she trained for the ministry. After she was ordained, she faced real difficulties in her marriage. This was not the sort of wife her husband, Jeremy, had married and lived with all those years. He felt hurt and neglected that, at a stage when he could have enjoyed a gentle domestic life and evenings with his spouse, she was concerned for numerous strangers in her parish and many other people seemed to depend on her and have a call on her time.

Wives of parish priests face stress from the many expectations laid on them. The congregation may look to them to lead women's organizations, to share the vicar's pastoral work, and to host innumerable church occasions. Some see their vocation as following those lines, but those women are becoming increasingly rare. More often than not, the vicar's wife has her own profession or vocation to fulfill, and this can lead to misunderstanding and to yet more pressure from the parishioners and within the vicar's family, providing material for work in spiritual direction. A director can be extremely helpful in teasing out and affirming a woman's true calling in such cases.

It is not part of the director's role to get in there and sort out other people's problems (to play Mummy and "kiss it better"), however strong the temptation may be. But an hour spent talking and listening, with an awareness of the presence of God in the meeting, can have a healing effect in situations like this. It helps to recognize openly that the callings to priesthood and to marriage are both from God; that both callings are real and true; and that in the nature of human relations, living out both callings can cause conflict. From these recognitions can come a change in attitude and some refinement in choices.

We need also to face the all-too-frequent difficulties in relations with the church hierarchy and the all-too-frequent failings in support networks. Two groups of clergy get a fair amount of interest from their bishops and others in the management of a diocese. One group consists of priests who are doing very well, whose parishes are successful, and who perhaps have a place within the team running things in the diocese, serving as a rural dean or on an important committee. The other group consists of priests who have their own problems and cause problems for bishops—whose parishes are failing, whose marriages are in trouble, or who show symptoms of crumbling under the pressures. A third group of clergy tends to slip through the pastoral care net. This group consists of the bulk of parish clergy, those who are just managing fairly well. People from each of these broad groups find that the time spent with a spiritual director can be very creative and beneficial, not to mention healing.

Priest Accompanying Priest

Clearly, priests who are accompanied by other priests enjoy certain advantages. The director has traveled some of the same ground and knows the geography. More than likely, she or he has had to cope with many of the same strains and work through similar situations.

However, priests who are directed by other priests may also face disadvantages. There is an interesting difference between spiritual direction and work consultancy, but often the boundary between the two is fluid. So much of the priest's story involves the events and relationships of his or her actual ministry that discussion—even advice—about these realities can often stray around the two disciplines. The function of an in-service trainer can also creep into the director's role, under the umbrella of the teaching aspect of spiritual direction.

Whatever its advantages or disadvantages, priest-to-priest direction has to happen against the background assurance that it is wholly for the benefit of the one who is seeking accompaniment. The direction encounter is never in any sense for expressing the power needs of the director.

Lay Director Accompanying Priest

Some priests seek direction from laypeople—either members of religious communities who are not ordained, or ordinary laywomen and laymen. People may feel that a lay director would not understand the special pressures that the clergy are under, but a good director can be there for anyone, even if the director's experience is not that of the person being directed. However, working with a lay director certainly can have disadvantages. One that can be very important is the layperson's lack of the formal power to grant absolution. Someone working with a lay director may need to pass on to a priest who can pronounce forgiveness, perhaps without going through the whole process covered in the time of direction.

The experiences of both lay directors and the people who come to them are positive. There is something nonthreatening about a lay director. He or she is not part of the system, and this independence gives a freedom and space to the encounter. The director is not a colleague or in a position of power. Both parties in the relationship are on a journey with God—one Christian, who happens to be a priest, coming to another Christian. The director is not a colleague or in a position of power. A lay-woman told me, "I hear a lot of things from priests. I am sure they would not want their weakest points known in clergy meetings." She added that being outside the system, a lay director is someone to whom a priest can come and confess.

A lay director lives out in the world and may be exposed to a rawness that does not penetrate the protection of a clerical collar. There is value in a layperson's relative unshockability. People respond differently to a layperson than to a professional person; there is a mystique about a doctor, psychologist, or priest, a barrier that does not surround a lay director. A person with a broad experience of life, gained through both direct personal interaction and the stories of others, can understand pressure. She or he knows what it feels like and can help clergy with their own particular stress.

As in any direction relationship, the question of suitability arises. What counts is the attitude. A lay director must approach accompanying a priest just as he or she approaches accompanying anyone else: here is a human being who wants a companion on life's journey. It can be a real advantage that the friendship is not fogged by a shared professionalism between priests.

Parish Life

Although they are committed to their work and express their willing and sometimes joyful acceptance of their calling, most clergy in most dioceses in England speak of a range of strains on their ministry and on themselves. The number of priests in full-time ministry is dropping, and the age profile of priests is getting older year by year.

Especially in rural areas, priests are accepting responsibility for larger, multi-parish cures. Not only does this mean that the work gets heavier; it also brings increasing isolation to a job that may already be lonely. In addition, many congregations are shrinking and comprise fewer young people in a society where organized religion holds less appeal. All these factors present plenty of reasons for despondency or even depression among priests.

Many parish clergy come to spiritual direction carrying the neurotic projections of those to whom they seek to minister. How they deal with those projections depends on their insight and skills. Some ministers have difficulty because of their own personalities, past hurts, and distorted perceptions. Although the director is not there to fix things, to make the person better, or to act as counselor, counseling insights and sometimes referral can help.

It can be hard for the priest to discern God's hand in some of the warped relationships, malicious people, or weird ways of church management that plague a vicar's life. Often, the only place the minister can face such trials is within the confidentiality of direction outside the hierarchy of the diocese or deanery.

Prayer

A Baptist friend to whom many ministers come for counsel tells how most of them find it hard to pray. They are so busy and so tired. His response is that if for them, prayer is just another segment in the pie chart, then they have missed the point. An Anglican director could echo that observation. Training colleges and courses will have prepared their ordinands in differing patterns of personal prayer. Although the classic tradition is for the priest to say morning and evening prayers daily, this is not widely observed. Evangelicals will have gained the habit of a quiet time daily, with Bible reading and prayer. Anglo-Catholics may still observe a daily mass, but it is not unusual to find priests who hardly ever achieve the rule of a regular half hour of meditation. For many, prayer comes up in direction as a source of guilt.

A director often meets clergy caught up in a dilemma. The public image of the church presents reflective prayer as important, but in reality, its value system demands more and more activity from people and gives little practical affirmation to those who seek quiet. An experienced director comments:

> Whilst prayer is presented as all of life for the Christian, most clergy (and ordinands) find that their busyness interferes with prayer. Although there is much prayer and support at college, few bring away a personal discipline. Few are consistently saying the Offices, which may say more about the Offices and the church's expectations of those trained than the clergy themselves. Some are faithful to this practice, but it tends to be those of a more Catholic tradition. Prayer is often intercessory and frequently takes place with others. The personal quiet waiting on God, the being available in the place of prayer for an encounter with God, is easily pushed out by the pressure of ministry. It is surprising to find that many do not have a pattern for prayer life, a "rule of life," or whatever phrase may be used. Much time can be spent in direction exploring and encouraging different ways of prayer as well as seeking an acceptable and useful way of life with meaningful time for reflection and relaxation. This area is not a major part of theological training even though priests and ordinands may acknowledge that all ministry is dependent on this essential personal relation with God, however it may be expressed.

In the first half of the twentieth century, Reginald Somerset Ward met similar pressures and responses among the priests he directed. His pattern for a rule of life was simple but tough. First came a rule of prayer, expressed as a commitment to a period of time, which he saw as a universal currency available to anyone. Second came a rule of rest, sleep, and recreation. Only third came a rule of work. Ward is credited with insisting that a priest take a regular weekly day off. The church institution pays lip service to the need for time-out and for retreat, but parishioners may have little understanding or sympathy for clergy who rightly recognize their own needs for space to renew their vision and energies.

Public worship forms are a large part of the priest's life. Presiding at the Eucharist, preaching, celebrating services of the Word, leading prayers, officiating at weddings and funerals—all these can be joyful expressions of an inner life of relating with God in prayer, or they can be heavy reminders of a tired emptiness within. Equally, the mutuality of give and response in church services can reinvigorate the priest, whereas flat, unresponsive worship can drain dwindling spiritual energy. Most priests can voice this range of perceptions and emotions only in spiritual direction. A director, as well as hearing and holding the priest, may well be able to point the way to oases where the priest who is dry and empty may be refreshed and renewed. Ministers may restore themselves by going on retreat, sharing in the good liturgy and fine music of a cathedral service, joining a course or workshop organized by in-service trainers, or pursuing a creative hobby or interest. Priests can also be greatly renewed and energized by simply worshiping without any responsibility for leadership, especially when the liturgy is good, as it may be at diocesan and other residential conferences.

Retreat does not feature as a regular part of many priests' spiritual pattern. They may have been on retreats in their training and in preparation for ordination, but they often need a spiritual director to explore with them how a retreat can enhance even the busiest and most fulfilling ministry, as well as refresh one that has become tired and anxious.

Women Priests

The year 2006 sees the twelfth anniversary of the ordination of women as priests in the Church of England. For many female priests, ordination was the culmination of decades of ministry as deaconesses and of waiting or campaigning for their eventual priesthood. It was a large part of a director's work to accompany these women through the hopes and frustrations, hurt and anger of that journey to fulfill a recognized vocation.

A few of the women ordained over the past eleven years had for a long time sensed a strong call to preside at the altar. Most found that their committed pastoral ministry was severely impaired because they were unable to celebrate the Eucharist with those for whom they were caring. Jennifer was one whose life followed that pattern. She speaks of the value of direction over her many years in ministry:

> I particularly value the support I've received, especially over all the women priest business. My director was someone I could come to, have a cry with, be angry, say whatever I was feeling, and know it was all right to be like that, because it really was serious stuff. He helped me to know it was OK to be where I was, in spite of the pain around it all. He helped me to go off and be joyful again. Looking back, that became very important to me, although it wasn't why I began spiritual direction. Direction has been a focus time when I could talk about how it was for me. Most of the time you've got to keep that locked up and get on with what you're there to do.

Since the first ordination of female priests, a new generation of women has followed the same selection and training as male ordinands. There are still, though, some limitations on their ministry. Some dioceses are more women-friendly than others. Parish councils have the right to refuse the ministry of women priests, many of whom tell stories of discrimination and hurtful rejection or aggressive rudeness. The number of women ordained each year matches that of men, but many of the women will be in self-supporting ministries rather than full-time salaried posts. Against this background it is clear that directors need a special sensitivity not only to the individuals with whom they sit but also to the situations in which those individuals live and minister.

Mixed ministerial teams of men and women are fairly new in the Church of England and can give rise to a number of problems that present themselves in direction. One such problem is instances of sexual attraction that surface when men and women are working closely in a ministry involving both care and confidentiality. Another is the opportunity for conflict in the home when spouses share a ministry. Andrew and Catherine had always seen their ministry as a shared one, he as vicar and she as vicar's wife, with all the duties that both Catherine and the people of the parish expected in the latter role. After Patricia came as curate, it was not long before triangular tensions began to appear. It took some months of patient listening and discernment for a spiritual director to identify and accept the strengths and weaknesses of the people concerned and to find creative ways for Andrew to relate as husband and priest, trainer and colleague.

Direction under Pressure from Authority

A priest friend runs a "matchmaker agency" for his large diocese, helping people who are seeking a director to find one. He reports that over half of his inquiries come from people who are in the process of discerning a vocation to ministry. They will have met with the diocesan director of ordinands or a vocational adviser; spiritual direction comes high on the list of recommendations from those counselors. Many of the introductions work well, but the occasional problems raise questions about the effectiveness of spiritual direction under duress.

Clergy who are having difficulties or have transgressed boundaries may be advised (or required) to undergo spiritual direction as part of their rehabilitation. In some cases, again, it works, but it is questionable whether this is really what spiritual direction is for.

Churchmanship

Although the desire for spiritual direction has in the past been more usually found among people of a more Catholic stance, directors are increasingly being sought out by Evangelical clergy. Frank is vicar of a busy suburban Evangelical parish. His story shows the need for a director who understands the demands of a life in ministry and who is sympathetic to different traditions.

Before I started with spiritual direction, I mostly dumped on my wife. For some time she'd had direction for herself. When there were difficulties in the parish, she was very supportive, but she also urged me to find a director. The title put me off for a while. Then I wanted a good evangelical who would know where I came from. For three years I went to a senior priest, who wasn't actually trained as a director, and found it good. I was able to talk honestly, with gentle prompting on his part, about the priority of a relationship with God and to see how central was a relationship of love. It was the start of facing up to the value of something like that and led on to taking the spiritual direction course. This helped me to be honest and vulnerable with other people. Then that priest retired and moved. I might have dropped the idea, but the course not only required me to have a director; it made me realize the need to be more honest and vulnerable, to be open to the importance of self-awareness in the spiritual life—which is what it's about! Now I go to a priest from a much more High Church background than my own, but I find that stimulating. He seems to appreciate where I am coming from.

Conclusion

Spiritual direction is one of many forms of help and support for the clergy. In theory, priests work in an environment that is designed to provide them with pastoral care. Bishops, archdeacons, and rural deans have it as part of their responsibility to be aware of the needs of their clergy and to do what they can to meet those needs. But the numbers involved and the pressures of other commitments often cause them to fail in this respect. So other systems are set up to help priests in some dioceses: regular annual appraisals, departments for continuing ministerial education, mentors, and work consultants.

Working alongside these official or quasi-official agencies is the informal network of spiritual directors. It is becoming more widely recognized that there is real value in a minister's taking time to sit with another person in the presence of God to reflect on her or his journey as a Christian and as a priest. Spiritual direction is in no sense a mass movement in the Church of England, but it is gathering strength.

PETER BALL is a priest in the Church of England. Now retired, he has a fulfilling ministry in spiritual direction, retreats, workshops, writing, and Sunday liturgies in neighboring village churches. Previously he served parishes in the London diocese and was for six years a canon residentiary and chancellor of St. Paul's Cathedral. His books cover two topics, the adult catechumenate and spiritual direction. His latest is *Introducing Spiritual Direction* (SPCK, 2003).

The Spiritual Elder:
The Early Desert Tradition
and the Eastern Orthodox Way
John Chryssavgis

Author's Note: Spiritual direction has never been an exclusively male prerogative. Nevertheless, over the centuries, it has unfortunately been restricted mostly to men in the Christian East, perhaps primarily as a result of popular confusion with sacramental confession, which remains the prerogative of male ordained clergy. Spiritual mothers are certainly in a minority, as reflected in their less frequent reference in the ascetic literature through the centuries, but they clearly have their rightful place in the early monastic desert as well as in the vision of more enlightened leaders in the past and present. While I have made every effort to be more inclusive in my general remarks, the language of this article ultimately represents the overall historical reality and predominant current practice in the Orthodox Church.

The issue of obedience, along with the attendant critical matters of authority and forgiveness, as well as of free will and self-will, are central concerns in the spiritual direction of the human soul. What is ultimately at stake in the matter of obedience is a person's ability to experience freedom in communion with the living God, as opposed to pursuing a separated, autonomous, noncommunal existence.

Such, then, is the context of spiritual direction in the Orthodox tradition. Through a personal relationship with disciples, the spiritual elder hands down Christ himself. In this relationship, the entire structure of the church is revealed as nothing other than interpersonal love in Christ. Thus, the elder's loyalty to and love for his or her children provide a creative way of tradition, a striking embodiment of spiritual authority. In the elder, the directee seeks to encounter a paradigm of spiritual integrity and human authenticity, and in turn seeks to give nothing of himself or herself, for it is Christ who lives within (cf. Gal 2:20). "I give only what God tells me to give," observed St. Seraphim of Sarov, a beloved spiritual guide of the Orthodox Church.[1]

In this respect, the figure and function of the spiritual elder illustrate the two levels on which the church is understood as existing in this world: the hierarchical and the spiritual, the outward and the inner, the institutional and the inspirational, ultimately the organizational and the charismatic. In this sense, the *geron* (in Greek) or *staretz* (in Russian) exists alongside the apostles. Although not necessarily ordained to be a presbyter through the episcopal laying on of hands, the spiritual elder is a prophetic person who has received a unique charisma from the Spirit of God. There is, however, no formal act of appointment for the spiritual elder. Although the elder pursues the blessing of the bishop, it is the disciples who in fact point to and reveal the elder as a human being pregnant with God.

This dialectic or tension between establishment and charisma, between priestly and prophetic function, has never really been resolved in the Christian East but has profoundly characterized the life of the church at least since the age of Constantine. If not always harmonious and facile, this tension has been a creative force. The monastic "flight" to the desert and the parish planted in "the world" are equally essential and complementary. Neither is without its weaknesses: the world continues to be an unadmitted temptation and idol for those in the city, whereas monasticism gives rise to individualism and extremism. Nevertheless, together they preserve the integrity of the gospel message. Monasticism remains a symbol of the Kingdom, which is "not of this world," while the parish reminds the church that Christ is present "where two or three are gathered in [his] name" (Matt 18:20).

The uneasy reconciliation of charisma and institution especially prevails in the early desert, where personal obedience to a chosen elder precedes all formal power relations. The spiritual elder's authority is legitimate inasmuch as the same elder is in turn subjected to and embodies the spiritual tradition of the church in its entirety. In this regard, it has been noted that "there is one thing more important than all possible books and ideas, and that is the example of an Orthodox *staretz*, before whom you can lay each of your thoughts and from whom you can hear not a more or less valuable private opinion, but the judgment of the Holy Fathers."[2]

The Spiritual Elder

The great Russian Orthodox writer Fyodor Dostoevsky offers us a description of the elder, such as he had experienced in the person of Father Ambrose:

> What is such an elder? An elder is one who takes your soul, your will, into his soul and his will. When you choose an elder you renounce your own will and yield it to him in complete submission, complete self-negation. This novitiate, this terrible school of abnegation, is undertaken voluntarily, in the

hope of self-conquest, of self-mastery, in order after a life of obedience, to attain to perfect freedom, that is from self; to escape the lot of those who have lived their whole life without finding their true selves in themselves.[3]

Such an elder merits the title "Spirit-bearer" precisely because of the struggle to be led as perfectly as possible through the immediate guidance of the Holy Spirit, rather than through individual powers or ambitions. This was the authority promised by the Lord himself, who said, "What you are to say will be given to you at that time; for it is not you who speaks but the Spirit of your Father speaking through you" (Matt 10:19–20). The genuine spiritual elder in turn becomes a spiritual leader, assisting in the rebirth and regeneration of others into the life of the Spirit. As an ascetic and martyr, then, the elder is called to "give blood and receive the Spirit."[4]

Orthodox tradition, of course, recognizes only one Father, who is "in heaven" (Matt 23:9), "from whom every family [spiritual or natural] takes its name" (Eph 3:14). It likewise affirms the bond of sharing and solidarity, which develops through the spiritual begetting of others into the body of Christ. Thus Arsenius, the disciple of Symeon the New Theologian (d. 1022), is able to describe the relationship with his own spiritual father as a life-giving bond:

> I am dead to the former world. How should I return backwards? I have a father according to the Spirit, from whom I receive each day the very pure milk of divine grace. I am referring to my father in God. He is also my mother since he has begotten me in the Spirit, and he warms me in his embrace as a newly-born baby.[5]

The spiritual elder gives birth to disciples through and in the Holy Spirit. The spiritual guide is, in this way, the servant of the Spirit—ever invoking and ever waiting upon the Holy Spirit. "Without the Holy Spirit, shepherds and teachers would not exist in the church," claims St. John Chrysostom.[6] It is the Holy Spirit who legitimates the authority of the elder; or rather, it is the Spirit who reveals the authority of the elder as authenticity of love. For the Spirit is the Giver of life in all its forms: personal, interpersonal, communal, ecclesial, and hierarchical. "God is love" (1 John 4:8). The Spirit of God makes possible true unity in diversity, ultimately reconciling freedom and authority in the church.

The Notion of Obedience

The way of reconciliation between freedom and authority contradicts the way of the world and is only gradually discerned by means of a change in one's patterns wrought through obedience. It is inimical to the life in Christ for one "to act in isolation," as John Climacus, the seventh-century author of *Ladder of Divine Ascent*, says; it is always "less damaging" to do things wearing the garb of obedience and service, allowing Christ to govern one's life "without danger."[7] Obedience means carrying one's cross with joy, knowing that one is actually taking part in Christ's crucifixion—itself an act of obedience. Climacus adheres to the notion of obedience as expressed by one of the Egyptian desert elders, Abba Hyperechios: "Obedience is the best ornament of the monk. He who has acquired it will be heard by God, and he will stand beside the crucified with confidence, for the crucified Lord became obedient unto death (Phil 2:8)."[8]

Disobedience, on the contrary, forms a barrier between humanity and God (Eph 2:14). John Climacus characterizes obedience as a form of inward "martyrdom," while the Great Old Man, Barsanuphius of Gaza, speaks in the fifth century of "a shedding of blood." It is a "witness" or "confession" that allows one actually to see God,[9] while the demons try to separate us from God and render obedience useless.

Understood from this perspective, obedience is an absolute response: one gives everything away and receives only in proportion to such giving, as a reciprocal gift, without merit or effort. Moreover, obedience is almost unconditional. Even if the physician's prescription is wrong, taken in obedience it will heal.[10] At times, obedience even seems to be taken to the point of the absurd and irrational; but it is "not illogical."[11] The fourth-century desert fathers stress an almost blind obedience, even to behests that are ostensibly absurd—John the Dwarf is ordered to water a piece of dry wood—or even apparently immoral—Abba Saio is ordered to steal. By the same token, the desert dwellers stress fidelity and promptness in obedience: Abba Mark was copying the letter omega when his elder called him and he left the letter unfinished.[12] The pain experienced as a result of such surrendering and sacrificial obedience is likened by John Climacus to an anesthetic given by the physician while the patient undergoes the cure, and so the burden of obedience ultimately becomes a painful way of reconciliation and an uncomfortable way toward spiritual comfort for the monastic.

Obedience, however, is not completely unconditional. It can only be efficaciously broken when it comes to questions of faith. There is a quaint story told of Abba Agathon in the Egyptian desert, who was once tested by certain monks:

> "Aren't you the Agathon who is said to be a fornicator and a proud man?" The elder accepted the criticism. "Aren't you the Agathon who is always talking nonsense?" The abba again accepted the charge. "Aren't you Agathon the heretic?" The elder protested, saying: "The first accusations I assume for myself, for that is good for my soul. But heresy is separation from God, and I have no desire to be separated from God."[13]

The liberating effects of obedience, which are enhanced by related disciplines, such as fasting and prayer, allow the monastic to "breathe" God, while at the same time simplifying the spiritual struggle against the vices. Obedience, moreover, is even able to mitigate the effort in struggling. Ascetic authorities claim that those living in obedience are attacked by only some of the classical vices, whereas "hesychasts"— understood here as those living in isolation and stillness—must face the challenge of all the vices. It would seem that, for John Climacus, the practice of obedience in community constitutes a protective, preparatory stage, whereas silence in seclusion marks the ideal, more advanced condition.[14] In general, obedience is appreciated as playing a key role in undoing the destructive willfulness of fallen human nature and as leading to repentance and purification.

To repent is to redirect one's intellect, will, and actions toward God: it is an act of obedience to God, mediated by the spiritual elder. It marks a new condition, a transformation. Obedience means obedience unto death, and even beyond death. The monk Akakios, in obedience to John the Sabbaite, overcomes the fear and barrier of death itself through obedience. He is said to obey even from his grave. Obedience becomes a promise of resurrection. To be thus resurrected is to be transfigured in divine light: "I have seen those who shone in obedience."[15]

The Relationship with the Spiritual Elder

The Christian meets God by way of the margins of self-renunciation, in the paradox of self-subjection to a spiritual elder. "Whoever seeks to save his life will lose it, and whoever loses his life will preserve it" (Luke 17:33 NKJV). The Christian lives in light of this precept. One gives oneself away in Christ; and one learns how to do this through relationship with one's elder. "Do you know someone who has fallen?" asks the renowned Palestinian elder Dorotheus of Gaza. "Well, you can be certain that this person has trusted oneself."[16]

This surrender is no easy task. The ascetic needs at times to go to extremes in cutting off his own will and acquiescing to the will of God. The ascetic must go to extremes because of the extremity of the fallen, self-enclosed condition. A limitative situation requires limitative measures. Obedience to one's spiritual elder is not like the submission that one is subjected to in the world, for it exists in the context of love. Without this special personal relationship, one gains nothing but a feeling of guilt from obedience. Such guilt defeats the purpose of obedience, which is spiritual liberation.[17]

As in the case of one's bodily father or mother, the spiritual child loves and respects the spiritual father or mother. Their relationship, however, is not biologically but spiritually based. Barsanuphius of Gaza observes that the spiritual father and child are "of one soul" in eternal love. For the monk or nun, the spiritual life becomes one's whole life and the monastery one's home. The diverse virtues constitute one's family, and one's father or mother is the one who serves as one's friend and "accomplice" in this labor. Barsanuphius goes still further, claiming that the elder does more for us than we do. The elder is the person to whom one must not be ashamed to confide everything. To confide is to confess, to throw off all disguise in the search for truth. In this way, cleansing and purification begin to occur.

The relationship with one's spiritual elder may also include confession in the sacramental sense, if the father is also an ordained presbyter. However, ordination is not always taken for granted in the tradition. Nowhere, for example, does John Climacus indicate that the spiritual elder should be in priestly orders. Indeed, there is no evidence that the author of the *Ladder* himself was actually ordained, though he clearly was regarded and respected as a spiritual father. Similar cases are to be found in fourth-century Egypt, where Abba Anthony and many other Fathers were not priests. The same applies in the tenth century to Symeon the Pious, the spiritual father of Symeon the New Theologian, and also to the twentieth-century Staretz Silouan, neither of whom were ordained presbyters. In the West, too, there is no evidence that, for example, Benedict of Nursia was in orders, while Francis of Assisi was a deacon but not a priest.

It bears reiteration that the spiritual elder does not aim at imposing rules and punishments, even in his or her admonitory role. Although "a [good] manager" for one's disciples, the spiritual elder is above all "an archetypal image," "a rule," and "a law": he or she does not prescribe rules but becomes a living model, not so much through the speaking of words as through the setting of a personal example. "Be their example, not their legislator,"[18] advises Abba Poemen, and Abba Barsanuphius writes to a disciple, "I have not bound you, brother, nor have I given you a commandment, but an advice; so do as you wish." This is the freedom that characterizes the elder, who need not necessarily be old in age; instead, it is one's overall attitude that reveals "everything that is said and done as a law and a rule for the community."[19]

The Spiritual Elder as Sponsor

In a unique and refreshing passage, John Climacus describes the spiritual leader as *anadochos*, the term used for the sponsor or godparent at the sacrament of baptism and signifying the one who assumes responsibility for another.[20] The source of this doctrine is Pauline: "We who are strong ought to put up with the failings of the weak" (Rom 15:1). Abba Barsanuphius writes to a disciple, "I assume and bear you, but on this condition: that you bear the keeping of my words and commandments."[21] The spiritual elder does nothing less than to take on full responsibility for the souls of others: "Thus, there is an assuming of spiritual responsibility (*anadoche*) in the proper sense, which is a laying down of one's soul on behalf of the soul of one's neighbor in every way."[22]

Such *anadoche* may be complete, as Barsanuphius of Gaza and John of Sinai suggest; but it may also be partial. Barsanuphius responds to another called spiritual child: "I care, then, for you more than you do; or rather, it is God who cares. . . . But if you want to cast *everything* on me on account of obedience, I accept this too."[23] Yet the spiritual elder may choose to undertake responsibility only for the sins of the past or those of the present. In *Sayings of the Desert Fathers*, Abba Lot remarks, "I will carry half of your fault with you." Thus the spiritual leader lifts burdens, assuming personal responsibility for them. This is strikingly illustrated by the following anecdote recounted in the *Ladder*: "The old man . . . smiled, lifted the brother, and said to him: 'My son, put your hand on my neck.' The brother did so. Then the great man said, 'Very well, brother. Now let this sin be on my neck for as many years as it has been or will be active within you. But from now on, ignore it.'"[24]

The physical gesture of placing one's hand on the neck of one's elder may point to a ritual practice of penance in the early church, preserved in the present custom of the priest laying his hand on the penitent's neck during confession. The act, however, primarily implies love and solidarity with humankind, for the elder assumes the suffering of others, bearing the cross of Christ (Luke 14:27). Nonetheless, the spiritual elder should never endeavor to lift burdens that exceed one's capacity, for the spiritual elder will account for all one's spiritual children at the Last Judgment (cf. Ezek 3:20). "If it is a difficult struggle to account for oneself," states the *Life of St. Pachomius*, "then how much more so is it to account for many?"[25]

Still, the spiritual elder would prefer personal damnation to the condemnation of one's disciples. Although John Climacus himself does not actually develop this argument, it is certainly implicit in the *Ladder* and can be found explicitly stated both in the earlier literature as well as in the later Patristic tradition. The biblical source is Moses' earnest petition to God on behalf of the people of Israel: "Oh, these people have committed a great sin, and have made for themselves a god of gold! Yet now, if You will forgive their sin—but if not, I pray, blot me out of Your book which You have written (Exod 32:31–32 NKJV)."

In like manner, the Apostle Paul writes to the church in Rome, "I wish that I myself were accursed from Christ for my brethren" (Rom 9:3 NKJV). Echoing this sentiment in sixth-century monastic Palestine, Barsanuphius the Great prays to God, "Master, either take me into your Kingdom with my children, or else wipe me also off your book."[26] And in tenth-century urban Constantinople, Symeon the New Theologian likewise guarantees to his disciples, "I will die if God overlooks you [my child]. I will hand myself over to the eternal fire in your place if he deserts you."

Such utterances, of course, not only echo God's reply to Moses in Exodus (32:32–33) but especially highlight the power of the loving prayer of a righteous person, as the spiritual father or mother is called to be and should be. Thus the prayer of the elder "avails much" (Jas 5:16 NKJV). In particular, however, these passages ultimately reflect the atoning love of the perfect One, "who knew no sin to be sin for us, that we might become the righteousness of God in Him" (2 Cor 5:21 NKJV).

Spiritual Direction as a Way of Love

In opening up to a spiritual elder, one allows the divine Other into the whole of one's life. One cannot achieve this alone. It is necessary to allow at least one other into the deepest recesses of the heart and mind, sharing every thought, emotion, insight, wound, and joy. For most people this is a difficult venture. We are today taught and encouraged from an early age to be strong and assertive, to handle matters alone. Yet for the tradition of Orthodox spirituality, such a way is false. For we are members one of another, not islands.

People need others because often the wounds are too deep to admit; sometimes the evil is too painful to confront. The sign, according to the Orthodox tradition, that one is on the right track is the ability to share with someone else. This is precisely the essence of the sacrament of confession. To seek God may be an abstract search; to acquire purity of the soul may be an arbitrary goal; but to seek and find one's neighbor is to discover all three: God, purity, and the other. "Life and death is found in one's neighbor."[27]

Through confession, one discovers the abyss of sin and the mystery of grace alike. Repentance should not be seen in terms of remorse but rather in terms of reconciliation, restoration, reintegration, and wholeness. Confession is not some transaction or deal; it defies mechanical definition and cannot be legalistically reduced merely to the act of absolution. Thus confession is no narcissistic self-reflection. Unless sin is understood as a rupture in the "I-Thou" relationship of the world, then *metanoia* may lead to paranoia. Confession is communion; it is being able to say, together, "our Father." It is the sacrament of Eucharist lived out day by day.

During the Reformation, far too much emphasis was laid on guilt and remission; previously, the problem was obedient submissiveness to institutional authority; and today, although death, guilt, and institutionalism are less obvious and threatening, yet they gnaw away in the form of frustration and anxiety. This is the age when people die of boredom and meaninglessness. Yet we are always in the context of meaning in life. The ultimate content and reference point of meaning lies in the knowledge and vision of God in and through the other. We all have a need to overcome the fear of death. So when a parent says to a child that "everything is all right," she or he is actually making a metaphysical statement. Similarly, when one confesses to an elder, one is in fact resurrecting Christ; and when one believes in God, one is no longer "afraid, for [God] has overcome the world" of death through love.

Spiritual Qualities of the Director

Some ascetic writers refer to the spiritual elder as a "gymnast" or "trainer." Others prefer to use such words as "abbot," "guide," "shepherd," or similar pastoral terms. In what follows, I shall briefly explore the spiritual director as guide, physician, teacher, and icon.

The Spiritual Elder as Guide

The spiritual elder is one's precursor, a forerunner in the way of salvation, having first entered personally into heaven and seen Christ, thereupon calling us to taste and see Christ for ourselves (cf. Ps 34:8). If the spiritual director has not personally encountered and known Christ, then in the words of Basil the Great, "he is a blind guide, leading to the destruction both of himself and of those who follow him."[28]

In the *Ladder*, the spiritual elder is likened to Moses, who led the Hebrews out of Egypt; we, too, have need of "some Moses" to take us by the hand and guide us to the Promised Land of freedom. It is a self-deception to presume that one may rely on oneself in this endeavor, even if one possesses all the wisdom and strength of the world (cf. Joh 5:30), "for angelic strength is needed for the solitary life."[29] Even in the solitary life, separation without obedience can become a way of self-servitude, whereas the seed

and fruit of obedience are experienced as freedom in harmonious concord. For John
Climacus's contemporary mystic, Isaac the Syrian, only in obedience is one truly free.[30]

A number of recurring metaphors are used in ascetic literature to express the idea
of guidance. The early sources speak of a guide for the blind (cf. John 9:1–15), shepherd for the flock, leader for the lost, father and mother (cf. I Thess 2:7) for a child,
nurse for the needy, friend for the desperate, and navigator for a ship. As the author of
the *Ladder* puts it: "I shall be surprised if anyone will be able by himself to save his ship
from the sea."[31]

The Spiritual Elder as Physician

When speaking of spiritual direction, John Climacus normally prefers therapeutic imagery: "We need a director who is indeed an equal to angels . . . a skilled person,
a physician."[32]

The spiritual elder is an experienced physician who knows, for instance, how to
remove splinters without enlarging the wound. For another Sinaite elder, Anastasius,
the spiritual elder must be experienced in the art of healing.[33] Sin is equivalent to disease or illness, and so we must enter the hospital of confession where the spiritual elder
makes us inwardly whole by prescribing medication, by bandaging, cauterizing, even
amputating when necessary. Trust in the spiritual elder's judgment should be equal to
confidence in the diagnosis of a physician. We are often incapable of detecting our
own disease, as Basil the Great observes.[34] Naturally, a physician can only heal us if we
expose our wounds to him. Therefore, the monks in the monastic community visited
by John Climacus at Alexandria noted down every sin or sinful thought in a notebook,
which they showed to their elder.[35] Anyone who confesses one's pain is near to health,
says Isaac the Syrian.[36]

For his part, the spiritual elder—impelled by "goodness" or by "good pleasure"—
must see his or her "patients" through to the completion of their healing process. Such
goodness is identified by the author of the *Ladder* almost with "a good sense of
humor" (cf. the reference to Moses in Acts 7:20, also cited by John Climacus). Abba
Barsanuphius wants the spiritual elder to be "free from anger."[37] Cases can occur, however, that will test the optimism of the spiritual elder, when the physician will even cause
despair. His powers are limited, and certain degrees of illness cannot be healed but by
angels or by God. Not everyone is up to the task of a confessor. Indeed, "not all of us
are required to save others," says Climacus.[38] It is a vocation that presupposes vision—
the gift of discernment or insight, and dispassion, without which the correct remedies
cannot be administered. A spiritual elder may also give away so much that he or she is
left spiritually dry, "empty-handed" as it were, unless continually refreshed and replen-
ished by God's grace. The fact, therefore, that one is spiritually gifted is not of itself sufficient for assuming the responsibility of an elder. The *Vita Antonii* illustrates well the
notion that the spiritual elder is called directly by God, or else indirectly through others. Those who have chosen him as their elder break down Anthony's door.[39]

The Spiritual Elder as Teacher

As one who has received wisdom from above, the spiritual elder is preeminently a teacher. There is no need of books other than those received through personal experience, written "by the hand of God."[40]

In the East, the church never formally condemned unofficial, extra-ecclesiastical charismatic leadership. While accepting institutional authority, monks, for example, could challenge even Patriarchs in the name of the truth. In fact, a charismatic atmosphere seems to have especially prevailed in the desert, where personal obedience to an elder or teacher preceded all institutionalized ecclesiastical power relations.

The teacher not only should be adorned with the virtues of "guilelessness" and "zeal" but should be, above all, rigorous and exacting, "for this also is the sign of a good Shepherd" who is concerned that the Last Judgment may not prove severe for the spiritual flock.[41] Gregory of Nyssa says that the pedagogue applies "wounds to one and to another advice, to one praise, while to another something else." And Isaac the Syrian corroborates: "One who combines chastisement with healing chastises with love."[42]

The Spiritual Elder as Icon

The spiritual elder stands vicariously not only in the place of the spiritual child before God but also in the place of God before the spiritual child. The elder's commission and hope for our salvation is Christ's very command and desire.

Envisioning thus the spiritual elder as a living icon of the living God, ascetic theology regards obedience to one's spiritual guide as though it were directed to God himself. The spiritual father must be a servant of God, who is our real Father. As scripture states: "Call no one your father on earth, for you have one Father—the one in heaven" (Matt 23:9). In the Orthodox tradition, the first part of this statement is understood not literally but as giving emphasis to the second part, namely, that God is the source of our existence. The spiritual elder, then, whether as father or mother, does nothing more than speak the word of God to the sons and daughters of God.

The desert fathers believe that God looks for nothing from beginners so much as renunciation of self-will through obedience to one who is advanced in the life in Christ. Thus it is sometimes said that if someone has faith in another and hands oneself over to that person in complete submission, one does not need to worry about discerning God's will but can entrust oneself fully to the care of one's spiritual elder.[43] God will then honor one's intent, which is not to reach mystical heights or to have command of prayer but to mortify the will, to die to this world through obedience to a spiritual elder who can, by God's grace, further our resurrection from this life. For John Climacus, this remains valid even if the spiritual elder is not a particularly "spiritual" person. God can speak through literally anyone!

... even if those consulted are not very spiritual. For God is not unjust, and will not lead astray souls who with faith and innocence humbly submit to the advice and judgment of their neighbor. Even if those who were asked were brute beasts, yet he who speaks is the immaterial and invisible One.[44]

Such is the burden of "blind" obedience advocated by the ascetic Fathers. It is not blind in the sense of being pointless or misjudged. It is the risk of faith and the transparency of love, which lead Abraham, "not knowing where he was going" (Heb 11:8), to offer his son as a sacrifice because God asked him to. It was the same risk and transparency and trust in his father that led Isaac to contribute to and cooperate in his own sacrifice, even carrying the wood to kindle the sacrificial fire. In a similar way, the relationship with one's spiritual elder incarnates the relationship with God, a relationship that "allows" for unconditional obedience to the former as an offering to the latter.

As has been noted before, there is a "protective" element in this relationship. We are "covered" by its grace from pitfalls. The spiritual elder, in fact, is present even in his or her absence; the spiritual protects even when he or she is not there. We surrender to the spiritual elder in imagination, or rather in trust, as we trust in God. Our very salvation hinges and depends on this. In the New Testament period, Christ was in person on earth. Now, following our Lord's ascension and the gift of the Holy Spirit to his body on earth, we must obey Christ through and in others. We must surrender to one who is his living image, one who intercedes to God on our behalf. Indeed, it becomes, in a sense and most paradoxically, preferable to sin against God than against one's own elder: "For when we anger God, our director can reconcile us; but when [our elder] is incensed against us, we no longer have anyone to make propitiation for us. But it seems to me that both cases amount to the same thing."[45]

There is, then, a line of continuity between God and the spiritual elder. God is inscrutable but meets us face-to-face in another, in the spiritual elder. In this encounter, all the ambivalent areas of personal commitment converge: obedience, trust, self-abnegation, recovery of oneself, and ultimate liberation. These areas always remain ambivalent, for none of them provides a basis for complacency and self-assurance. The link itself with the spiritual elder provides no "guarantee" for unblemished spiritual life. This is a gratuitous gift offered by the Holy Spirit, which we may or may not accept and cooperate with. If we accept it, the gift commits us, and like all true commitment, this one cannot but be unconditional and enduring.

By presiding over our spiritual pathway, the spiritual elder moreover acquires a priestly function, offering us to God in an act of sacrifice, preparing and leading us into the Holy of Holies. This is a form of consecration to a priesthood in the world around us and within us. As "intercessor," the spiritual elder expresses the ontological priesthood entrusted to all people by virtue of the divine image according to which we have been created and by virtue of the divine grace through which we have been baptized.

Whether ordained to the sacramental priesthood or endowed with the "royal priesthood" (1 Pet 2:5, 9), as all Christians are, the spiritual elder becomes the disciple's

supreme intercessor and guide. The calling is shown to be part of one's personal relationship with God and with one's fellow human beings. Whichever dimensions of spiritual direction we may consider—the elder as priest, as intercessor, as healer, as teacher,
as guide, or as icon—it remains that the phenomenon of spiritual direction, as indeed
that of spiritual generation and spiritual formation, spells the supremacy of the personal over the impersonal. It is not by chance that John Climacus displays such a great
interest in the spiritual elder and disciple as human persons having unique qualities and
particular relations. The preeminence of the personal over abstract rules and ordi-
nances has always been and will ever be a sign of life in Christ as this is known in the
Orthodox spiritual experience and traditional expression.

Conclusion

In the absence of a spiritual elder, one may turn to religious communities with
an established tradition of prayer and silence. Much discipline and personal formation may be received from an ordered daily rule of prayer and liturgy, of labor and
recreation. This appears to have been the chief way in which many persons in the history of spirituality gained inner maturity. The powerful presence of spiritual elders—
who have passed away and whose memory still guides and guards a particular monastic
community—can be evoked at all times and in all places by those who know how to
trust and who wish to learn to love.

It is, in this respect, especially significant to recognize the *flexibility* that characterizes the relationship between elder and disciple. Some spiritual leaders may be
endowed with rare gifts of the Spirit, while others are simply able to provide the fundamental guidance required. Some disciples may need to contact their spiritual elder
frequently, whereas others may be inspired by infrequent visits. One must never forget
the *dynamism* of the personal encounter. The New Testament righteous prophet,
Symeon the Elder, held Christ only once in his arms; the great preacher of the divine
incarnation, John the Forerunner, met Christ only on a single occasion; and the woman
most admired by the ascetics of the desert, Mary of Egypt, received communion but
once in her life.

Of course, if a suitable elder cannot be readily found, then the Orthodox tradition encourages one to turn to the reading of scripture and the writings of the church
fathers.[46] The crucial point is always to look outside and beyond oneself, to open up
oneself, to begin to trust another. For healing will come only once one learns to love,
when one is willing to bear the burdens of others and assume responsibility for others.
Through this openness, one receives the power to transform the whole world, to the
last speck of dust. Nothing is any longer trivial: everything is perceived, in the light of
Mount Tabor, as uniquely contributing to one's spiritual formation and salvation. Then
one no longer has expectations of a spiritual elder—imagining or demanding him or
her to be of a particular type or reflect a specific model—but only of oneself.

A spiritual elder is to be sought in prayer and repentance. Should one not find
such an elder, then there still remains the call to prayer and repentance. Even if any

identification is drawn between Christ and the spiritual elder, yet it is always Christ who remains the true icon of the Father. It is to Christ ultimately that one is opened, laid bare for diagnosis and therapy. If you find a spiritual guide, writes Symeon the New Theologian, tell him your thoughts; if not, then simply raise your eyes constantly to Christ.[47] The spiritual elder is the living image of Christ and begets us into the life in Christ. The same Symeon concludes: "Secure a father—through love and faith and desire. Become attached to him as to Christ himself, so that you may be united by him and in him to Christ and show yourself to be a partaker and co-heir of his eternal Kingdom and glory, praising and magnifying him with his Father and his All-Holy Spirit."[48]

Rev. Dr. John Chryssavgis studied at the University of Athens (Greece) and the University of Oxford (England). He was professor of theology at St. Andrew's Theological School in Sydney (Australia) and at Holy Cross School of Theology in Boston (USA). He is the author of *Beyond the Shattered Image: Orthodox Perspectives on the Environment* (Light and Life 1999), *Soul Mending: The Art of Spiritual Direction* (Holy Cross Orthodox Press 2000), *Cosmic Grace—Humble Prayer* (William B. Eerdmans 2002), and *Light through Darkness: The Orthodox Tradition* (Orbis 2004).

Notes

1. Valentine Zander, *St. Seraphim of Sarov* (London: 1975), 32.
2. See Kallistos Ware, "The Spiritual Father in Orthodox Christianity," *Cross Currents* (Summer/Fall 1974): 296.
3. Fyodor Dostoevsky, *The Brothers Karamazov* (trans. C. Garnett; New York: Modern Library, n.d.), 27.
4. Cf. B. Ward, *The Sayings of the Desert Fathers* (Kalamazoo, Mich.: Cistercian Publications, Longinus V, 1985).
5. Cited by I. Hausherr, "Vie de Symeon le Nouveau Theologien," in *Orientalia Christiana* (Rome: 1928), 61.
6. *Patrologia Graeca*, volume 50, column 463.
7. *The Ladder of Divine Ascent* (Brookline, Mass.: Holy Transfiguration Monastery, 2001), Step 8, 20; also *Step* 28, 27 and 56. See also John Chryssavgis, *John Climacus: From the Egyptian Desert to the Sinaite Mountain* (London: Ashgate, 2004).
8. *Sayings*, Hyperechios 8. For the linking of obedience with the Cross, cf. Cassian, *Conf.* XIX, 6.
9. *Step* 4, 10; 15, 6 and 33. The reference to Barsanuphius is *Letter* 254.
10. *Steps* 26, 21; 25, 49; and 24, 14. The notion of obedience as "blind" will be discussed below.
11. *Step* 4, 111.
12. See *Sayings*, John the Dwarf 1. John Cassian speaks of "indiscussa oboedientia" in *Inst.* I, 2, 4; and *Conf.* XVIII, 3.
13. See *Sayings*, Agathon 5.
14. *Step* 27, ii. 9.

15. *Step* 4, 111.

16. *Teaching* 5, 6 PG 88: 1680B.

17. Regarding such guilt, cf. *Ladder, Step* 4, 42.

18. *Sayings*, Poemen 174.

19. Basil, *Sermo Asceticus* 3 (PG 31: 876BC).

20. *Step* 4, 104.

21. Barsanuphius, *Letter* 270. The English edition of *The Letters of Barsanuphius and John* (translated and edited by John Chryssavgis) is forthcoming in two volumes from Catholic University Press. A selection of the correspondence may be found in J. Chryssavgis, *Letters from the Desert* (St. Vladimir's Seminary Press: 2003).

22. John Climacus, *Letter to the Shepherd* 57. See also *Sayings*, Lot 2.

23. Barsanuphius, *Letters* 39 and 169. For carrying half the weight, see Barsanuphius 168; for forgiveness of all sins since birth, cf. 202 and 210.

24. *Step* 23, 14.

25. *Greek Life*, 132.

26. Barsanuphius, *Letter* 110.

27. *Sayings*, Anthony 9.

28. *Reg. Fus. Tract.* 25, 2 (PG 31: 985).

29. *Step* 1, 14; *Shepherd* 93 and 100.

30. *Steps* 27, 12; 26, 111, 45.

31. *Step* 15, 56.

32. *Step* 1, 15. Medical imagery is found in *Steps* 8, 23; 23, 1; and 4, 28.

33. *Quaestiones* 6 (PG 89: 369–372).

34. *Reg. Brev. Tract.* 301 (PG 31: 1296).

35. *Steps* 4, 32, 70, and 13.

36. Isaac the Syrian, *Mystic Treatises*, 7.

37. Barsanuphius 23. The reference to the *Ladder* is from *Step* 1, 33.

38. *Step* 3, 5.

39. Athanasius, *Life of Anthony* 14 (PG 26: 864).

40. *Shepherd* 5–6 and 20. The parallel here is with the tablets given to Moses on Mt. Sinai.

41. *Shepherd* 30. The reference here is *Shepherd* 7.

42. Gregory of Nyssa, *On . . . Two Gods* (PG 46: 300).

43. *Sayings*, Ares 1.

44. *Step* 26, ii, 2.

45. *Steps* 4, 126; and 1, 14.

46. See St. Nil Sorsky, "The Monastic Rule," quoted in G. Fedotov, *A Treasury of Russian Spirituality* (London: 1950), 96.

47. *Ethical Discourse* VII, 399–405.

48. *Epistle* III, 824–34.

Rural Spiritual Direction

Loretta Ross

On this Holy Ground
Each falling leaf
Is a living story.
The Sanctuary made up for lost time last night. It's been two years since my last visit—two
years since I have "bothered" with the sacred. Big mistake. I've never encountered so many
bumps in the night. Screechings, scurryings, sniggers, and of course, George, our resident lake
leviathan, splashed his way into my life. I slept on the porch after being welcomed by coyotes
and an owl at the end of the dock just after dark. I think I experienced them getting their dinner later on. But you know it was a joyous fecundity that was brought to me after my weeping on the dock for the sorrows of human imprints on the earth. Thank you, Holy Ground,
for absorbing my tears and anguish and turning them into woodpeckers and wavelets, a star-
filled night, and new roots growing out of my own feet.

Joan

I found this entry in the little book in the hermitage the other day. Guests
often leave poems, notes, and stories in the book—testimonies of what they have seen
and heard during their stay in the pasture. These eyewitness accounts like Joan's speak
eloquently of the role of place in the process of spiritual growth.

The setting and environment in which spiritual direction occurs may have significant influence on the direction session and the quality of an individual's attentiveness
to God. Early in my ministry I offered spiritual guidance in urban settings, but for the
past sixteen years I have been listening to souls in a rural Kansas town. Some of those

sessions take place in my living room in a big old house on a quiet, shaded brick street. Others occur eight miles out in the country in a one-room hermitage on a lake. There, through my own experience and the observations and journal entries of guests, I have increasingly seen the ability of the setting itself to become a powerful spiritual guide.

From the desert fathers to the women of fourth-century Rome (who fled the city's corruption to pray in the Holy Land) to Thomas Merton's travels to the Himalayas, the role of environment and setting figure significantly in many stories of spiritual growth. One directee tells me how trapped and closed in he felt while living in the mountains of Kentucky; another speaks of her fear of the wide star-filled sky and openness of the prairie. A seminarian confides his longing to be in the country, where he could look in any direction and see natural landscapes and walk on breathing earth not smothered by cement.

The Bible is often specific about the setting of divine and human encounters— wilderness, plain, mountain, garden, river, sea, upper room, tent, cave. One can read *Dakota*,[1] Kathleen Norris's spiritual geography, and see the power of place in her growing consciousness of God. The Incarnation and its sanctification of creation, its specificity and its historicity, further remind us that *where* things happen is important. Encounters with the Holy and deepening intimacy with Christ occur not in some ethereal abstract realm but in the time and space of this earth. And it seems to me there is no better place to experience that than a nondescript pasture in Kansas.

How does a rural setting inform and affect a ministry of spiritual direction? How might it contribute to or shape it? How might it detract or undermine it? In answering these questions I will look at two broad areas: (1) some qualities of the rural setting that seem to inform the experience of the directee and director; and (2) the role of the director in the rural setting. I will particularly focus on my experience in the setting of a secluded hermitage in a pasture on a small lake.

Qualities of a Rural Setting That May Inform the Experience of the Directee

Effort

The hermitage takes some work to get to. Most of my directees live in cities, and some drive up to four hours to come here. A few come from more distant parts of the country. This setting requires something of you. Once you manage to find Holton, Kansas, USA, you have to take a highway east of town for eight miles, then turn down a dirt road that may be muddy, snow-packed, or dusty. There may be delays if you get behind a tractor hauling hay or come across a calf who broke through a fence. Then you will have to stop at the gate, get out of the car, unlock and open the gate, drive in, and run back to close the gate. Next you may have to wait while the calves curled up on the lane awkwardly come to their feet and gaze at you curiously. Cows are rarely in a hurry. They take their time clearing a path for you in the pasture they clearly see as their own.

The nature of the pasture requires us to slow down and step around the cow pies. When you come to the country, you come to it on its terms. You will likely be asked to do some accommodating. For example, there is no running water in the hermitage. An ample supply of water is provided, but you will have to heat it up if you want it hot—and use the outdoor privy. Before we put in the gas furnace, a stay in cold weather meant a guest needed to build and maintain a fire in the hearth. Then there are the elements: the hail, wind, and lightning that combine to form ice storms that occasionally blow out the power transformer. There are the critters. A lot of bugs live in a pasture, as well as wild turkeys, coyotes, rabbits, herons, and, yes, a snake or two. I may meet something I cannot impose my will upon or manipulate and control with a flick of a switch, a phone call, or a trip to the mall. I learn again who really is in charge and how futile my efforts are to continuously impose my will upon reality.

To me, holy ground, as the place of encounter between mortals and God and the place where we receive our mission, ought to be hard to get to, on the far side of some wilderness—which, of course, can be in the city or country. The point is that something is asked of me, I have been taken a bit out of my comfort zone, and I have come face-to-face with some things I may be taking for granted. One guest put it like this: "I had a lot of time to reflect on our ecological codependency in a profoundly positive way. I like the idea of the privy and bottled water. The cabin lacked for nothing, and tender loving care was evident at every turn."

Ordinariness

The simplicity and poverty of the cabin in the pasture may encourage a simplicity of spirit and the safety and freedom for us to be honest with ourselves and God. There is nobody to impress here. No one will mind if you track in mud on the stone floor or spill your tea on the porch. The cozy hermitage and pasture are unpretentious, unspectacular, unmanicured. I never seem to get around to fixing the hole in the screen door. The beavers moved in last fall and cut down a lot of the willows around the lake. The branches lay scattered helter-skelter. Once in a while I am tempted to do landscaping, fix up the place more, install a pretty facade. So far I have resisted the urge to make the hermitage any more than what it is.

> Here is what I want you to do: find a quiet secluded place so that you won't be tempted to role-play before God. Just be there as simply and honestly as you can manage. The focus will shift from you to God, and you will begin to sense [God's] grace.[2]

This paraphrase of Matthew 6:6 by Eugene Peterson in *The Message: The New Testament in Contemporary English* speaks of the sort of setting that invites us to remove some of our defenses, take off our shoes, and make ourselves at home in creation.

After a guest has spent some time in the pasture, I often marvel at the softness in his or her demeanor. Bodies are relaxed and seem lighter. Faces look younger, fresh, and open. The striving, stress, and pretense have fallen away. As we discover the wonder and grace of a lowly pasture, we may also see the grace in our own imperfect selves and experience the relief and freedom that come with self-acceptance.

The Absorbent Earth

I spent Good Friday at the cabin and it was the most wonderful way I have ever spent this day. I felt so much union with God, joy, and love. I received so many insights into Christ's passion and felt what it means to be redeemed. My heart is cleansed of toxins, stress, alienation, and sin.

Carol

The pasture heals and cleanses. The absorbent quality of the earth receives our tears and rage, our fatigue and sin, with generous mercy. Taking my cue from the Good Shepherd, I sometimes encourage guests to lie down in the green pasture for a while and let their pain and agitation drain into mother earth. The ego and spiritual pride that puff us up are deflated as we find ourselves more grounded and connected to the earth.

The plowed fields of furrowed earth teach humility. Humility means literally fertile ground. As Anthony Bloom writes,

The fertile ground is there, unnoticed, taken for granted, always there to be trodden upon. It is silent, inconspicuous, dark, and yet it is always ready to receive any seed, ready to give it substance and life. The more lowly, the more fruitful, because it becomes really fertile when it accepts all the refuse of the earth. It is so low that nothing can soil it, abase it, humiliate it; it has accepted the last place and cannot go any lower.[3]

The fields and pasture suggest to us that the last place isn't really so bad, that it is good to come down where we ought to be, and that a posture of receptivity bears much fruit.

Medium of Revelation

Easter Morning. Went for a walk yesterday and saw a turtle making its way across the huge pasture. I also read something last night that said having a foot on the path is to accept moving at the pace of a turtle . . . (not my pace or the world's pace) but God's pace and rhythm. It is a day of surrendering and letting go—so renewal can take place. This is a beautiful place to do that among the wind, trees, birds, water, and feel a part of what life is really about. Thank you, God.

Alex

Many of us first come to know God through the created order—through nature, beauty, art, music, and other people. We glimpse God through the cracks, a glimmer here, a flicker there. We sit in the cleft of our life's experience, peeking at God's backside.

> Pouring out thousand graces,
> he passed these groves in haste;
> and having looked at them,
> With his image alone,
> clothed them in beauty.[4]

In this stanza from *The Spiritual Canticle*, John of the Cross wrote of the creation as a reflection of the Beloved, who, having only passed by, leaves a divine imprint on all that is. The rural setting bears the imprint of Christ. Guests frequently comment on the ways God spoke to them through nature on their drive to Holton, as well as at the hermitage.

What a crowd! Red-winged blackbirds with Mr. and Mrs. Cardinal, mourning doves harmonizing with the bullfrogs. The silent heron calling us to stillness. A lone turtle on the float. And the snake: now in the tree (how does it hold on to the trunk?), now speeding across the water. And then darkness, a crack of thunder, and blustery rain through the night. So with our souls.

Sandy

The pasture affirms that the earth and all who dwell in it belong to the Creator and are subject to the Creator's will. The heavens truly declare God's glory. The pasture is not the only means of revelation for an individual, but it becomes a privileged mode because of the expectant, seeking heart of the one who comes. An unfamiliar setting may shake us up enough to create openness. I notice in some guests a reverence as soon as they get out of the car and begin the walk up the hill to the cabin. Now this pasture is no holier than their own backyard. What may be different is their expectation, their active desire for and intention to draw closer to God, and the presence of a sister pilgrim who has witnessed Christ's presence in this place and lives to tell the tale.

A pair of bluebirds so intent upon each other and their task within the birdhouse on the fence north of the cabin. They mated outside their house, then darted in. Once as she sat on a wire over the house, he sat down beside her and quickly dropped a piece of food in her mouth. What a happy honeymoon couple! I watched them over two hours and enjoyed being a human being, rather than a human doing.

Marianne

For a pasture or anything else in creation to be a means of revelation of the Divine to us, we must bring an expectant heart and the capacity for wonder. We must be curious and brave enough to let go of the tasks at hand and turn aside with Moses to see the great sight. We must be free enough and surrendered enough to venture away from the siren song of the duties and responsibilities of our lives. Prayer is radical, counter-cultural action. There are many obstacles to such turning aside. I am often impressed with what a difficult and fearful thing it can be to come before God in this way. I feel awe and respect for those who come to the cabin, who dare to dawdle about a pasture and watch hawks circling in the heavens.

Role of the Director in a Rural Setting

Host

When people arrive for spiritual direction, I usually drive with them out to the hermitage and show them around. As we walk from the parking area up the gentle rise to the hermitage, I hear the sound of giggles in the trees. I sense an exuberant delight and expectation in the angels I like to think dwell in the treetops. "Oh look, wake up. Somebody's coming!" they whisper. "Run and get Jesus."

Whatever the setting, a spiritual guide offers hospitality, welcome, and an environment of safety. In the pasture I also make introductions. "Here is the lake, the wind, the grasshopper. Say hello to the rabbit. Shake hands with the sunset. Keep an eye out for the heron." After a brief orientation and time for me to learn a few things about the guest, I may pray something like, "Christ, here is Jim. He has come a long way. He is tired and anxious about his work. He is a little uncertain about what to expect. So be gentle and help him to feel at home. . . ." Then, "Jim, God dwells here. Christ is eager to be with you and to love and support you. Sometimes God likes to play tag and hide-and-seek. You may discover God's words to you in the most amazing places." We determine when to meet next. I often pray for the person's protection; and then I tiptoe away and let Jim and Jesus be alone.

I usually return later in the day or the following day for a session. This gives the pasture time to speak to the guest, and the guest time to shed some anxiety and become more centered.

Sometimes people arrive so exhausted and overwhelmed that they need time to refresh their bodies with rest and gentle activity before beginning spiritual direction. When a guest stays overnight or for several days, I check on the person briefly each day. This checking, though not what I would call formal spiritual direction, often becomes a mini-session as a guest asks questions or tells me about what he or she has been seeing.

As I sit with someone on the screened porch and we gaze out at the lake shimmering in the sun and watch the breeze sway the willows, we are drawn into the profound silence and peace that accompany the presence of Christ. It is not unusual when I return to the hermitage for someone to say a little apologetically, "I haven't opened my briefcase or read or done anything but sit in this rocking chair and look out the window the whole afternoon."

"Ah," I think, "very good. Much progress has been made!"

Foster Attentiveness, Noticing, and Naming

Chickadees. Woodpeckers galore. A female cardinal rests in my hand after flying into the window. She recovers. Opossum, late twilight, silhouetted against last light on a branch. 3,000 geese headed south, moving at about 35 miles per hour at 35,000 feet. A coyote who sounded like he spoke French. Accidentally impaled snake on east door, gave it communion.

Susan

The setting in which we offer spiritual guidance becomes the guide as we allow it to speak and teach us. City, ghetto, village, mountain, or seaside—each holds the promise of encounter, healing, redemption, and sanctification. I am always eager to hear which voices in the pasture spoke to individuals, which creatures showed themselves, which cried out, what sacred sightings were given.

I watched the awakening of the day. I watched the reflection of the clouds mirrored from the pond's surface. I watched the cardinal on the limb outlined against the morning light. I watched the squirrel high in the tree jump from limb to limb with ease. I watched the finches come to feed, bright yellow flashing. I watched the heron skim over the surface of the pond. I watched concentric circles widen outward when a fish jumped. I watched as a turtle head broke the surface to feed on bugs. I watched as the leaves swayed and danced, tethered to the limb. I listened to God as he spoke to me through the wonders of his creation as I watched.

Marianne

The Greek word for "prayer," *proseuche*, means to hold to, be intent on, devote oneself to, pay attention. "Attention" from the Latin, *ad tendere*, means to stretch. To give the gift of our attention to God stretches us out of ourselves toward something beyond us. Christ draws us to the Real as we turn aside to see the great sight with Moses at the burning bush. Prayer, in part, is that turning aside to see and to be stretched out of myself and my preoccupations toward the Great Mystery. In this context what I pay attention to forms part of the content of my prayer.

To encourage this turning aside to see and listen, sometimes I leave these words from Franz Kafka out on the table in the hermitage:

It is not necessary that you leave the house. Remain at your table and listen. Do not even listen, only wait. Do not even wait, be wholly still and alone. The world will present itself to you for its unmasking, it can do no other, in Ecstasy it will writhe at your feet.[5]

Some persons come to pray expecting deep insights, fancy theophanies, visions, and other pyrotechnics. A gentle reminder that God most often visits us in the simplest, most ordinary things of our lives can free us to see our experience through new eyes.

Epiphany. The frozen pond gurgles and gasps for breath underneath the silent sheet of ice. The stars flirt with all those who take them as their blanket. I learned about containment; from the fire dancing with the elementals I learned love.

Jan

As one might work with a dream by suggesting an individual retell the dream from the point of view of the various persons and objects in the dream, one may approach encounters with nature in the same way: What do you suppose the hawk had to say to you? If the raccoon you startled had a message for you, what might it be? This approach opens us to the imaginative level of experience, invites playfulness, and places us in the company of the psalmists who wrote of trees clapping their hands and mountains skipping like rams.

Witness to Another's Testimony

Autumn. Each visit helps reset my priorities and expands my awareness and attention. This time was joyful, restful, and healing. There is always a cleansing and new beginning. I came with an agenda and immediately had to let go of it. I feel more sensitized to the beauty and holiness of things and people all around me.

Duane

What I notice and pay attention to, and the meaning and significance I give it, becomes a mirror of myself—my projections, transference, and what might not yet be conscious or integrated in me. What matters and what counts to me helps me to know myself, and in telling another I become a witness for my own truth. Part of my role as director is to hear the testimony, to receive and honor what another has seen.

Revelation is incomplete until it has been shared with others. God brings a larger agenda than simply entertaining us with a burning bush. The cries of the suffering ones have risen to God's ears. God is intent on justice, redemption, healing, and love. We may be about to become the answer to someone else's prayer. Prayer and encounter with God equip us to be servants and bearers of the promises of God to others. Part of my role is helping persons to consider the larger significance of their experience and their truth for the realm of God.

This has been a Sabbath time and a safe and nourishing space for experiencing solitude and silence in communion with God. I am so filled with the peace and joy that this place and time have provided me. I fervently pray that because of this experience others with whom I live and love will benefit from it as well.

Kate

The rural setting has its limitations. Remoteness, the lack of plumbing, the absence of a phone, goldenrod, and chiggers make a pasture less than ideal for some individuals.

Some of the people I work with never come to the pasture. Solitude is not appropriate for all persons or all phases of our journey. Others prefer not to drive a long distance.

Holy ground, whether we find it in the country or in the city, summons us to turn aside, to pay attention, to see and be seen, and to share with others what we have seen. Joan wrote, "Each falling leaf is a living story." The rhythms of the pasture and its fearless cycles of death and rebirth teach us to let go and trust. To me rural spiritual direction is telling and listening to the living stories of our surrender into the Great Story of God's redeeming love for this world.

LORETTA ROSS is a Presbyterian minister and director of The Sanctuary, a center for prayer in Kansas. She offers spiritual guidance, leads retreats, and publishes a quarterly reflection on the spiritual life, *Making Haqqodesh* (the Holy Ground). Her publications include *Letters from the Holy Ground: Seeing God Where You Are* (Sheed & Ward, 2000). Portions of this book have been excerpted in other publications. Her poetry appears in several books, including Richard Rohr's *Hope against Darkness: The Transforming Vision of Saint Francis*. She has published in numerous periodicals, including *The Christian Century*, *Theology Today*, *Weavings*, and *Presence: An International Journal of Spiritual Direction*. Loretta's chancel dramas are produced widely in churches in the US and abroad.

Notes

1. Kathleen Norris, *Dakota* (New York: Houghton Mifflin, 1993).

2. Eugene Peterson, *The Message: The Bible in Contemporary Language* (Colorado Springs: NavPress, 2002), 1754.

3. Anthony Bloom, *Living Prayer* (Springfield, Ill.: Templegate, 1997), 98.

4. St. John of the Cross, *The Collected Works of St. John of the Cross* (trans. Otilio Rodriguez; Washington, D.C.: ICS Publications, 1991), 472.

5. Franz Kafka, *The Columbia World of Quotations* (Columbia University Press, 1996), number 31951, www.bartleby.com.

Riding the Monsters:
Spiritual Direction with People Who Live on the Street

River Sims

What image do you have of spiritual direction? You might think of a quiet room with a burning candle or of people who seek out a director because they want to grow in their relationship with God. There are the kinds of images that come to my mind when I think of spiritual direction: It is late at night in a dark alley; two people are sitting on blankets. The "directee" is "tweaking," high on speed or high on heroin. On a street corner a young sex worker awaits a "date." These may not be the images that come to many people as typical times of spiritual direction. The directees are filled with their personal "monsters" that terrify them and often terrify others. A friend commented to me when I began my certificate program in spiritual direction, "Why are you wasting your time and money? You won't use those skills with these guys." I have used my skills as a spiritual director for nine years—just not in the traditional manner.

Join me in the world in which I do ministry. It is a world of drug dealers, pimps, and young, homeless sex workers. All the directees I serve abuse drugs, and all "ride the monsters." I invite you to look at spiritual direction as a gem that has many facets. I invite you to move radically beyond the traditional model of spiritual direction. Elementally, spiritual direction involves being a companion, a fellow traveler, and, most important, a listener. Listening is spiritual direction; in the sharing of life stories, it is possible to see God at work.

By listening, spiritual directors find the "monsters" that have wounded and crippled many young men and women for life. And in "riding these monsters" with them, directors can learn that they are the same monsters that everyone deals with:

In the deeps are the violence and terror of which psychology has warned us. But if you ride these monsters deeper down, if you drop with them farther over the world's rim, you find what our sciences cannot locate or name, the substrate, the ocean or matrix or ether which buoys the rest, which gives goodness its power for good, and evil its power for evil, the unified field: our complex and inexplicable caring for one another, and for our life together here. This is given. It is not learned.[1]

You will be introduced to a variety of people whose names have been changed and in whom I see the crucified body of Jesus. On my office wall are their pictures, which for me are icons, the windows through which I encounter the very face of Jesus.

Immersion/Solidarity

If we do not care for our bodies, and if we do not find a rhythm of life we can sustain in the years to come, it is not worth us being here. Our job is to stay. It is too easy to come and live among the poor for the experience, to exploit them for our own spiritual ends and then leave. What we have to do is stay.[2]

Twenty-year-old Tim was talking to someone one day and commented, "River is one of us." Thirty-year-old Paul commented to me, "I respect you because this is not your job; it is your life. You don't come here and leave us and make money off of us." Recently a gentleman approached me about volunteering, and I asked him why he would like to work with street kids. He replied, "Helping the poor gives me energy, it makes me feel alive, and it helps me appreciate what I have." Last year a young man applied for an internship because it would "look good on my résumé." Jean Vanier says that to work with street people means to come and "stay" in some form or another, not come and exploit the experience for personal purposes. The people with whom I work know when someone is real and genuine, and they respond to them accordingly. To commit time to doing spiritual direction with someone who lives on the streets means to commit to live in some form of solidarity with that culture.

My vocation is to live in voluntary poverty in the midst of those I serve in the Polk Gulch area of San Francisco. My living arrangement is one room. I share a bath. My home is similar to the single-occupancy hotels in which many of my people live. Most people will not choose or may be unable to live as I live, so close to the people on the streets. There are other ways to "come and stay." It is possible to develop a practice of committing time to a ministry of direction with street people and "hang out" in the area where they live. It is possible to just simply "hang" and be a presence. Over time you will be amazed at what develops. A commitment to street people can be taken further by living simply and then giving what is left over to the poor.

Another way to "come and stay" is to look at personal areas of poverty. One seminary student with whom I was doing direction asked me, "How can I identify with the poor, even come close to understanding what it means, when I am a child of wealth?" My suggestion to her was that she come to see her own poverty in her privilege, that like many of the poor on the street, she may never move out of her lifestyle. This young woman had a childhood of abuse and depression. I encouraged her to look at her monsters and thus see herself as a fellow traveler. Everyone travels the path of life; everyone is broken in one way or another and rides the same monsters—people simply deal with the monsters differently. Everyone is in the same boat.

Live in the Gray Areas

One afternoon I sat with and listened to a young man, Sean, who had been raped the night before. When he was finished speaking, he asked, "Aren't you going to tell me what to do?" I responded, "No, you have to let that come from within you." Sean laughed and said, "Whew, you are the first person who does not try to tell me what to do."

Listening is the key to spiritual direction. With people on the street, this skill must be applied within the context and parameters of their lives. Listening needs to be attuned to the gray areas of life and done with a nonjudgmental approach.

Eric, seventeen, asked me one day if I would pray that he not get picked up for "boosting" (stealing) that day. We talked, and I prayed that God would protect him during the day. I made no judgment on the request, understanding that in his eyes this was his only way of survival. To me it was no different than the request uttered by a man during the prayers of the people in a local congregation who asked that we pray that his house sell at a higher price.

Jason, nineteen, considers me his spiritual mentor. We see each other daily but meet intentionally weekly to talk. Jason is from the Midwest. He struggles with his sexual orientation and uses speed heavily. Jason makes his living as a sex worker and speed dealer. He asked me one day how much education it takes to become a priest; I told him seven years. The young man laughed and showed me a card from the Universal Life Church saying he was an ordained minister. It only cost him five dollars. He thought it was funny that I had to go to school in order to be ordained. Jason shares his struggles—his life with an abusive stepfather, his depression. He feels God's presence when he is on speed.

Twenty-year-old Kenny woke me up early one morning in tears when he found out his young daughter might be dying on the East Coast. Kenny is a heroin abuser and a sex worker. He has a long history of emotional and physical abuse. As we seek ways to get him home, he talks of God in his life, of how much he disappoints God and how God must be punishing him. As I turn the talk to grace, Kenny describes my relationship with him as a presence of God in his life.

In each case it would be tempting to make a judgment, to find ways of "fixing" the young person. Ultimately, spiritual directors must live in the gray areas, must be able to sit with people and accept them as they are, and must be able to see their activities as a part of their world of survival. For me what most call "sin" is simply taking the wrong path, for which people suffer the consequences. I often ask, "How has this [whatever the behavior is] affected the quality of your life?" I talk with the person about the consequences without judgment.

Riding My Monsters

When I live in the gray areas with other people, I ride their monsters with them and find myself riding mine as well. To live in the shadow side of a person also confronts me with my shadow side. For example, my history is shaped by my struggle with sexual identity issues. I, too, spent some time as a prostitute. All of the darkness around those issues I see in the people I work with, and I am aware of my potential for returning into the shadow. In other words, when I "ride the monsters with others," I am brought face-to-face with monsters in my life, those shadows that I fear may engulf me. I see not only their worst possibilities but mine as well.

Several years ago I sat in court as nineteen-year-old Shane confessed on the witness stand to the murder of a "john," a client who tried to rape him. He was trying to avoid the death penalty. As Shane described the brutality of the murder, I found myself surrounded by evil and darkness. I was riding his monster with him and also my own deepest fears of violence and death.

My shadow side is confronted when listening to people whose world is full of violence, abuse, and despair. I must have a sense of my center in that process. In order for me to know the center of my life, I ground myself in the daily Eucharist and praying the Liturgy of the Hours. The stories that I hear are scary, painful with much darkness, but they are powerful with God's presence at work in them. In the deepest of the darkness, I find the power of good, the power of God.

Riding the Monsters to Transformation

The day of Shane's confession was the culmination of a long journey he and I had taken together. We had known each other for six years. I met him when he first came to Polk Street at age thirteen, hanging out in the bars. He came from a conservative southern California family and had been emotionally abused from the time he was six or seven. He is a young man who is artistic and brilliant, and under the right circumstances he could have accomplished much. He was struggling with his sexual orientation. During the six years I saw Shane grow up, he manipulated his way through one system after another, lied and hustled his way on the street. He would tell me often that I was the one person who never gave up on him. Shane's family was Southern Baptist. All his life he was preached homophobia and "thou shalts." His early years shaped his image of God; his God punished homosexual thoughts and actions, a God whom he had to please. He transferred this image onto the men in his life.

Through the years we talked a lot of God. Shane always had a well-marked Bible. We would discuss scripture, especially those passages dealing with homosexuality. Over time Shane began to see a God of grace and forgiveness because he experienced that, even at his worst, I would be there for him. Other people often said I was one of the few people with whom he was truthful, largely because I offered no judgment.

Shane rode a monster of confused sexuality, and he sought to tame the monster through the use of speed. Shane bragged to me that he never had to be sexual with any of his "clients." Like most adolescents, Shane thought he was immortal and knew everything. One day a man with whom I was familiar picked him up. This gentleman was wealthy and had influence, and his particular fetish was to get a young man high on speed, tie him up, and rape him. This man took Shane home with him and proceeded to follow his normal pattern, but this time the young man got loose and in fear and rage stabbed him multiple times and killed him. Shane then stole his car and was picked up two days later in Texas.

For the next year Shane attempted to lie his way out of his situation and told me that because he was so "cute" any jury would believe him. As time moved on, it became obvious to Shane that he was headed for death row. I worked with him and encouraged him to tell the truth on the stand and to own up to what had happened. He was eaten up by guilt, even though he tried to cover it with arrogance. Others said he was a sociopath, but my experience was that he was a young man so at war with the monsters within that he did not know whom he could trust or what he should do. Shane was honest with me from day one. We talked on a regular basis over the next two years. He began to see that real freedom would come through his confession and that his confession could possibly save him from the death penalty. Through the process of deciding to confess and actually confessing in court, Shane talked of his experience of God as one of unconditional love and forgiveness. Shane is now in prison serving twenty-five years to life. We talk and visit regularly. Over these past four years, I have seen him grow more at ease with himself. He now experiences a loving presence of God in his life. This boy's story is painful and dark, but in that darkness is goodness and God.

Jimmy, another young man from southern California, was thirteen when I met him. He was the product of a broken home, struggling with sexual identity and mental health issues. He found a good friend in speed. The drug made him feel good, gave him energy, and took away all of his cares. Jimmy, too, made his way through the system, and finally the system simply tired of him. Like so many, Jimmy became totally on his own on the streets. He and I met one night while he was out trying to make money. Jimmy found a safe haven in me, and for the past nine years he and I have been companions on the way. From the first time I met Jimmy, he has been very expressive about his spirituality. He tried everything, from pagan to Wiccan to fundamentalist, and now he is a believer in a God of grace.

Jimmy found himself in and out of jail, like most of my kids do, for petty crimes. One night he and a friend became really high on speed and stole a car. They hit and killed a man walking across the street. For three years he tried to avoid taking responsibility. We talked a lot about life, its sacredness, and how wholeness comes from accepting responsibility. Jimmy wrote the following poem for me to share his journey.

DAY OF RECKONING

Today was truly one of the most difficult days of my life.

I sit in a courtroom and listen to a family tell me how much they hate me, how I am such a terrible person, how I should be dead instead of their relative.

Most would take offense to some of the words they said to me today.

Yet I understand—Should I be dead? Am I a terrible person?

In their eyes, yes, I am a monster and anyone else would feel the same when a family member dies a horrible death.

However, in the eyes of my family and those who truly know me, I am a beautiful person.

A person that loves and is capable of being loved.

A truly intelligent person.

A person of indescribable courage and stamina, and who deserves to start over.

Fallen to a terrible situation, a tragic accident.

A victim of circumstance in the eyes of some.

A murderer in the eyes of others.

Everyone involved here is a victim, including myself.

I don't want to sound selfish to say such things, but it hurts me too.

If you must be angry with someone, let it be the Creator, because it is He who decides when and where one shall pass.

I came back from court today and soon fell asleep.

I am haunted with the nightmare of the mother of the deceased making her statement in court.

Only in my dream she screams it instead of cries it.

Followed by her pulling a gun from her coat and shooting me through my left eye.

I am outside my body as I watch her disintegrate.

Then I awake, dinnertime. Yet if dreams only last a few seconds, then where did all those hours go before this terrible nightmare?

Absolute peaceful slumber.

And so follows the story of my life:

Peace followed by complete and utter destruction, then restored to a sense of peace.

I am now in the third stage of my life.

And so it shall stay.

But for all of this, still I am sorry.

This is my day of reckoning.

(October 29, 2002)

The stories of Shane and Jimmy illustrate the essence of spiritual direction with people on the street. Spiritual direction is a commitment to a journey of listening and companioning, and it is a commitment to riding monsters. My commitment in spiritual direction is one of being a continual presence with the "directees," being willing to journey with them in their darkness, and being willing to stay with them and not abandon them. I must do so without judgment and see each person as he or she is— a broken child of God and the very image of Jesus. In the deepest darkness of others, I see my own deepest darkness. In riding their monsters, I ride my own. By riding my monsters, I get in touch with those gifts that allow me to be their companion. By experiencing my darkness and remembering my suffering, I can identify with them as fellow human beings.

Have you never thought of killing someone you were angry at, stealing something, or acting out some weird, kinky sex fetish? Everyone has, and when you face the monsters, you acknowledge your darkest capabilities and stand on the brink. This edge is a place of grace. It helps me to know that my companion and I are simply fellow travelers. How can I judge? I may be able to decide that the consequences are not worth the action, but I realize it is only this thin line that separates me from a person on the street. As Will Campbell, noted Baptist minister and civil rights activist, is fond of saying: "I know that God has forgiven me, for God forgives all bastards, and I am the biggest bastard of all." By acknowledging my oneness with humanity, I find the power of God most at work. I become a companion on the way.

Holding the Hope

During the year 2002, I celebrated memorial services for thirty-two young men and women, the oldest of whom was twenty-seven. The young men and women I work with are called "fatalities" by the system because they are incorrigible, they do not follow the rules, and for the most part they will either remain on the street or die young. My call as a spiritual director is to hold the hope, to be threatened with the resurrection. As a counselor, I know that I am often a container for people's anger and fear and also their hope. When those who are hurting cannot hold their anger, their fear, or their hope, I hold it for them.

> Accompany us then on this vigil
> and you will know what it is to dream!
> You will then know
> how marvelous it is
> to live threatened with Resurrection!
> To dream awake,
> to keep watch asleep,
> to live while dying
> and to know oneself resurrected![3]

In the same way, spiritual companions for people on the street hold the hope. Like the author of the poem above, spiritual directors allow themselves to be "threatened with Resurrection" and hold on to the promise of the Risen One, that in death of any sort there is life. To be "threatened with Resurrection" is to know that everyone is in God's hands, that all will be well in the end.

In that confidence, I move forth in taking risks, going where others may fear to tread, and working for justice in radical ways. For me this risk-taking has meant doing needle exchanges, living from day to day not knowing where my next meal might come from, and being a presence in a nontraditional manner with people whom others tend to fear. To be "threatened with Resurrection" means to be in community with others and get my hands dirty, knowing that there is life in God through the resurrection.

Conclusion

Spiritual companioning with street people is a call to set aside traditional expectations and to "ride the monsters" while holding on to hope. It is a call that is both challenging and fearful. It will threaten spiritual directors with resurrection.

RIVER SIMS is a priest of the American Catholic Church of New England. He has a Master of Divinity degree and a Doctor of Sacred Theology degree. Fr. Sims is the founder and director of Temenos Catholic Worker in San Francisco, California. Temenos is a pastoral ministry of presence to young adults and homeless youth in San Francisco.

Notes

1. Annie Dilliard, *Teaching a Stone to Talk: Expedition and Encounters* (San Francisco: Harper, 1988), 25ff.

2. Jean Vanier, *Community and Growth: Our Pilgrimage Together* (New York: Paulist, 1989), 105.

3. Julia Esquivel, *Threatened with Resurrection: Poems of an Exile Guatemalan* (Elgin, Ill.: Brethren Press, 1994), 35.

A Little Soul Work
Does a Hospital Well:
Spiritual Direction in Health Care

Gordon Self

Why is this happening to me?" For the third time, Tom pointed angrily at his watch, saying it was almost to the exact hour he was first diagnosed with kidney cancer—just one week ago. His surgery was scheduled for Monday, leaving us only this introductory meeting in the pre-op clinic Friday afternoon to talk about his fears and concerns and how he felt abandoned by God. Tom and his wife, Irene, admitted feeling bitter, blaming God for yet another family crisis, hitting them, proverbially, like a blow to the back of the head. "Where is this God when I need him?"

As a hospital chaplain, I have heard these questions often. Patients find themselves reevaluating priorities and meaning in their lives in the face of medical crises. Suddenly catapulted into the unknown, some are challenged to draw deeper from the well of their faith; others go in search for a God to call their own. Illness is the great leveler, having the power to stop us in our tracks, regardless of what side of the tracks we come from. We all look much the same in those open-backed hospital gowns.

In one week Tom's life had unraveled before him. He prided himself in having pulled the boat out at the lake, in addition to chopping and stacking wood the weekend he first noticed his symptoms appear. Now he was wondering if he would ever see his cottage again. For Tom and other patients, the distortion of self-image and identity makes illness difficult to embrace. We do not pencil illness in among the many "to do" items listed in our day planners, nor do we allow for the usual soul-searching questions that accompany hospitalization. More likely, illness is viewed as an unwelcome interruption in the rhythm of our lives. Unwittingly, the hospital has become the modern-day monastery, for it is within these walls that we size up the meaning and value of our lives.

Or at least it used to be. The current health-care reforms in Canada and the US have seen a growing number of patients moving through the hospital faster than ever before. Reduced length of stay, same-day admissions, and outpatient clinics have changed the profile of the general patient population. This in turn has altered the "window of opportunity" in my work as a hospital chaplain. Regrettably, there was only one chance to talk with Tom before surgery. Just seeing patients once is a gift, let alone spending adequate follow-up time to really listen to their experience. Let's face it, you have to be pretty sick to get into a hospital these days, and if you are admitted, you're often too ill to be able to delve into the spiritual questions aroused. Watch an episode of a medical drama, for example, and try to imagine quiet, contemplative "holy listening" unfolding amid bells, alarms, and the guttural sounds of patients throwing up!

Ministry to Patients

Called to both ministries, I have often wondered about the relationship between pastoral care and spiritual direction. Are these pastoral encounters in the hospital, fleeting as they may be, an opportunity for spiritual direction? Is the patient guided further along his or her spiritual path, analogous to someone in a car slowing down to ask a passerby on the street for directions?

Certainly these experiences can be no less sacred, unforgettable, and pregnant with meaning than the contemplative moments sitting opposite the directee in the sunroom of my home. In both environments God's purpose is more clearly discerned and a sense of direction gleaned. But my experience also tells me that many chaplain visits with patients are too transient to be adequately deemed "spiritual direction" in the formal sense of the term. My wife is always my reality check when it comes to patients' needs. After twenty years of nursing, she reminds me that some patients simply want to "get their big toe fixed." They're not here to talk about God.

Because their stays are so brief, many patients are barely aware of what those spiritual questions are while in hospital. A clearer sense of what's happened and the implications their illness holds often only comes after they've gone home. The reality is that many are in a state of shock. The concern is just to "get through" the proce-dure, to complete the test, to stabilize medications, and to go home. It's at home that the numbness lifts and the questioning begins. My father began to confront the spiri-tual dimensions of prostate cancer the day he finished his last radiotherapy treatment. Or as another cancer survivor declared when reflecting on his journey, "I came to the hospital to be cured. I went home to be healed."

This is not to say profound spiritual encounters are never shared during these short hospital stays. Like Tom, a person may face his or her deepest fears before sur-gery, or discover the strength of his or her faith in struggling to accept the diagnosis. It is now, at this hour, in this hospital room, that the patient needs someone to listen. Tomorrow might be too late. I have heard echoed in many such brief encounters the psalmist's cry, the anguish of lament, or the surprise and awe of God's grace simply by sitting next to the patient at the bedside, listening. Many such moments have lasting impact. The woman at the well comes to mind (John 4:7–30). Her brief exchange with Jesus challenged her to draw deeper from the well of her faith. Like the Samaritan woman, we often refer back to these watershed moments throughout our lives, continuing to unpack meaning.

The challenge for institutional pastoral care is to move where modern health care is moving—into the community. As more centers become known as "hospitals without walls," pastoral care departments are challenged to restructure and revision their own delivery of care to meet the patients where they are: hence "patient-focused care." But while pastoral care is invited to move in this direction, perhaps finding ways and means to accompany patients in a more traditional spiritual direction role, it's unlikely to happen in the current hospital milieu. Is there nevertheless still a role for spiritual direction in the modern hospital? For whom? In what context?

Ministry to Staff

The lament still sounds: "Where are you, God, when I need you now?" This time it is not the patient I hear crying out, but a staff member. Amid the endless sea of patients coming through the revolving door of the hospital, the staff remains the relative constant. It's staff members whom you really get to know; day in and day out, they come to work with their family problems, crises of faith, and search for meaning in this frantic world of health care. In fact, it was only when I finally heard Diane, a nurse, that my whole attitude and focus of ministry in the hospital changed. On a particularly busy pre-op clinic day, she sat down next to me in the chart room, frustrated and upset with trying to keep on top of things. She continued to vent, oblivious to my own distraction and frustration. "They don't understand. . . . How can they say we're doing good patient care when we're not! I have three patients coming back from surgery at the same time, while I'm trying to cover the rest of my assignment."

I didn't want to listen to this. I was too busy myself, needing to finish charting before I was called to see the next patient. But in that struggle something shifted. I was worrying about trying to chart, doubting anyone would ever bother to read it anyway, while a person was falling apart next to me. Whom was God calling me to be with in that moment? I felt guilty and, at the same time, surprisingly affirmed, resolving never to ignore the needs of the staff again. It is in the long-term commitment to ministering alongside the staff, while sitting next to people like Diane in the chart rooms of the hospital, that a chaplain begins to hear the deeper questions and sense the movement of the Spirit in the organization. This is the family I'm called to live and work with in the busy hospital world.

Although a recent hospital survey indicated a high degree of patient satisfaction with the services provided, a much different perception is held by the staff. Employees increasingly feel frustrated and powerless, pointing to the patients lining the hallways outside the emergency room waiting to be seen as a sign of a system gone very wrong. The discrepancy between what the mission and core values say and the reality of the staff's working experience have prompted some to ask, "Is our hospital losing its soul?" Having a mission statement in the corridors and a crucifix adorning the walls of patients' rooms is not enough. Feeling demoralized and devalued, staff members turn to their founders and to their chaplains for answers. They want to know if there is still something to believe in and whether, as staff, they can make a difference.

Finding a Living Mission

The health-care crisis throughout North America requires more than a nostalgic look back at where we have come from and what we stand for. This is a system undergoing major reform, including a long period of downsizing, bed shortages, hospital closures, and program deletions. This has undermined the morale of the staff as well as the public's trust in the health-care system. Spiritual direction in the hospital and, indeed, within any organization having survived the 1990s economic bust, requires sensitivity to this overall malaise.

It is revealing, nonetheless, that even in the midst of these difficulties, the hospital is still viewed as a corporate body with a soul. The question remains: If the hospital has a soul, is it not possible this same soul is also on a journey, one requiring the skill and grace involved in spiritual accompaniment? The growing interest in corporate spiritual direction would seem to argue a resounding "Yes." A hospital's soul, if in danger of being lost, presumably must first exist and, in turn, be one capable of guidance.

Mission awareness—which has been historically very important in faith-based institutions—requires more than a simple proclamation of statements. Arguably, this approach may have worked well in a relatively stable, overtly visible Christian culture, where reference to the founding story was enough to rekindle passion for the mission and to sustain the staff in its difficult ministry to the sick.

Today, however, a different religious culture exists. Sociologist Reginald Bibby has described the slow, steady decline of religious practices in Canada as a process of dismantling and fragmentation of the gods. He argues that Canadians no longer view faith as a system of meaning informing all of their lives. Instead, our culture has moved toward a religious smorgasbord of beliefs and piecemeal spirituality, lacking traditional values and roots. Bibby points out only 25 percent of Canadians attend church every week or more, less than half the reported number from the mid-1950s. By the year 2015 he projects only 15 percent of the population will be attending church regularly.

In this context, hospital mission activities relying exclusively on the founding story are no longer meaningful for many staff members. The founding story of the hospital is less effective and meaningful because it is no longer viewed as *the* story but only one story among many for people to identify with. Mission strategies must work with this current religious culture to help staff members integrate the many stories into a coherent whole—a story they can call their own. Appealing to historic or religious authority, without helping staff members to appreciate the meaning of the story for them today, simply won't work. This approach to mission runs the risk of being dismissed—at best, as quaint and tolerable; at worst, as preachy and offensive.

At the same time, it will do no good to throw the baby out with the bathwater. Despite the smorgasbord religious mentality, our roots and history should not be devalued. Bibby insists the greatest hope for religion is to transform culture, not mirror it, while remaining relevant and involved. Staying connected to the founding story is essential in critically interpreting corporate policy and decisions. The challenge is to own, celebrate, and claim our mission, articulating it in a language that can be understood. This must begin with the lived experience of the staff.

Mission Possible

In response to this challenge, I see signs of a meaningful mission language beginning to emerge. I believe this is a necessary foundation for spiritual direction in the organization, whether on an individual or corporate level. Mission activities in our hospital are slowly moving away from a nostalgic view to a more palatable "in the trenches with the troops" approach, in which a certain credibility and meaning can be felt.

Newsletter

Our hospital mission newsletter, for example, follows a "Dear Abby" question-and-answer format, drawing together comments heard in daily conversations with staff members. It is a nonthreatening way to acknowledge the various feelings of staff members who are trying to live out the mission in the midst of difficult circumstances. Letters signed "Perplexed" or "Feeling Unappreciated" or "Depressed and Disgusted" are answered using everyday language, trying to offer a little perspective without dismissing or minimizing the feelings expressed. Staff members feel someone is actually listening.

Staff members feel heard because their efforts are recognized and honored as a tangible manifestation of the mission at work. They are encouraged to continue making a difference, because by having their experience validated, staff members themselves feel different about what they do. We all need a little feedback. It is easy to give up when no one is telling us we're doing a good job.

Daisy Program

Other occasions arise when staff members are publicly acknowledged for their commitment to the mission. Long-service recognition, research and clinical breakthroughs, and communal ward blessings ritualizing a team's specialized care with stories, prayers, and celebration are all efforts to affirm the staff. But perhaps the most successful mission initiative has been the Daisy Program. Staff members who have gone beyond the call of duty are recommended by their peers for a "daisy," a brightly colored lapel pin designed in the symbol of the corporate founders. Those who have been given a daisy proudly wear it on their uniform, serving as an inspiration for other staff members to continue striving for excellence.

Staff Lunches

Staff members still need an opportunity to express their feelings and talk about their experiences, especially during this time of major change. Many health-care workers put their hearts and souls into their work, sometimes to their own detriment. It is not surprising, then, that the level of conversations among staff members moves to such depths. Recognizing this, we ventured to do some further soul work with an advertisement for a brown bag lunch, posing the following questions:

"Is it harder for you to come to work each day?"

"Do you wonder if you are making a difference?"

"Is [our hospital] losing its soul?"

We invited the staff to gather in the hospital for lunch once per week, sharing their responses to these questions. We asked how people felt sustained in their work and where they may have also experienced a diminishment of spirit. We noted that even if only a handful of people attended, advertising in such a way that named people's experience would be valuable and affirming.

Using a lectio-style format, we began with a story, purposely chosen so that it was both imaginative and inclusive. After a period of silence, the facilitator would invite participants to reflect on the story itself, helping notice and underscore their own felt responses. While some remained silent, opting not to return to subsequent sessions, others continued to come regularly, sharing openly their hunger for meaning and purpose in their hospital work. The facilitator reflected back what was being shared, not only in relation to the individual's experience but also in relation to the collective experience of the wider hospital community, helping to notice where we are being called as an organization.

As always, the timing of these gatherings is crucial. Some people are simply too busy or too exhausted to give more of themselves over a lunch period, even when the purpose of the gathering is for staff spiritual renewal. This is simply the limitation and reality of nurturing spirituality in the workplace.

We realized in these sessions that, although the staff has a good understanding of the hospital mission statement, nowhere did there seem to be an opportunity to explore with the staff how they personally feel called to live out the mission in their work. We believe this to be the next evolutionary step in mission. We should not only make reference to the mission statement but also explore with the staff their response to it as suggested in the pragmatic question, "What does this mean in terms of my daily work?" This is the sort of question one would normally want to explore with a directee.

We knew that our language of spirituality had to be inclusive, meaningful, and accessible in order to facilitate an integration of mission with the staff's everyday work life. Asking whether the hospital was in danger of losing its soul, for example, generated a lot of comments among those attending the sessions as well as in private conversations with other staff members who opted not to come.

Lisa, who had initially been quiet during the first two staff sessions, shared how she is now beginning to look at her job in a new way. She admitted having devalued her work, viewing her role as "just" an administrative assistant, not recognizing the impact she actually had on patient care. She affirmed herself in accurately transcribing and distributing information to other staff members regarding resuscitation and health-care directive policies. She saw how important her role was in ensuring quality patient care and promoting the mission of the hospital in a tangible way.

As for Lisa, these meetings have resulted in overall changes in the attitude of many staff persons toward tending to the spiritual health of the organization, beginning primarily with matters of self-care. I stopped running momentarily to listen to Diane in the chart room, hearing not only another human being but also the stirrings within my own heart. It allowed me time to simply breathe. Even chaplains know all too well the "demons of busyness"! It seems that daring to ask the important questions during the sessions invited the staff to take responsibility for putting a little soul back into the workplace.

On reflection, this opportunity to reclaim responsibility for the soulfulness of the institution has shifted the malaise and powerlessness felt by some staff members. In its place a renewed belief pervades that says, indeed, "we can make a difference." As in Bryce Courtenay's novel *The Power of One*, starting with one staff member at a time, a transformative energy is unleashed throughout the hospital, gathering the efforts of many into a more focused commitment. While individual staff members feel more renewed, the ultimate fruits of the Spirit are seen in quality patient care. By tending to the well-being of the organization, staff members are much healthier and better able to respond to the physical, emotional, psychological, social, and spiritual needs of patients. You can only give away what you already own.

Sharing the Wisdom, Sharing the Responsibility

What have we on the pastoral team learned from this experience? We recognize more seriously our mandate to continue ministering to the staff. Our pastoral care model has dramatically shifted to attend more closely to the staff's spiritual and emotional needs, including formal group sessions as described above. We have repeatedly noticed staff members' hunger for more than a therapeutic, "fix it" intervention. The availability of employee assistance and critical incident debriefing services has undeniably improved staff morale and mental health but has not satisfied this felt spiritual hunger. This malaise also has spiritual roots, thereby inviting a spiritual response. There is indeed a place for spiritual guidance in the hospital.

We also learned that attending to the spirituality of the staff has implications for leadership and corporate decision-making. The more staff members are attuned to the lived mission of the hospital, the greater the need to take responsibility for the decisions that affect the management of the hospital as a whole. Unleashing the prophetic voice demands sensitivity to how God may be speaking to us during our planning retreats and grand round presentations, instead of simply inserting bookendlike prayers at the beginning and end of meetings.

This attempt to enliven mission through spiritual accompaniment of the staff is seen closer to home, in dialoguing with our own pastoral care staff. Adopting periodic sharing circle experiences, modeled after North American aboriginal practices, has helped complement our regular staff meetings. As we sit together in a circle, a wooden "talking stick" is passed around to each person in turn. Whoever is in possession of the stick commands the listening ear of the whole group, empowering the individual to share his or her thoughts and feelings without interruption and with complete reverence. These experiences have attuned our ears to hear more clearly the needs and perspectives of our colleagues. This process has shifted the burden of leadership from one to all, as well as heightening responsibility for the spiritual health of our own department. Called to listen to the many hurting people in our hospital, we have for too long set out on this ministry limping, wounded by fear, mistrust, and criticism that can cripple even the most cohesive group. Attending to our own spiritual health as a community of chaplains has allowed us to be more attentive to the movements of others.

The rippling effects of our pastoral care department's communal discernment model throughout the rest of the hospital remain to be seen. Like the brown bag gatherings with hospital staff, our own soul work will have implications for the continued delivery of quality patient care. How? If only by more genuinely modeling a belief that God really is active and present in our lives, which is the difference in caring for patients. This is mission incarnate, characterized by a meaningful and gutsy response to the lived experience of patients and staff.

Transforming Corporate Culture

Not only does our hospital still have a soul, but given the brown bag sessions, sharing circles, mission newsletters, ward blessings, and brief chart room encounters offering individual support on the run, staff members have shown a greater ownership and commitment to take responsibility for the state of the hospital's soul. I don't want to paint a romantic picture here. We continue to be rocked by ongoing health-care reform and economic pressures. These won't disappear overnight. But it is easier coping with these demands knowing in a felt way the meaningfulness of our work. The mission is more than words on a page framed neatly on a wall, but a reality embraced, owned, and shared by the staff, who are the soul of this hospital.

Like many faith-based communities, we are relearning to take our mission seriously. We are challenged to tell our founding story in a creative and palatable way, allowing the Spirit to break in anew and transform our corporate world. Rather than lagging safely behind, mirroring culture, as Bibby warns, we are called to claim our prophetic voice and speak to the lived experiences of people in the language of the people. By attending to the spiritual needs of the staff, we have invited a deeper integration with the hospital mission, ultimately resulting in better patient care.

Recognizing that the hospital has a soul—and one precious enough to cause fear of its loss—has inspired others to care for themselves and one another, thereby preserving the life and spiritual health of the hospital. Indeed, a little soul work does do a hospital well.

Recommended Reading

Benefiel, Margaret. "Spiritual Direction for Organizations: Toward Articulating a Model." *Presence* 2, no. 3 (September 1996): 40–49.

Bibby, Reginald. *Fragmented Gods: The Poverty and Potential of Religion in Canada*. Toronto: Irwin, 1987.

————. *Unknown Gods: The Ongoing Story of Religion in Canada*. Toronto: Stoddart, 1993.

————. *The Bibby Report: Social Trends Canadian Style*. Toronto: Stoddart, 1995.

Catholic Health Association of the United States. *Chaplaincy: Moving Toward the Next Millennium*. St. Louis: C.H.A., 1997.

Craigie, Frederic C., Jr. "Weaving Spirituality into Organizational Life: Suggestions for Processes and Programs." *Health Progress* 79, no. 2 (March–April 1998): 25–28, 32.

McKinney, Mary Benet, OSB. *Sharing Wisdom: A Process for Group Decision Making*. Allen, Tex.: Tabor Publishing, 1987.

O'Donohue, John. "Spirituality and Leadership: Genuine Leaders Recognize the Sacredness of the Human Presence." *Health Progress* 79, no. 6 (November–December 1998): 31–34, 42.

Roche, James. *Spirituality and Health: What's Good for the Soul Can Be Good for the Body, Too*. Ottawa: Catholic Health Association of Canada, 1996.

GORDON SELF, MDIV, is a past member of the Coordinating Council of Spiritual Directors International. At the time of the writing of this essay, he served as a chaplain and mission team member at St. Boniface General Hospital in Winnipeg, Manitoba, Canada. He is now with Caritas Health Group in Edmonton, Alberta, Canada. As vice presidents of Mission, Ethics, and Spirituality, he is a regular presenter in the Caritas Leadership Program and teaches on the subect of corporate discernment and ethical decision-making. He is a Benedictine Oblate and is married with three children.

Widening the Lens:
The Gift of Group Spiritual Direction

Ann Kline

As any photographer knows, perspective can be a matter of how you focus the lens. In spiritual direction, we look at life through the lens of our individual relationship with God the way a photographer might focus on one flower in a field of daisies, the intricacies of one unique expression of creation. In group spiritual direction, the subject is still the same—the mutual desire of God for humanity, and humanity for God—but the focus is no longer one individual's relationship with the Divine. The lens now takes in more of the field, our perspective shifts, and, consequently, so does the broadness of our sense of God's presence.

In widening the lens, we come to see in our individual desire a deeper mystery and a more potentially unsettling significance. Coming so intimately face-to-face with God in each other, we come to know what Abraham Joshua Heschel meant by "a prophet is a man who is able to hold God and man in one thought, at one time, at all times."[1]

We come to understand in a more tangible way that our spiritual journeys are not ours alone. They form part of God's continuing flow of prayer in the world that encompasses us all.

In group spiritual direction we find ourselves joined in God's prayer, like those daisies grounded in the same earth, as we offer ourselves to it for the sake of each other. We open to the desire of God being lived out through each person and the group as a whole. This stance of intercessory prayer is at the heart of group spiritual direction and is what Douglas Steere called the social dimension of prayer: "There is something startling in the human situation that intercession brings out. Notwithstanding our ultimate aloneness and individuality, evident in the final core of freedom and responsibility in each of us, we are all bound up in the 'bundle of living.'"[2]

Living into this interconnectedness month after month can change our sense of ourselves in relation to all of life. It is a change that can have significant implications for how we are in the world and for the world we are helping to create. What starts as something we do for ourselves becomes something we do for the whole world.

A Process for Group Spiritual Direction

Group spiritual direction is a process in which people come together on a regular basis to assist one another in an ongoing awareness of God in all of life. At the Shalem Institute for Spiritual Formation in Bethseda, Maryland, we ask that people in group spiritual direction agree to

- commit themselves to an honest relationship with God,
- participate wholeheartedly in the group process through prayerful listening and response,
- open their spiritual journeys for consideration by others,
- meet with their group once a month for nine months.

Participants in group direction are drawn by their shared desire in God. Rose Mary Dougherty, SSND, a pioneer in group spiritual direction, wrote:

Having been touched by God's desire, [people in group direction] want to make their desire for God the determining factor of all of their choices, and they recognize that they need some help to do this. This shared desire of the group gives . . . coherence as well as a shared commitment to be there for one another in that desire. The group's primary task is to make the shared desire explicit and to hold one another in it.[3]

This is spiritual direction, not support, conversation, study, or therapy. It is an intentional process of prayerful attentiveness to God on behalf of each individual in the group.

The process of group direction helps to honor the prayerful intention of the group through a disciplined rhythm of silence and sharing. Meetings are facilitated either by a group member taking a turn in that role or by someone who is present solely to serve as facilitator. At Shalem group direction sessions, the time together starts with an extended period of silence to gather the group into the common desire for God. After the silence, the facilitator invites the first person to share as he or she feels ready. (Groups can choose how to determine who shares and in what order, from something systematic to waiting for the Spirit to move someone to speak.)

The group listens prayerfully without interrupting the speaker. Sharing draws from the experiences of living: work, health, relationships, prayer, community. Whatever the content, the focus is always on how God is seeking to meet the speaker within him- or herself and where the holy ground is. When the person is finished, the group allows a few minutes of silence to make space for a deeper response than a habitual reaction—to fix, explain, or judge, for example. The silence allows space for God's prayer for the person to be heard inside. Participants then share whatever questions or thoughts came out of the silence.

After the response time, there is another period of silence when participants pray for the person who has just shared and make space for the next presenter. The rhythm of sharing-silence-response-silence is repeated until everyone has presented. At the end of the meeting, the group reflects on its time together, not to revisit content but to notice anything that supported or obstructed its prayerful intention and thus what may be called for in how the group comes together.

The Stance of Intercessory Prayer

The heart of group spiritual direction is the stance of intercessory prayer each person assumes on behalf of the group. It is a stance of making oneself "radically available" to God on behalf of the others. This differs from what I understand as petitionary prayer. In petitionary prayer, we bring to God our hopes, desires, fears, and needs, with the faith that our hearts are heard in God even if the specifics of our wants are not realized. Petition is a passive prayer of trust in which we are enveloped in God's care.

In intercessory prayer we set aside our own agendas and desires. We ask, "God, what is your prayer?" We do not assume we know the answer. And in asking that question, we go further and offer ourselves to the prayer: "God, what would you have me do on your behalf?" In offering ourselves we trust in the continual stream of God's ongoing love long before that person or situation drew our attention, and continuing long after we turn away to other things.

We enter this prayer not knowing what may be asked of us. Sometimes we may feel a nudge to take a step outward in some gesture of healing or repair. Maybe we will just sense a call to pray. We may not even know why we feel the invitation to do what we do. We step into the flow of prayer not to divert it to our course of action but to make ourselves available to it. We immerse ourselves in God's movement of love and allow our response to be shaped by that current.

We offer ourselves to be used, in a prayer of *hineni*—"here I am." *Hineni* is not a statement of geographic information (here I am, but a minute from now I may be somewhere else). It is a presentation of self, what Abraham said to God when asked to take Isaac up to Mt. Moriah. In that offering of self to God, we know ourselves to be conduits of God's prayer, one source among many that could and will be used for God's purpose.

For Christians, this offering of availability enters into the prayer begun with the death of Jesus, the ultimate act of intercession that is still going on through the mind and spirit of Christ in us and in the world. For Jews, intercessory prayer can be seen as service to God in the continuing act of creation.

In Kabbalistic thought, the world consists of scattered fragments from God's original creation, a creation that shattered with the intensity of God's divine light and desire. Within each fragment are holy sparks, pieces of that divine light that we can release from the husks of material existence limiting their reach and return to their original state of wholeness in God. Raising holy sparks becomes an act of continuing creation, participating in God's desire for the world. In other words, we have the ability to repair the brokenness of the world and complete the task of creation. This process of *tikkun olam* (repair of the world) depends upon our ability to serve God's purposes, not our own. It is love of creation, of God, for God's sake.

Whether the imagery brings us into the mind of Christ or into a co-creative process with God, the basic understanding that we come to is the same: nothing is devoid of God. All of life is interconnected. Rabbi Abraham Isaac Kook also noted that there is nothing devoid of God's presence. He wrote, "One feels the divine force coursing the pathways of existence, through all desires, all worlds, all thoughts, all nations, all creatures."[4] It is to awareness of this divine coursing through all creation that we come in intercessory prayer.

Intercessory Prayer and Group Direction

Group spiritual direction brings us into regular and intimate contact with the force of God acting in and through all of creation, including each of us. In group direction we follow the instruction of Rabbi Kook, who enjoined us to "meditate on the wonders of all creation and the divine life within them. Not in some diluted form, as a mere performance distant from your vision, but, instead, know it as the reality within which you live."[5]

When we sit in prayerful attentiveness to each other's stories, we are struck by the echoes of our own stories and experiences. Often participants will remark that they get as much, if not more, from the stories and responses of others as the responses to their own sharing. It is not unusual at the end of a meeting for participants to note that related themes emerged, quite unintentionally, in the stories. A theme such as forgiveness, gratitude, or the struggle for authenticity may interweave like veins through all the sharings, calling attention to the shared life of prayer. Each story, unique in itself, becomes like one plane on the same prism reflecting God acting from myriad perspectives but flashing with the same deep longing and truth.

After sitting together month after month, something may happen to a group. It can cease to be merely a group of individuals, each pursuing separate journeys, grateful for the illumination of their paths given by the care and attention of other group members, and come to be something more. At the beginning, each individual in a group is more aware of being like a separate spoke in a wheel, focused at the far edge of the circle where his or her life is like a series of turnings in the course of daily events. At this point, discernment is mostly about us in relation to God.

As time goes on, however, a group's attention can be drawn more and more from the perimeter of the wheel to the center that unites all the spokes. The motive force of all that turning might be sensed as something not of themselves but also not outside themselves. A new entity can then emerge from the depth of shared loving concern that has been allowed to flow through the prayer of the group. It is the heart of the group, the group as an entity in itself. It is Spirit.

"Mays" and "cans" pepper this description because not all groups experience such evolution. Sometimes we can collude subtly with each other to avoid diving for the true treasure we profess to seek, preferring to remain in the safer shallows of our experience. We can affirm, support, and lift each other up to the point that discernment of God's true movement becomes lost.

Instead, we float in a pleasant haze of feeling spiritual without being Spirit seekers, unwilling to venture into the darker depths that call us away from our complacency. To get back to the wheel, we can prefer to stay on the outer rim rather than look to the center and see the illusion of our separateness from God and each other. However, when a group holds each member to its original intention—the faithfulness of each member to his or her own unique journey—"accountability" for our desire can be the very prompt we need to head for deeper water.

When the whole of the wheel, its interconnectedness, becomes more and more evident, discernment can change from "us in relation to God" to God in relation to us. We can see more and more of God looking for us in the events of daily living and the underlying desire living within us, and become less preoccupied with seeking some fleeting sense of personal experience. We can cease to see ourselves as the sole concern of God and instead see our lives as part of God's greater concern for the world.

A point can come for members of a group when intercessory prayer is more than a "practice" performed at particular times in particular ways. A connection is made between what happens in the group and what happens in life. We can come to see, through the process of the group, that how we are and what we do is felt in and becomes the life of God. We are ready then for intercessory prayer to become a way of life. As Abraham Joshua Heschel said, "Prayer must not be dissonant with the rest of living. The mercifulness, gentleness, which pervades us in moments of prayer is but a ruse or a bluff if it is inconsistent with the way we live at other moments."[6]

The receptive and attentive way we are in group spiritual direction ripples out from that center to affect all of our relationships. We find ourselves listening more, offering less advice, and being more freely available to people, from our families to the stranger on the street we pass with a smile. We find ourselves more appreciative of life as it is. This is a countercultural way of being. As we model this in our relationships, then those relationships must shift and respond to new stimuli.

Dreaming in League with God

All spiritual direction has a prophetic edge. It is a process that calls us to truths at odds with the norms and temptations of the culture we live in. It asks that we claim a love greater than our own desire and make hard choices in the name of that love.

Group spiritual direction is no exception. It has implications for social change that are at once subtle and far-reaching. Once we change from being people who see God somehow removed from us, or somehow ours alone—an object of desire, rather than being alive in that desire—we can recognize the active presence of God in all of life. And then we cannot live in the world in the same way. We cannot use paper with abandon without seeing a lack of regard for the trees that were its source. We cannot eat a banana without awareness of the land, rain, sun, and people who made it possible for us to eat. We cannot be quite as impatient with a new grocery store clerk, knowing ourselves to be part of the same ongoing life of God.

Group spiritual direction is a subversive process that can, if we let it, oust us from our comfortable seat at the center of the universe. This is the inevitable effect of a life of intercessory prayer. Kenneth Leech wrote:

> The understanding of prayer is crucial to the understanding of social change. There is no split between spirituality and social responsibility . . . prayer is "a consciousness of [humanity's] union with God" and an awareness of one's inner self. Self-knowledge, as all the mystics insist, is the beginning of sanctity, but it is only a beginning. There must be a movement beyond self to God, a real transformation of consciousness.[7]

Intercessory prayer prepares us for that transformation, and group spiritual direction helps ground that awareness in all of our life. Group spiritual direction prepares us, as Abraham Joshua Heschel said, to "dream in league with God":

> At the beginning of all action is an inner vision in which things to be are experienced as real. Prayer, too, is frequently an inner vision, an intense dreaming for God—the reflection of the divine intentions in the soul of [humanity]. . . . We anticipate the fulfillment of the hope shared by both God and [humanity]. To pray is to dream in league with God, to envision his holy visions.[8]

This is not a quick or dramatic process. Prayer has more the power of a snail than that of a bulldozer—one inches slowly and patiently toward life; the other crashes through. It may not be possible to measure such change. Perhaps one might be able to say, as one participant did, that she knew group direction was having an effect when she looked around a crowded sanctuary one day, saw other group members, and realized that the whole room was full of God. Perhaps the only sense of what the group has meant will come in the freedom to claim a desire now recognized to be planted in the hearts of all by the God who desires us all.

The Dalai Lama said that while seeking social change through individual transformation is difficult, it is the only way.[9] Group spiritual direction provides communal grounding for that transformation to occur. In individual direction, we come to know that God is in our lives. In group direction, we come to know that our lives are lived together in God.

ANN KLINE has been facilitating spiritual diretion groups for many years. A spiritual director, retreat leader, and author, she has led programs in prayer and spiritual direction for the Shalem Institute for Spiritual Formation, the Elat Chayyim Spiritual Retreat Center, and various organizations and congregations in the Washington, D.C., area. She is the co-founder of Lev Tahor: A Center for Jewish Soulwork, in Kensington, Maryland. Her writing has appeared in *Spirituality and Health*, *Presence*, and in the anthology *The Lived Experience of Group Spiritual Direction*, edited by Rose Mary Dougherty, among other publications.

Notes

1. Abraham Joshua Heschel, *Moral Grandeur and Spiritual Audacity* (New York: Farrar, Straus & Giroux, 1996), 399.

2. Douglas Steere, *Dimensions of Prayer* (New York: Harper & Row, 1963), 66.

3. Rose Mary Dougherty, *Group Spiritual Direction: Community for Discernment* (New York: Paulist Press, 1995), 37.

4. Abraham Isaac Kook, quoted by David S. Ariel in *Spiritual Judaism* (New York: Hyperion, 1998), 27–28.

5. Abraham Isaac Kook, quoted by Lawrence Kushner in *The Way into Jewish Mystical Tradition* (Woodstock, Vt.: Jewish Lights Publishing, 2001), 15.

6. Heschel, *Moral Grandeur*, 261.

7. Kenneth Leech, *True Prayer* (London: Sheldon Press, 1980), 83.

8. Heschel, *Moral Grandeur*, 353.

9. His Holiness the Dalai Lama, foreword to Thich Nhat Hanh, *Peace Is Every Step* (New York: Bantam Books, 1991), vii.

Spiritual Companioning within Small Christian Communities

Helen Marie Raycraft, OP

The time is surely coming, says the Lord GOD,
when I will send famine on the land;
not a famine of bread, or a thirst for water,
but of hearing the words of the LORD.

—*Amos 8:11*

These prophetic words, written more than twenty-five hundred years ago, are still true today. People are starving for the Word and the living reality of Jesus Christ in their lives and families and are searching for spiritual nourishment and guidance.

Two realities confront the church today: the extreme individualism that has become a way of life in modern society and the divorce of faith from ordinary family and social life. Yet, in the midst of what appear to be very negative factors, a quiet revolution is occurring deep within the hearts of many. People are crying out for community and are being graced as they reach out for one another. They are discovering the value of bonding together as believers in Jesus to pray, to share scripture, and to tell their own stories that flow from the living Word. They are nourishing that hunger deep within by listening and accompanying one another on their journeys of faith.

Within Roman Catholic circles, small faith communities—Basic Ecclesial Communities—are steadily multiplying in the lives of ordinary believers through the United States and the world. The Roman Catholic bishops of Latin America convened in Medellin, Columbia, in 1967 and recognized the promotion of basic ecclesial communities as one of the principal ways to evangelize the masses of unchurched people. Since that time, these communities have been multiplying throughout the world and have become a very hopeful sign for the future of the church. Here in the United States, these communities are increasing rapidly among Hispanics. The United States Bishops Committee on Hispanic Affairs recently published a guide, *Communion and Mission*, for pastoral leaders working with Hispanic communities.

The basic community is a small group of people who come together on a regular basis, many of them meeting once a week in their homes to pray and read scripture; to grow in bonds of love, forgiveness, and unity; and to serve one another and the broader community through evangelization and working for social justice. Relating faith stories and life experiences around the Sunday Gospel is the heart of these small communities. People break open the Word for one another by honestly talking about their joys and sorrows, successes and failures, sickness and struggles in the midst of the daily realities of their lives. Testimonies of gratitude for God's provident care accompany petitions for urgent needs in their families and neighborhoods. This is carried on with an alive, expectant faith that God accompanies them and gives them signs of his love.

Salvation History of La Paloma Community

La Paloma is a small faith community that has been meeting weekly since 1978 in McAllen, Texas, a city on the Texas-Mexico border. When I first moved to McAllen, I began visiting the people in the impoverished barrio called La Paloma. Many residents of that area did not want their neighborhood to continue to be called by that name because of the violent reputation it had acquired. After the neighbors began to meet regularly as a small community to pray and share their faith stories, their lives began to change and the environment in the neighborhood was gradually transformed. They then began to honor the name of their barrio, La Paloma, which means "dove" and refers to the Holy Spirit. Today if you visit the neighborhood, people will proudly tell you their area is called La Paloma. The neighbors have reclaimed their barrio through the transforming effects of the small faith community.

A group of fifteen to twenty adults gather at each other's homes on a rotating basis to sing, thank, and praise God for God's faithful love; to plead together for their personal and communal needs; and to look at their lives in the mirror of the readings from the Sunday Eucharist. The Word of God is powerful in their midst. Henri Nouwen describes it this way: "The full power of the word lies, not in how we apply it to our lives after we have heard it, but in its transforming power that does its divine work as we listen."[1] The Word is both life-giving and healing as it is proclaimed in their lives. Nouwen continues, "The Word of God is not a word to apply to our daily lives at some later date; it is a word to heal us through, and in our listening here and now."

During the past years this little community of La Paloma has radically changed the lives of hundreds of people, not only the active participants, but also their families, their neighbors, and others whose lives they have touched. The majority of the people are very poor, many living in rented homes and relying on government food programs.

La Paloma Reaches Out

La Paloma has been an evangelizing force in beginning at least five other groups in the nearby area. As members move or reach out in the workplace, others have expressed an interest in sharing the Word of God with them. La Paloma continues to grow and thrive. The members of the group fought together so that their neighborhood and homes would not be consumed by a huge development project. They were also actively involved in a voter registration project in the surrounding area.

The most permanent force during these years of being community is that they have been for one another the compassionate presence of Jesus Christ. They are *hesed* reaching out in a loving, merciful, faithful way not only to their members but in a rippling effect way beyond what they ever could have imagined. They have accompanied others in their pain and loneliness, their grief and anguish. They have been able to be this compassionate presence of Christ for one another because of their faith, their dependence upon God and interdependence on each other, their fidelity in prayer, and their contemplation of the Word together. "Has not God chosen the poor in the world to be rich in faith and to be heirs of the kingdom that he has promised to those who love him?" (Jas 2:5).

As a community of faith, La Paloma has been a ray of hope when people have telephoned them for prayer during times of family crisis and tragedy. They have brought comfort to the families of two of their own members who have died from cancer and another who was killed in a hit-and-run accident. Chronic illness is very difficult for everyone, especially for the very poor, who often have inadequate health insurance and access to quality health care. Illness compounds the poverty cycle. This faith community has been a source of strength for the sick and the dying. The sick continue to participate in the gatherings whenever possible, and they often meet in the home of someone who is disabled. Several people in the community struggle as members of their families are ravaged by drugs and alcohol.

Lupe was a member of the La Paloma barrio. As a single mother who lived with her mother and daughter in a one-room trailer, she earned her living by making and selling tortillas in the neighborhood. When I first met Lupe, she was a very angry woman who felt cheated by God because of her poverty. I invited her to participate in an open-air retreat that I led for five evenings on her neighbor's front patio. During the week she began to experience God's total love and acceptance of her as a woman through the community's response to her and her story. In opening herself to this love, a deep process of inner healing began within her. She was able to forgive her husband for abandoning her and take the beginning steps in learning to love herself and others. She became an active member of the small community that the neighbors began as a result of the retreat.

Lupe spent the last two years of her life struggling with cancer. God granted her one desire to see her daughter graduate from college. People who visited her to console her during her illness left her home with an awareness of God as she shared her own faith and acceptance of her illness. She died as an evangelizer among her people, as one who had experienced the mystery of God with her neighbors in the context of the small faith community.

Another woman, Maria, struggled with diabetes for many years, and finally her leg was amputated. Her sickness and disability have not isolated her from the group. The community members regularly visit her, bring her Communion, and pray with her. They meet at her home when it is her turn to host the weekly session. Recently I returned to McAllen and met with the people for lunch and a celebration. They decided to gather at the home of Mario, a bedridden man who has been a leader of their group. There is a profound recognition of the presence of God among them through the sick and suffering.

Communal Spiritual Direction

The members of the La Paloma community and many ordinary poor people do not have the luxury of a spiritual director. Although they may not have the time or money to assist at a weekend retreat, they also long for God. They yearn to have someone listen to them, and God is providing this in a communal way through the experience of small faith communities. They challenge us to new understandings of spiritual direction. The community experience stretches the commonly held image of spiritual direction beyond the individual approach and into companioning communities in their faith development. For the spiritual director, the challenge is to journey with a community of people in their vocation of transforming their families, their neighborhoods, and their workplaces.

In my own ministry as a missionary, I have had the privilege of accompanying hundreds of small faith communities in the United States for twenty years and several years previous in Latin America. To be able to listen to people tell their faith stories, to be present in their lives during moments of crisis and deep suffering, and to celebrate with them in moments of birth and joy has been an evangelizing experience for me.

I am awed by the hunger and thirst that people have for God. They are willing to make great sacrifices in order to be able to participate in retreat days or formation classes. Many couples who are both working to make ends meet struggle in being faithful to their own personal prayer time and prayer within their families. Some have learned to read because of their desire to know the Bible.

As people immerse themselves in scripture, a desire for contemplative prayer is born, and the spiritual director's task is to gently guide and nourish. As they are invited to ponder the stories about the reign of God and the parables, they learn to listen to their own understanding of the Word as they hear it within themselves. In the welcoming environment of small communities, the faith stories that they share with one another open their mind and hearts, leading them to listen in a more attentive way to the mysteries of God.

Raquel is an elderly widow who is recognized within the neighborhood and the parish as a woman of great wisdom. When she speaks, everyone listens. She spends many hours each day listening to the living God who dwells within her, and as she visits the sick, she shares a peace and sense of the presence of Jesus with them. As people like Raquel and others relate their search for God, they have inspired me in my own prayer to plunge more deeply into the scriptures. I am humbled by their yearning to understand the Word of God and share it with others.

Visiting the elderly, praying, and reading the Sunday scriptures with them is a ministry that has developed among the various small communities. Since many of the homebound do not read or their eyesight is failing, they welcome these visits. As people reach out tirelessly to minister to one another and accompany one another in the Christian journey, they overcome their timidity and hesitancy to share their faith.

As I have formed and accompanied hundreds of small faith communities among Hispanics, my own spirituality and my way of understanding spiritual direction have changed. I have learned to listen to the Spirit of God speaking in individuals and especially through the community as a whole. This contemplative listening has called me to an openness to the mystery of God within the community, a receptivity to God speaking through them. People within small faith communities inspire one another to maintain a rich prayer life, to delve into the Word of God, and to reach out in diverse ministries. When Lupe was dying of cancer, the whole community enabled her to walk that journey. They sustained her hope and held her until the moment of her final "yes." Mario's disability has affected not only his wife and family but the members of the community as they see the face of Jesus in his suffering.

These groups possess a new, creative, and transforming energy. As spiritual directors, we need to accompany them, listen to them, and be willing to be transformed by them. As small faith communities continue to develop and become normative of Christian life, we will need to acquire new pastoral skills in spiritual guidance in order to work more effectively with networks of communities as they discover together a new way of being church.

What are some of the qualities we will need? A knowledge of group dynamics and leadership skills are helpful in working with the shared leadership of the communities. A sensitive listening to the participants and the group as a whole is essential to perceive the movement of the Spirit in each person and the group as a whole. A gentle encouragement of people as they tell their stories helps them develop the confidence needed to share those moments with others without dominating the time together.

These communities are forming people in a holistic, communal spirituality that permeates every aspect of their lives: prayer, family, neighborhood, work, and parish. Spirituality therefore is not just a personal faith journey; each community develops its own salvation history. The small community is a new way of living, a new way of seeing, a new way of being, a new way of life as a community of believers in Jesus Christ. Base communities are the seeds of a new way of being church and the beginnings of a new civilization.

Recommended Reading

Boff, Leonardo. *Ecclesiogenesis*. Maryknoll, N.Y.: Orbis Books, 1986.

Lee, Bernard, and Michael Cowan. *Dangerous Memories*. Kansas City, Mo.: Sheed & Ward, 1986.

McKenna, Megan. *Not Counting Women and Children: Neglected Stories from the Bible*. Maryknoll, N.Y.: Orbis Books, 1992.

————. *Parables: The Arrows of God*. Maryknoll, N.Y.: Orbis Books, 1994.

Raycraft, Helen Marie, and Ralph Rogawski. *Fruit of Our Labor*. San Antonio: Oblate Communications, 1980.

Raycraft, Helen Marie. *Seeds of Hope: Hispanic Spirituality in the Basic Ecclesial Communities*. Austin, Tex.: Dominican Missionary Preaching Team, 1994.

HELEN MARIE RAYCRAFT is a member of the Sinsinawa Dominican Congregation and the Dominican Missionary Preaching Team, which is based in Asutin, Texas. She holds a master's degree in education and counseling and a Doctor of Ministry in spiritual direction. She has ministered with basic ecclesial communities for more than thirty-five years and is the author of several books, one of which is *Seeds of Hope: Hispanic Spirituality in the Basic Ecclesial Communities*.

———————————

Note

1. Henri Nouwen, *With Burning Hearts* (Maryknoll, N.Y.: Orbis Books, 1994), 46.

The Coming Out Process
in Spiritual Direction

Peg Thompson

My church is coming apart at the seams because we can't agree on whether to adopt a gay-welcoming policy. Some people are saying really horrible things about gays and lesbians. If they knew I am a lesbian I don't think they'd say these things, but since I'm not "out" I have to listen to a lot of hurtful statements without being able to talk about how I feel. I'm scared to come out in this atmosphere. And why should I have to? I love my church, but this really hurts. I don't know if I can continue to be a member.

My partner and I want to have a commitment ceremony, but our church says clergy can't perform them for same-sex couples. This really makes me mad, but there's nothing I can do about it, I guess. Why should straight couples be able to get married in our church when we can't? We love each other just as much as they do!

I think I might be gay. Does this mean I'm going to hell? I feel like I'm going crazy. I don't want to live a lie, but I'm afraid I'll be condemned by God if I come out.

These are some of the many dilemmas gay men and lesbians face as they enter into the coming out process and encounter their own and others' religious beliefs, policies, and communities. As spiritual directors, we will be called to companion them in each stage of the coming out process.

Each gay man or lesbian experiences the process of coming out in his or her own way. This journey is shaped by the temperament, family experience, and spiritual/religious history of the person. But perhaps even more profound, given that same-sex orientation is a stigmatized and marginalized identity, the coming out process is shaped by conditions in the broader cultural context. Directors may tend to forget that many of the gay and lesbian people we meet with have experienced at least three different cultural eras. The past thirty years have seen tremendous change not only in whom gay and lesbian individuals understand themselves to be but in how society perceives and treats us.

Think of three generations of gay and lesbian people. Those roughly sixty-five and older entered adulthood in a time when being beaten up by police and citizens alike was a real possibility and one that usually went unpunished; when jobs were routinely lost when workers were found to be—or even accused of being—gay; when being gay was labeled "perversion" and gay men and lesbians were lumped in with pedophiles. The vast majority of church denominations, local churches, and clergy openly condemned homosexuality as sin and abomination. Many in this generation have spent much of their energy "passing" as straight people: denying and hiding their relationships, lying about what they do on weekends, marrying people they were not in love with, living a double life. While many of them have come out, others are just now coming to understand their sexual orientation—many after decades-long marriages and children. For these people, often in their fifties, sixties, and seventies, coming out is both a tremendous liberation and a poignant struggle with shame and loss.

Gay men and lesbians now in midlife—roughly ages forty to sixty-five—reached young adulthood in the era of the gay liberation movement, a time of dramatic social change. In this generation, coming out—at least in some parts of one's life—became somewhat of a psychological imperative for many. But internalized homophobia is a major factor in coming out, both for them and their parents. Coming out necessitates dealing with the resulting shame that has accumulated over the years. And even now, when people decide to come out, they risk being cut off from friends and family, having their partnerships go unrecognized, and being defrocked or kicked out of their spiritual communities. In many communities, gay men and lesbians still face the threat of violence and hatred and have the same alternatives as people born thirty years earlier.

Persons now in adolescence and young adulthood are reaping the benefit of the changes wrought by the gay liberation movement. Lesbians appear on the cover of *Newsweek*; homosexuality is no longer considered a diagnosable mental illness; major corporations provide partner benefits for gay and lesbian employees; same-sex marriages are legal in the United States in the state of Massachusetts (at the time of this writing). There are churches that explicitly welcome gay men and lesbians, as well as those who serve them primarily. There are theologies and biblical scholarship that support those of all sexual orientations and debunk previous antigay scriptural interpretation. There are still many challenges and much heterosexism facing us, some of the most daunting within the church itself. However, many young people come out to themselves as adolescents and then to others at home and school without much negative consequence. It is only as they meet the wider, still quite heterosexist society that they encounter prejudice and hatred.

As spiritual directors, we will be working with persons from all of these groups. They will have quite different approaches to coming out and will need directors who can work with them wherever they are. This may involve us in our own inner work, for we, too, have been shaped by our generations' cultural and religious heritage. We may have to confront our own fears, biases, prejudices, and misinformation in order to walk with our directees in the coming out process.

A core reality for gay men and lesbians is that we are marginalized and oppressed in society. From a Christian point of view, this puts us squarely in the focus group of Jesus' ministry—and thus of our own ministry as spiritual directors. The very fact that lesbians and gay men must "come out of the closet" stems from this fact. Without marginalization, there is no closet.

Homophobia and Heterosexism

"Homophobia" is a term often used to describe hostile reactions to lesbians and gay men, their culture, or their behavior. "Internalized homophobia" refers to that hostility taken into the self-image, emotions, and values of gay and lesbian people who have grown up and live in a homophobic society.

In recent years, the term "homophobia" has been critically examined for two reasons. First, antigay attitudes are not phobias in the clinical sense, and are often not even based in fear. And second, the term focuses attention on the attitudes of individuals rather than on the reality of a deeply rooted social and cultural prejudice against nonheterosexual persons.

More recently, the term "heterosexism"[1] has been used as an alternative to homophobia. It has been defined as the ideological system that denies, denigrates, and stigmatizes any nonheterosexual form of behavior, identity, relationship, or community. Cultural heterosexism, like racism and sexism, permeates all parts of society. Consider "don't ask, don't tell," a governmental manifestation. Or the fact that our educational system is in a major battle over the teaching of gay and lesbian history, literature, and arts. Or the fact that only one mainstream Christian denomination (United Church of Christ) permits ordination of "practicing" gay men and lesbians. The term "practicing" is in itself heterosexist. No one would consider distinguishing heterosexuals who would be allowed to express their sexuality genitally from those who would not. Implicit in the term "practicing" is the idea that nonheterosexual persons are pathological, spiritually or psychologically, but could be acceptable if only they did not "practice" their pathology. "Love the sinner, hate the sin" is probably the most blatant "theological" version of this idea.

"Psychological heterosexism" is the individual expression of cultural heterosexism, manifested through hostility, feelings of personal disgust, and condemnation. It is also expressed behaviorally, though verbal abuse, discrimination, and physical assault. In a heterosexist culture, psychological heterosexism is not regarded as wrong or as needing to be stopped. Just as no one is free of racism, everyone in our society is heterosexist to one degree or another.

In this context, "internalized heterosexism" could be understood as the self-hate, shame, rage, and self-injury that result from growing up and living as a nonheterosexual in a heterosexist society. Messages of hate, inferiority, mistrust, judgment, and disgust abound about nonheterosexuality in our society; there is no way to filter them even as an adult, let alone as a child.

Stages of Coming Out

Within psychology, there is vigorous debate about models of coming out. As I have pointed out, the social climate for coming out has radically changed, thus calling for new and reworked models. In addition, many early models were created from gay men's experience and need to be reexamined for lesbians. People of color and those with working-class backgrounds are bringing their own cultural experiences to the discussion. Finally, there is concern for individual variations in experience as well. Consequently, I will be outlining a composite process which, it must be understood, takes as many individual variations as there are individuals. No special "goodness" is attached to going through all the stages and reaching the "highest" stage. We all go at our own pace, work within our personal resources, and face our own struggles.

Note that friends and family members of gay men and lesbians also go through their own coming out process. These books may be particularly helpful to parents, spouses, siblings, children, and friends of gay, lesbian, and bisexual people during the coming out process:

> Borhek, Mary. *Coming Out to Parents: A Two-Way Guide for Lesbians and Gay Men and Their Parents.* Cleveland: Pilgrim Press, 1993.
>
> Buxton, Amity Pierce. *The Other Side of the Closet: The Coming-Out Crisis for Straight Spouses and Families.* New York: John Wiley and Sons, 1994.
>
> Corley, Rip. *The Final Closet: The Gay Parents' Guide for Coming Out to Their Children.* Miami: Editech Press, 1990.
>
> Fairchild, Betty, and Nancy Hayward. *Now That You Know: What Every Parent Should Know about Homosexuality.* San Diego: Harcourt Brace, 1998.
>
> Schaar Gochros, Jean. *When Husbands Come Out of the Closet.* Birminghampton, N.Y.: Haworth Press, 1989.
>
> Troiden, Richard R. "The Formation of Homosexual Identities." *Psychological Perspectives on Lesbian and Gay Male Experiences.* Edited by Linda D. Garnets and Douglas Kimmel. New York: Columbia Press, 1993.
>
> Welch Griffin, Carolyn, Marian J. Wirth, Arthur G. Wirth, and Brian McNaught. *Beyond Acceptance: Parents of Lesbians and Gays Talk about Their Experiences.* New York: St. Martin's Press, 1996.

Awareness of Differentness

As a little girl, I always felt different. I didn't want a cowgirl outfit, I wanted a cowboy outfit. I didn't see why I couldn't wear jeans to school. I liked to play with boys instead of girls because girl play was so boring. Who wants to have little doll tea parties and dress up like Mommy? I liked to play baseball and practice the high jump and build forts.

Children who later understand themselves as nonheterosexual usually experience themselves as somehow "different." Both boys and girls experience internal conflict between role behaviors expected of them—for example, dating persons of the opposite sex, using makeup, showing interest in cross-gender play—and what they prefer. At this stage, this feeling of being different usually remains undefined and unnamed. It is usually not attached to a gay or lesbian identity either because sexual expression is not a part of the young child's experience or because the child has not yet learned the terminology of sexual orientation.

What we learn about ourselves in relation to God and religion during childhood is the foundation for our later spiritual life. In some churches, we learn that homosexuality is a sin and homosexuals will go to hell for it. In others, we learn that the life path for "normal" people is either heterosexual marriage or celibacy. In other churches none of this is taught; in fact, nothing is taught about homosexuality. Thus nonheterosexuals are rendered invisible in the context of the sacred.

As spiritual directors, we are called to help people tell the story of their lives. When we are companioning gay men and lesbians, these early teachings—and the feelings that go with them—are a major part of what stands in the way not only of a self-affirming nonheterosexual identity but of greater intimacy with the Holy.

Identity Confusion

All through high school and college I was attracted to other men, but I dated girls because I wanted to fit in. At my high school in rural Nebraska, I can tell you, no guy would go to the prom with another guy! It wasn't even something you thought about. Then when I went to the university, I found the gay and lesbian club. I wanted to check it out and I didn't want to. I didn't want to find out I was gay, but I wanted to know that there were other people like me. I was so mixed up and scared.

Here the individual (at whatever age) has a dawning awareness that the sense of difference in the first stage may be related to a nonheterosexual identity. The sense of difference takes the form of questioning: Who am I? What do these differences mean? Am I really straight? Or am I gay or lesbian or bisexual? For many people, this stage takes place during adolescence or early adulthood. However, it may take place at any age.

Identity confusion also arises when persons who have identified themselves as bisexual, for example, realize that they are actually gay or lesbian or vice versa. Since throughout life we have new experiences and process them internally, sexual orientation must sometimes be reevaluated based on new information.

Societal stigmatization prolongs the period of identity confusion because it prevents people from discussing and exploring their sexual desires, experiences, and feelings with others for fear they will be ostracized, judged, fired, persecuted, or physically harmed. Despite the progress of recent decades, no member of a sexual minority can feel completely safe when he or she begins to explore or question sexual identity.

Lesbians and gay men must cope in daily life with the anguish and fear of identity confusion. They may use denial: "I'm not gay, no way." They may seek to convert themselves to heterosexuality—with or without professional "help"—and to eradicate all same-sex behaviors, feelings, and fantasies from their psyche. It might be helpful to note here that in 1997 the American Psychological Association passed a resolution that strongly reaffirmed that homosexuality is not a mental illness. In addition, it stated that there is no sound scientific evidence of the efficacy of so-called reparative therapies, in which therapists seek to convert gay people to heterosexuality. The resolution calls on psychologists to "respect the rights of individuals, including sexual minority clients, to privacy, confidentiality, self-determination, and autonomy."

At this stage they may choose to avoid interests, people, or information relating to nonheterosexual orientation. They may immerse themselves in heterosexual relationships to prove to themselves and others that they are straight. They may even adopt antigay political and personal values and verbally or physically attack those who are gay, lesbian, or bisexual. Or they may avoid the struggle of identity formation through the use of alcohol and other drugs to numb themselves to the conflict. Some lesbians and gay men at this stage use redefinition, telling themselves and others that theirs is a special case of falling in love with this particular person, or that they are just experimenting with a temporary identity. They may claim to be bisexual or ambisexual when they are not. Or they may claim that their same-sex behavior was just a result of being drunk or high.

Identity confusion represents what we in spiritual direction would call a time of discernment. It is in this spirit that we best companion directees. They need to sift and sort all the conflicting messages and behaviors and try to claim the deeper spiritual truth about their lives and who they were created to be. We help them best when we stay present, despite how painful it is to be present to these self-denying behaviors, and try to keep a connection with all that is sacred in this individual and his or her story. If we can focus on the part of the directee that is afraid, angry, or mixed up, but still beloved by God—rather than on the behavior that is so self-hurtful—he or she may find a way to be compassionate about his or her own dilemmas as well.

When we companion people in a state of identity confusion, they are often in tremendous pain. Their lives are carrying them forward into a new self-identity that is internally painful and externally judged as wrong. We may feel a powerful urge to rescue them by helping them get back into the closet or to liberate them by pushing them to come out. But we need to ground ourselves in the love of God for all those God has created and trust that holy listening means hearing the story and staying with the emotions and conflicts it involves. Lesbians and gay men need to tell their stories, and there are few places they can safely tell them. It is the sacred trust and privilege of a spiritual director to provide such a place.

Sometimes a referral for counseling is needed to help the individual cope with the stresses and symptoms of identity reevaluation—depression, anxiety, suicidal thoughts, self-destructive behaviors. Such referrals must be made to carefully chosen, experienced therapists who are gay or lesbian, or at least gay/lesbian-sensitive. Because of the intense vulnerability to shame at this stage, directors must take care to ensure that directees understand the referral is in support of their process, not because you see their sexual orientation as sick or disturbed.

This is not the time (if there ever is a time) to take an objective or neutral stance in relation to spirituality. When clients cite scripture or church dogma in support of their internalized heterosexism, it is our job to offer them information about other options. For example, if the directee cites passages about men lying with men (Leviticus 18:22 and 20:13) as evidence that they are an abomination before God, it is our responsibility to offer other perspectives.

Directee:	I know I might be gay, but how can I say it when it means I'm going to hell?
PT:	Where did you learn that being gay meant you would go to hell?
Directee:	It's right there in the Bible, in that thing about men who lie with men being an abomination.
PT:	Did you learn anything else like this?
Directee:	I know there are other passages like that. I heard them in church when I was a kid. And our minister was always lumping homo-sexuals in with perverts and adulterers and all those other people who were going to hell if they didn't repent. But I don't feel like I can repent. I can't help who I am.
PT:	Did you know that there are people who have done a lot of work on those scriptures and believe that they weren't about being gay or not gay?
Directee:	(Laughs.) Yeah, they're probably going to hell too!
PT:	I'd be glad to give you some information to read if you're inter-ested in knowing more.
Directee:	OK, I'll look at it.

Similarly, we can introduce the reality that there are churches that have decided to welcome gays, lesbians, and bisexuals, and that even among those who belong to churches with antigay theologies, there are individuals who do not agree.

It is often helpful to directees at this stage to recommend scripture passages that affirm God's unconditional love. I suggest Psalm 139:1–18 and 23–24; Isaiah 43:1–7; and Romans 8:38–39 as texts for meditation and prayer. It may be helpful for directees, especially those who have taken in the scriptures commonly used to fuel anti-gay beliefs, to memorize one or more of these passages and say it as a daily prayer.

There are a few books I sometimes suggest at this stage as well. If there is a biblical component to the internalized heterosexism, *Word Is Out* by Chris Glaser (out of print) and *The New Testament and Homosexuality* by Robin Scroggs (Fortress Press, 1984) may provide alternative analysis and information. *Is the Homosexual My Neighbor? A Positive Christian Response* by Letha Dawson Scanzoni and Virginia Ramey Mollenkott (HarperSanFrancisco, 1994) can provide a scriptural and theological foundation for gay- and lesbian-affirming spirituality.

It is often helpful to suggest some of the many books of coming out stories as well. Among those that I recommend are the following:

> Barber, Karen, and Sarah Holme, eds. *Testimonies: Lesbian Coming Out Stories*. Boston: Alyson Publishing, 1994.

> Savin-Williams, Ritch C., ed. *And Then I Became Gay: Young Men's Stories*. Nashville: Rutledge Press, 1997.

> Stanley, Julia Penelope, and Susan J. Wolfe, eds. *The Coming Out Stories*. Watsonville, Calif.: Crossing Press, 1989.

Although the following books are out of print, they are also helpful if you can find them:

> Curtis, Wayne, ed. *Revelations: Gay Men's Coming Out Stories*. New York: Alyson Publications, 1994.

> Umans, Meg, ed. *Like Coming Home: Coming Out Letters*. Austin, Tex.: Banned Books, 1988.

These stories provide "grist for the mill" at this stage—directees can bounce off others' stories to clarify their own.

I frequently suggest that directees express their dilemmas and struggles at this stage by writing letters in their journal to God, Jesus, or a person they trust. This writing can then become part of what is shared in the next session.

Acceptance

I got to this place where I said to myself and God, OK, OK, I guess I'm gay after all. This was kind of an "I give up" moment. I didn't feel all that great about it, but at least I could quit lying and hiding and drinking and get on with my life.

The third stage of coming out is *acceptance*. Here an individual begins to acknowledge that his or her feelings and behavior probably mean that he is gay or she is lesbian. This is a calmer appraisal of one's history and feelings, combined with new information about other gay men and lesbians in the community and in history. Here is the beginning of what we often call "coming out to myself." This is a great divide. We are moving from a position of "culture is right; there is something wrong with me" to one of "this is the way I am; perhaps culture is not right." Self-definition has begun, and questioning everything we have learned follows right behind. Avoidance strategies gradually subside and there is movement into the next stage, identity assumption.

Identity Assumption: Claiming a New Identity

It was a strange process. The more lesbians I met, the more I saw the lesbian in myself as really pretty OK. I found a lot of women I really liked and respected. Rather than avoiding everything about the lesbian community, I began to want to learn more, to meet more people, to take part in some of the social gatherings in the gay/lesbian/bisexual community. I actually started to have fun as a lesbian.

"Identity claiming" is the beginning of the more overt process we normally think of as "coming out." Persons at this stage affirm an identity as gay, lesbian, or bisexual. Often this is an attitude of toleration, not necessarily pride or affirmation. They seek contact and connection with the gay/lesbian/bisexual community. They often experiment more frequently with same-gender sexual partners. Greater segments of their social life take place in the gay/lesbian/bisexual community.

These contacts with others are like the yeast in the loaf. As it ferments, it transforms the worldview of the coming out person. In the spiritual arena this is often a time of vigorous questioning, challenge, and change. Everything that has been learned spiritually may seem to have been contaminated by heterosexism. There is often a shift in relationship with the Divine: directees may cut off their relationship with God, feeling that the "God" they embraced before was associated with intolerance and religious bigotry and must be kept at a distance. Or their connection with the Divine may be rekindled through participation in new, more inclusive faith communities. Or they may discover their relationship with God for the first time.

Some directees question a sin-and-salvation theology, asserting that they don't think being gay or lesbian makes them sinners. They may become intolerant and rejecting of "organized religion" in a global way, understanding it as an institution that has contributed to their oppression. They may be angry that the church does not (with a few exceptions) ordain those who are "out" gays and lesbians or allow them to marry. They may stop worshiping, seek a different community of faith, or enter a period of experimentation with various faith traditions. They may even seek out a new spiritual director!

As a spiritual director, I try to listen to all of this with as much serenity as I can—resisting the tendency to defend God or religion and/or to show my agreement with directees' critiques. This is a time for directees to speak their own truth, however changeable, and to listen to how it sounds. It is a time to challenge the religious structures that have kept them from the wholeness they are just now claiming and to rebuild a relationship with the Divine and with spiritual community that does not force them to choose between their deepest nature and full participation. For me as director, it calls for radical trust that "God is doing a new thing" and is guiding me and directee alike.

Sadly, this is all too frequently a time of abandonment and rejection by trusted members of faith communities. In my own small, primarily nonheterosexual church, there are many men and women who tell excruciating stories. One woman, for example, was expelled from her church and forced by her minister to turn in all her Bibles. She hid her most treasured one, but her mother ferreted it out and gave it to the minister as well. Another was dismissed from her ministry in a church when she was "outed" by a congregant. Another was sent away from a monastery where he had lived for ten years when found sleeping with another monk. Another, a church organist, was fired immediately after he confided in his clergyman that he thought he might be gay. These are stories that need to be told in spiritual direction, grief that needs to be felt, anger that needs to be expressed. Our empathic listening and loving responses are needed to bear witness to God's love and God's outrage about these acts done in God's name.

In particular, directees at this stage question, reframe, and often reject theologies and pseudotheologies used to oppress gay/lesbian/bisexual people. Some need to reevaluate the sin-and-redemption motif in Jesus' journey, no longer feeling sinful because they are gay or lesbian and thus no longer in need of redemption. I find *Original Blessing*, by Matthew Fox, and *Meeting Jesus Again for the First Time*, by Marcus Borg, can be helpful reading when directees are exploring these issues. If theologically inclined, they may embrace a liberation theology instead, a theology that focuses on Jesus' ministry as one of justice and liberation rather than salvation. The theology of "love the sinner, hate the sin" comes under fire for the same reason, not to mention its tone of condescension. The dogma in some churches that it is not sinful to be "homosexual" as long as one does not express it genitally causes great pain and must be reevaluated.

It is helpful to directees at this time in their lives to have access to books that affirm a gay/lesbian/bisexual spiritual path. I keep them on hand to loan to directees, since they may be hesitant in their own communities to go into a bookstore and buy or order them. I recommend the following:

Glaser, Chris. *Coming Out to God: Prayers for Lesbians and Gays and Their Families and Friends.* Louisville, Ky.: Westminster/John Knox Press, 1991.

Frontain, Raymond-Jean, ed. *Reclaiming the Sacred: The Bible in Gay/Lesbian Culture.* New York: Harrington Park Press, 1997.

McNeill, John J. *The Church and the Homosexual.* Boston: Beacon Press, 1993.

———. *Taking a Chance on God.* Boston: Beacon Press, 1996.

O'Neill, Kathleen, and Craig Ritter. *Coming Out Within: Stages of Spiritual Awakening for Lesbians and Gay Men.* San Francisco: HarperSanFrancisco, 1992.

Although the following books are out of print, they are also helpful if you can find them:

Dean, Amy E. *Proud to Be: Daily Meditations for Lesbians and Gay Men*. New York: Bantam, 1994.

Edwards, George R. *Gay/Lesbian Liberation: A Biblical Perspective*. Cleveland, Ohio: Pilgrim Press, 1984.

Glaser, Chris. *Coming Home: Reclaiming Spirituality and Community as Gay Men and Lesbians*. San Francisco: HarperSanFrancisco, 1991.

Nugent, Robert, ed. *A Challenge to Love: Gay and Lesbian Catholics in the Church*. New York: Crossroad Publishing Co., 1983.

As directees stir the pot, we can get bumped—even those of us who are also non-heterosexual. Their questions can threaten our own theologies, our own churches' doctrines. We can be confronted with heterosexism in ourselves. To work with these directees in the deepest spirit of our tradition, we must be willing to open up to new ideas, new challenges, and new self-awareness. It is our responsibility—not our directees'—to educate ourselves to work with them as we would with any other cultural group. We must read the literature of the gay/lesbian community, learn more about the scriptures that are misused by heterosexist Christians, study theologies that make room for everyone in the reign of God, and gather a network of consultants.

It is also critical that we are willing to face our own inevitable prejudice and ignorance and to learn and grow through it. Here again, it is our responsibility—through honest self-confrontation, supervision, prayer, our own spiritual direction, worship, self-examination, and forgiveness—to heal ourselves of prejudice.

Directees in this period of their lives need lots of ideas, people, congregations, theological reflections, and contacts. They use these to bounce off of, almost like sonar, in order to know where they are. To be most helpful, we need to have a referral network of therapists, clergy, and consultants. I keep in my office information about churches and retreat centers that have policies of actively welcoming and affirming nonheterosexual worshipers, and those whose members are primarily gay/lesbian/ bisexual. Several mainline Protestant churches have a process that allows a congregation to designate itself as gay-welcoming. In the United Church of Christ, these are called Open and Affirming (ONA) congregations; in the United Methodist Church, Reconciling; in the Evangelical Lutheran Church of America, Reconciled in Christ congregations; in the Presbyterian tradition, More Light. In addition, chapters of Dignity, for Roman Catholic gay men and lesbians, and Integrity, for Episcopalians, provide spiritual and personal support for lesbian and gay people. Directories of these churches and organizations may be obtained from the respective denominations as well as through Internet sites. Metropolitan Community Church (MCC), a predominantly gay/lesbian/bisexual church, has congregations in many cities across the USA.

Affirmation and Celebration

I love being a gay man. I think that's what God created me to be. It's not something to over-come or something that I need to be saved from. It's a beautiful, loving way to be a person. I feel most alive when I'm with others in the gay/lesbian/bisexual community. I can be com-pletely myself there—just as I was meant to be.

Here, being gay or lesbian is adopted as a way of life. Long-term relationships often begin or are committed to once this decisive self-affirmation is in place. It could be expressed this way: "I celebrate my sexual orientation, and in the context of spiri-tuality, I understand it to be the essence of what I was created to be." There is a new sense of freedom, happiness, and contentment with oneself. Now individuals choose to come out to a much broader group of people and even to let their sexual orienta-tion be known publicly (as in the case of professionals advertising in gay/lesbian/ bisexual publications). Now heterosexism is clearly seen as what is wrong, and the fully authentic, self-affirming, and whole person as what is right.

Directees at this stage of coming out require a director who is as unambivalent about their sexual orientation as they are, one who can truly celebrate their relation-ships, their communities, and their spiritual path. If they are with a director who can-not, they will often make a change at this point.

Activism

I see a lot of things about the world that need to be changed. Now that I'm clear about myself and I love myself, my lesbian self, I feel called to work on political change for people in the gay/lesbian/bisexual community—gays in the military, access to marriage as a right for everyone, things like that.

At this stage gay men and lesbians move from awareness of oppression to action in the world to change it. In the spiritual realm, this is work for justice. Justice-making may be expressed through a wide range of services and activities—from lobbying leg-islative bodies to offering volunteer services to persons with HIV and AIDS to mak-ing films and writing books. In this stage there is a new energy for connecting with others to improve the lives of gay men and lesbians, as well as bisexual and transgen-der persons, by building coalitions and working through the inevitable conflicts that arise from various groups' needs and political stances. For some, the activism stage opens out into an awareness of gay/lesbian/bisexual persons as only one of many marginalized groups. These people may devote their energy to bettering life conditions for persons in other groups.

Coming Out Never Ends

Because we live in a heterosexist society, gay men and lesbians face coming out dilemmas constantly. They come up when we change jobs, meet new relatives, talk about our partners to people we don't know well, have a commitment ceremony, move to a new neighborhood, or meet new people. Each of these encounters may reactivate the coming out process. Shame or anger may resurface and need to be worked through yet another time.

When coming out seems dangerous or inappropriate in a particular context, gay men and lesbians employ coping strategies as needed. Sometimes we merely keep information about our sexual identity close to the vest. Teachers and other professionals who work with children, and those who live in areas where many people are antigay, are likely to adopt this strategy as needed. Sometimes we act in gender-appropriate ways and neither announce nor deny our sexual orientation. Gay men and lesbians who work at the higher levels of professions and corporations, and many others, may adopt this strategy.

Each such incident may provoke intense feelings: anger that one has to deal with this situation at all; fear of harm; determination to be oneself and let others deal with their prejudice. The spiritual director can be a supportive and affirming presence when such situations arise.

Conclusion

Coming out almost inevitably involves spiritual and religious issues. It asks us to reevaluate and reposition ourselves in relation to religion—doctrine, scripture, community, clergy—and spirituality—integrity, prayer, images of God, relationship with the sacred. At every step there are choices to be made, choices that fundamentally alter the course of the interior life as well as the exterior. Spiritual directors can be vital companions in the discernment and self-affirmation process of coming out. Doing so, we work as witnesses to God's love.

PEG THOMPSON, PHD, is a licensed psychologist practicing in St. Paul, Minnesota. She offers psychotherapy and spiritual direction as well as consultation and inservice training for both therapists and spiritual directors. She also serves as an adjunct faculty member at two local graduate schools. When not working, she can often be found in her garden or on a trout stream—or dreaming of being there.

Note

1. Gregory M. Herek, "The Context of Anti-Gay Violence: Notes on Cultural and Psychological Heterosexism," *Journal of Interpersonal Violence* 5 (1990): 316–33.

Hallowing Our Diminishments: Spiritual Guidance in Later Life

Susan P. Sihler

Pierre Teilhard de Chardin, in his classic, *The Divine Milieu*, speaks of the first half of life as divinizing one's activities and the second half of life as hallowing one's diminishments. The opportunity and challenge for the spiritual director or guide is to companion persons in the second half of life, through the process of coming to see their diminishments as holy and consecrated, as an opening to a deeper life in God.[1]

We are living in a culture that is rapidly growing older. We hear phrases such as "the graying of America." Western culture has been one that denies aging and death and elevates youth, activity, and vitality. We have not been provided with positive models for the second half of life—growing toward old age with a sense of acceptance and grace. Growing older brings the "threat" of losses—physical, emotional, relational, economic, vocational, and social. But growing older can also be "reframed" as a time of great opportunity and growth in the spiritual realm.

In this essay, I will look at tools that will help us do this reframing. I will also explore some of the qualities that can help a spiritual director or guide be more present to directees who are in later life. Finally, I will articulate some opportunities and challenges that seem to be particularly appropriate for this time of life.

Frameworks for Looking at Spirituality in Later Life

Because little has been written in the specific area of spiritual guidance and later life, we will look to both psychology and spirituality for frameworks in which we can understand the challenges and struggles of growing older.

The Second Journey

The depth psychologist C. G. Jung presented the notion that, for persons in midlife and beyond, problems are essentially spiritual rather than psychological. "A person in the second half of life . . . no longer needs to educate his conscious will, but . . . to understand the meaning of his individual life and needs to experience his own inner being."[2] The most important task of the second half of life is personal and spiritual growth.

Gerald O'Collins's book *The Second Journey* gives us a viable image of the second half of life. We spend the first half of life establishing ourselves in the world, accumulating earthly possessions, satisfying our ego needs in terms of role, status, and position. Mid to later life is a time to rethink and rediscover. O'Collins uses the Emmaus story (Luke 24) as his metaphor for the second journey. He says that as the disciples on the road to Emmaus encountered Jesus, they were able to rethink and rediscover and, in turn, were also rediscovered by Jesus.[3]

We may think we know who we are, but as we enter the second journey, we have the opportunity to discover new aspects of ourselves—to become reacquainted with parts of ourselves that have been hidden from us during our years of striving and acquiring. O'Collins says that "Christians on a second journey always travel with Christ, even if they are not aware of that 'stranger' with them. By sensing his presence they will definitively identify themselves."[4] Our identity becomes rooted in Christ as we see Christ and the scriptures as a mirror for any suffering or diminishment that we endure.

Second journey people must die to be reborn. Rebirth can be harder than birth because it often involves a stripping away and an emptying out of things that once seemed to fill us. Sally is a directee whose "death" and "rebirth" came in the form of undergoing a serious surgical intervention, celebrating her sixtieth birthday, and realizing how lifeless her marriage of thirty-five years had become. Her world is both falling apart and being recreated. She will no longer have her big house; she is giving up some of the financial security that her husband's retirement income would have afforded; she is dying to many of the things that used to matter. Sally will face retirement alone but with a stronger sense of herself and a personal integrity that was lacking as she trudged toward later life in a loveless marriage. The death of her marriage is bringing a rebirth of a self that had long been buried. Christ is her companion as she journeys into the next stage of her life.

Scripture gives us various stories about the need for conversion or rebirth on this second journey, which I would call the "journey inward" or the "journey of the spirit." Recall the question of Nicodemus: "'How can anyone be born after having grown old?' . . . Jesus answered, 'Very truly, I tell you, no one can enter the kingdom of God without being born of water and Spirit" (John 3:4–5).

Our place of hope on this second journey, this spiritual journey, is in God. Consider the words of the psalmist:

LORD, let me know my end and what is the measure of my days; let me know how fleeting my life is. You have made my days a few handbreadths;

and my lifetime is as nothing in your sight. Surely everyone stands as a mere breath. Surely everyone goes about like a shadow. Surely for nothing they are in turmoil; they heap up, and do not know who will gather. And now, O Lord, what do I wait for? My hope is in you. (Ps 39:4–7)

All that seemed important in the first half of life takes on a different meaning if we allow ourselves the experience of rebirth as we enter into the second journey. The earthly/worldly seems far less important, and the spiritual or otherworldly takes on increasing importance. This second journey work is important and necessary in order to move into the third journey, which involves aging and moving through the last years before death.[5]

The Desert

Another helpful framework as we look at the spiritual journey of later life is the rich imagery and metaphor of the desert. Scripture, the example of the early desert fathers and mothers, and the writings of the Christian mystics and contemplatives exemplify the power of the desert.

It was in the desert, barren, unpredictable, surprising, that the people of God were to learn the lesson and privilege of dependence upon Yahweh in the simplicity of naked faith. It would be in the desert that renewal would take place, there that the wastes would rejoice and blossom like the rose, there that waters would flow again (Isa 35:1–6). Throughout human history, religious and secular, the desert has played a crucial role.[6]

Renewal stories tell of God calling Abraham into the desert of the unknown; of Moses leading the Israelites' exodus into the desert wilderness; of Elijah journeying into the desert and finding God in the solitude and stillness of the cave at Horeb, and returning to Mt. Carmel for periods of solitude; of John the Baptist as "a voice crying in the wilderness"; and of Jesus being led by the Spirit into the wilderness, where he experienced temptations. Throughout his ministry, Jesus also sought solitude in deserts and lonely places, instructing his disciples to follow his example.

In Western culture in particular, later life can be a silent time and a time of struggle for meaning, for validity, and for a rightful place in society. Because of this, later life can be experienced as a desert time. The desert metaphor represents not only a place of silence but also a place of struggle. Across cultures, late life presents the struggle of physical decline and the sense of loss and loneliness that comes with the death of one's companions. Death can be viewed as the ultimate desert, the unknown, the stilling of human life as we have known it. But in this silence and void lies the paradox—and therefore the opportunity for both spiritual guide and older person—of knowing God in a new way. Entering the desert with its stillness and its struggle is a way of preparing for that ultimate meeting with our God through death. To again

quote Teilhard de Chardin, "Death is the sum and consummation of all our diminishments. We must overcome death by finding God in it. And by the same token, we shall
find the divine established in our innermost hearts, in the last stronghold which might
have seemed able to escape his reach."[7]

Erik Erikson: Psychosocial Development

Turning from a spiritual to a psychological framework is helpful as we develop
frameworks for spiritual direction in later life. Psychologist Erik Erikson has divided
the life cycle into eight stages of psychosocial development, from infancy to old age.
Each stage is designated by a primary task or struggle and a potential virtue to be
gained when the task is completed or the struggle resolved. Resolution of a stage prepares a person for a successful outcome of the task or struggle presented in the suc-
ceeding stage.[8] Two stages are pertinent to this essay.

Generativity vs. Stagnation

The seventh stage, "Adulthood" (ages thirty-five to sixty), is especially important
for living a fruitful old age. The struggle in "Adulthood" is between generativity and
stagnation (self-absorption). If unresolved, we fool ourselves with a false generativity
that hides in busyness, or we become indifferent and enter old age withdrawn by self-
absorption; either frenetic activity until physical health no longer allows it, or a sense
of self-pity, complaining, unreasonable demands on others, loneliness, and meaninglessness. Resolved, we enter the final stage of life with a sense of caring, which is the
virtue to be gained in the seventh stage of life. This caring, which is the outgrowth of
generativity, is seen as caring for the next generation and for leaving a better society and
environment to them.

With persons over the age of sixty, the early stages of the direction relationship
may involve a "life review." Greta, a seventy-eight-year-old retired missionary, came to
spiritual guidance first needing to talk through the hurts of childhood coming from a
rigid and emotionally unpredictable minister father. She looked back at her forty years
on the mission field and her difficulty with close relationships, not only with peers, but
also with God. She had spent her life working for God, but she felt no closeness with
God. As she began to make connections between her "earthly" and "heavenly" fathers,
she recognized how much she longed for a loving God. The life review helped her connect, grieve what she had missed, and begin to move into a relationship with a more
loving, intimate God.

Integrity vs. Despair

Erikson's eighth and last stage, "Old Age," involves the struggle between integrity
and despair. If this task is unresolved, we enter a state of melancholy. Resolution
brings the virtue of wisdom. "Wisdom is detached concern with life itself in the face
of death itself. It maintains and learns to convey the integrity of experience, in spite
of the decline of bodily and mental functions."[9] At this stage the life review process

helps a person assess how one's life has been lived and then come to terms with it. The person often comes to spiritual guidance wanting to take a life inventory and see where God fits in at this stage of change.

My friend and colleague in the Shalem Spiritual Guidance Program, Sister Mary Frances Lottes, wrote a paper titled "Spiritual Guidance and the Elderly." As a person then in her sixties, she wrote:

> At some time during our sixties, most of us tend to look back at our lives and to see how all that we have experienced fits together. . . . We try to see as a whole the tapestry that the threads of our lives have woven. . . . We need to face our lives, even the darknesses, own them, accept them, ask for forgiveness, and then entrust them in confidence to the loving mercy of God. As we move through this life review and offer it to God, we can let go of past hurts, angers, resentments, myths about ourselves and life. It is in this way that we can integrate our lives . . . and with trust and confidence put our energy into facing each moment of the present. . . .
>
> In our struggle to achieve integration we must fight against the enemy, Despair. Despair tells us . . . that this period of Old Age is meaningless, that we are a burden to others and have nothing to contribute to others or to the world. We seem to be condemned to isolation and loneliness. . . . We are not given a choice about whether or not we will age, but we do have a choice about how we will age. The challenge of old age is to be truly active in the sense of accepting old age, appropriating it, giving it meaning, and integrating it into oneself as a person. If we engage ourselves in the struggle, we can hope to arrive at the grace of Old Age which is Wisdom.[10]

Later life is a time of both stillness and struggle, a time of rebirth, and a time of coming to terms with the meaning of our lives. These understandings are necessary for a spiritual guide called to work with older people. At a time when the directee's physical health may be failing and his or her contributions to the material world seem all but over, the vast and rich expanse of inner space may be experienced as rich soil for both the directee and his or her spiritual guide.

Qualities of a Spiritual Guide Working with Later Life Directees

Margaret Guenther, in the last paragraph of *Toward Holy Ground: Spiritual Directions for the Second Half of Life*, writes: "The aged among us are rare parchments, waiting to be read by those of us who will take the time to listen. We are honored to sit in their presence. And these rare parchments may indeed show us how we, ourselves, God willing, might grow up to be rare parchments too."[11] How privileged, but how challenged, we are as spiritual guides to listen to these rare parchments who are our directees.

Throughout her book, Guenther weaves various qualities needed for guiding persons in later life. Following is a composite of her thoughts and some of my own.

Age of the Director

That the spiritual guide has moved into the tasks and questions of the second half of life is more important than his or her chronological age. Margaret Guenther asks, "So what is the second half of life?"

> It is when we are finally grown up . . . when we have developed an aware-ness of mortality . . . our perspective changes and we are amazed to realize that some things just don't matter anymore . . . we are able to embrace ambiguity . . . and there is a knowing that is almost a numinous experience. This is the knowing of profound understanding, of the grasp of hidden connections. This is the knowing of insight and wisdom. . . . The knowing that characterizes the second half of life is open to mystery, drawn to the depths, and ready to risk.[12]

Those of us called to accompany people who are in later life must be willing to be with all of the issues (as they pertain to our personal lives) that Guenther raises in the above excerpt. Our willingness serves as an indication of our readiness to walk with the elderly.

Willingness to Listen

You may say, "Well, of course." Any spiritual guide knows that at the heart of our ministry is listening, but listening with an older person is different. We are listening to people come into wholeness and completion. This may be the last chance they will have to be listened to on this earth.[13] Sometimes they are still struggling with relation-ships that need to be put in place (Erikson's Integrity vs. Despair). Many continue to wrestle with images of God, as Greta did when she made connections between her "earthly" and her "heavenly" father. Several of my older directees have experienced very distant, fearful relationships with a judgmental male God. In order not to fear death, they need to discover solace in a loving, accepting God.

Guenther refers to the spirituality of the aged as a "spirituality of storytelling." Telling their story breathes life into a time of closure and seeming diminishment. They need to review their lives and need to talk about their approaching death.[14] Listening to persons who are weaving the final tapestry of life cannot be done in a hurry. Directors also need to anticipate and prepare for hearing loss in some of their elderly directees. Over 40 percent of persons over age seventy-five have some degree of hear-ing impairment.[15] Allowing sufficient time in your schedule to be totally present to the hearing-impaired person is a must; listening and speaking simply take longer in this context. Speaking slowly and enunciating clearly are also required.

Facing of Our Diminishments and Death

As directors, we must face ourselves and know ourselves. We need to know how much we can tolerate in the way of illness. We must face our own mortality and befriend it if we are to minister creatively to those who are facing their own death. We need to continually evaluate and work on this if we are not entirely clear about it.[16]

My older sister has had Parkinson's disease for twenty-six years. In its early stages, I could deny that she had a disease that would eventually ravage her body; the symptoms were barely perceptible, and she was able to continue her work as a church musician. In the last few years I have had to come to terms with more dramatic changes in my sister that are resulting from this disease. As her posture becomes more stooped, her falls more frequent, and her ability to perform household tasks almost nonexistent, I have had to accept that she will never recover and will become more and more helpless. As I observe her physical diminishment, I recognize that some day that could be me. A part of me wants to continue to deny and to not visit her so that I don't have to face this truth. But a stronger part of me pushes me to be with her diminishment simply because I love her. I am also aware that my presence with her prepares me for what I someday may face.

Willingness to Deal with Loss and Simplification

As spiritual guides we try to help people learn the art of nonattachment and to order their lives in relationship to the internal vs. the external. But if we are going to offer spiritual direction to people in later life, we must prepare ourselves for the starkness and simplification of their environment, relationships, and interior life as they become "stripped down" in preparation for death. It is important for us to be clear with ourselves about our feelings of anxiety and apprehension about hospitals, retirement centers, and nursing homes before we enter this environment to offer spiritual guidance.[17]

Some familiarity with the grief/loss process and the stages of grief as described by Kubler-Ross and others would be especially helpful to the director. Acknowledging the feelings of anger, depression, and denial that are a necessary part of grieving needs to be a part of the director's understanding and process.

Although my directees usually come to my office, I had a recent experience with a woman named Marianne, who, in the course of six months, had both knee and brain surgery. During this time she was unable to come to my office, and in order to continue direction, I visited her both in her small apartment and in the nursing care section in the retirement center where she lives. Many of us offering spiritual guidance to older people will find ourselves being called upon to change the environment of "place" to adapt to the health needs of the person we are serving.

Awareness and Understanding of Depression

Older people often experience depression as they face their physical diminishments. When we find ourselves feeling bored, unusually tired, or resistant, we may be absorbing some of their depression. We need to acknowledge this to ourselves, seek supervision when it feels appropriate, and try not to promise or expect more than we can realistically give. We will also want to be sure that the person is getting adequate medical and mental health services so that we can then focus on the spiritual.

Challenges and Opportunities for Spiritual Guidance in Later Life

"The goal of spiritual direction is to help a person become more open to the Holy Spirit in the events of life which summon that person to continued conversion and towards deeper communication with God."[18] Sister Mary Frances says about her own aging:

> The events of life as one grows into old age can be very trying and challenging. One is pushed to the edge of the mystery of life, but that is where God can work more effectively in us. It is a call to another conversion experience. A spiritual companion can be of great support and assistance at this time, aware all the time that it is God who is doing the leading and giving grace to the person to follow.[19]

The diminishment of the body and the growth of the spirit are the paradoxical gifts of growing older. As we become empty to the things of this world, we are opening ourselves or "hallowing ourselves"[20] to be ultimately united with Christ. Our death will become a new birth. We have many wonderful verses in scripture that can reassure us. "So we do not lose heart. Even though our outer nature is wasting away, our inner nature is being renewed day by day. For this slight momentary affliction is preparing for us an eternal weight of glory beyond all measure, because we look not at what can be seen but at what cannot be seen; for what can be seen is temporary, but what cannot be seen is eternal" (2 Cor 4:16–18).

Silence, Solitude, and Surrender

Many of the "practices" that we recommend to our younger directees, such as silence and solitude, become almost natural accompaniments to the person in later life. The "noise" of an active life is moving into increased silence. Sometimes the loss of spouse, friends, and other family members brings increased solitude. With support from their spiritual guides, directees can be gently challenged to see these experiences not only as times of loss but also as invitations from God to growth in the Spirit.

Jane Thibault, in an article titled "The Spiritual Call of Later Life," tells of a woman who had been very busy in her earlier life and at the age of sixty-seven was widowed. She came to counseling saying that she was finding little satisfaction in any of her previous activities and feeling that there was "something more" to life than what she had experienced. She craved something, but she didn't know what this might be. Through spiritual guidance she discovered that this "more" was God. She had never really "met God," and she longed to do so.[21] One of our tasks as spiritual guides is to help people take that next step of surrender—falling into the arms of God and becoming intimate with God. One of the gifts of later life can be coming to experience and appreciate God's presence in the depths of one's being.

The invitation to encounter God as lover, dwelling within the soul, is one of the special opportunities of later life. The development of this relationship requires time, and retirement provides us with the freedom to choose how to spend large amounts of our time. We used to think that contemplative life was possible only in a monastic environment, but more and more we are seeing that anyone can practice the contemplative life, and later life affords the space and time for it.

The lessening of our attachments to the world that can come with later life prepares us for deeper attachment to God. The spiritual call of later life is to intensify our relationship with God, to develop a deeper intimacy with God, to journey inward to God, and finally to make our dwelling place with God. In doing this we die gradually to the world, and our ultimate death becomes not something to fear but the final union for which we have longed.

Contemplative Prayer

The call to a deeper relationship with God often evokes a different kind of prayer, known as contemplative prayer. Many people spend their whole prayer life talking to God, but they have never stopped to listen. As spiritual guides, we are teachers and mentors, helping those in later life welcome and become comfortable with this "listening prayer." Contemplative prayer prepares us for old age, helping us learn how to willingly put ourselves into the dark spaciousness of God's love, trusting that God will work in us whatever we need.

Spiritual Life Review

When seen from a spiritual perspective, the life review can become part of the spiritual direction relationship, framed as a process of continual conversions and identified as a series of "dyings and risings as a way of living," daily and yearly in relationships and exteriorly. We die often before we die forever.[22] We may find comfort in realizing that as we enter into later life and prepare for our own death, we have already experienced deaths and resurrections in many ways.

Ministry of Prayer

No matter what our age or state of health, the world needs the energy of our prayer. Intercessory prayer—praying for those close to us, our world, its leadership, the poor and oppressed—can be a powerful ministry. People in later life who begin a ministry of intercessory prayer may find a renewed sense of purpose and freedom, in part because the activity is not adversely affected by physical diminishment. A spiritual director can offer guidance to directees in later life that supports this ministry.

Catherine is a woman of retirement age and is a serious prayer who is in a spiritual guidance relationship. She belongs to two prayer groups and has an ongoing list of persons, which changes from time to time, for whom she prays daily. She has had some serious personal health problems, but each difficulty has strengthened her belief in prayer and her resolve to pray for others. I expect that Catherine's ministry of intercessory prayer will continue until she breathes her last breath. People know how seriously she accepts this calling and often ask her to pray for them.

Group Spiritual Direction

Most people seek spiritual direction midlife when they are beginning the second journey, the journey of the spirit. Persons in later life may feel more comfortable beginning spiritual guidance in a group setting, which may seem less threatening. Senior adult groups within churches or retirement home settings would be ideal places to introduce group spiritual direction and to build trust for those who might later like to move into individual spiritual guidance. You might begin a Bible study group that looks at passages about God's promises and growing older; you might begin a contemplative prayer group or have a spiritual retreat for people in later life.[23]

Conclusion

To be a spiritual guide to those in later life requires a willingness to venture into the spaciousness and emptiness that come with the growing detachment from the things of this world and entrance into the vast unknown. Teilhard de Chardin sees the final invitation as that moment of hallowed diminishment when we become one with God through death.

> Grant that I may willingly consent to this last phase of communion in the course of which I shall possess You by diminishing in You. . . . When the signs of age begin to mar my body (and still more when they touch my mind), when the painful moment comes in which I suddenly awaken to the fact that I am ill or growing old; and above all at that last moment when I feel I am losing hold of myself and am absolutely passive within the hands of the great unknown forces that have formed me, in all these dark moments, O God, grant that I may understand that it is You (provided only my faith is strong enough) who is painfully parting the fibers of my being in order to penetrate to the very marrow of my substance and bear me away within yourself.[24]

What greater privilege could we have than to be an earthly companion to those who are at this point of their sacred journey.

Recommended Reading

Bianchi, Eugene C. *Aging as a Spiritual Journey*. New York: Crossroads Press, 1989.
Devoy, Juliana. "Spiritual Direction: Being Artist with God," *Spiritual Life* 34, no. 4 (Winter 1988).

Fischer, Kathleen. *Winter Grace: Spirituality for the Later Years*. New York: Paulist Press, 1985.

————. *Autumn Gospel: Women in the Second Half of Life*. New York: Paulist Press, 1995.

Harris, Maria. *Jubilee Time: Celebrating Women, Spirit and the Advent of Age*. New York: Bantam, 1995.

Kenel, Mary Elizabeth. "Birthing the Elderly Self." *Human Development* 16, no. 3 (Fall 1995).

Koenig, Harold G., MD. *Aging and God: Spiritual Pathways to Mental Health in Midlife and Later Years*. Binghamton, N.Y.: Haworth Press, 1990.

Luke, Helen M. *Old Age: Journey into Simplicity*. New York: Parabola Books, 1987.

Nouwen, Henri J. *Our Greatest Gift: A Meditation on Dying and Caring*. San Francisco: Harper, 1994.

On Hallowing One's Diminishments. Pendle Hill Pamphlet 292. Wallingford, Pa.: Pendle Hill, 1990.

Rupp, Joyce. *Praying Our Goodbyes*. Notre Dame, Ind.: Ave Maria Press, 1987.

Yungblut, John R. *The Gentle Art of Spiritual Direction*. New York: Amity House, 1988.

SUSAN P. SIHLER holds an MSW from the University of Minnesota and completed the Shalem Institute program in spiritual guidance. She has practiced as a clinical social worker in the mental health field for the past forty years. She began her work in spiritual guidance seventeen years ago and now has a solo practice in psychotherapy, spiritual guidance, and retreat work in Asheville, North Carolina.

Notes

1. Pierre Teilhard de Chardin, *The Divine Milieu* (New York: Harper, 1966).

2. C. G. Jung, *C. G. Jung, Psychological Reflections: A New Anthology of His Writings* (ed. J. Jacobi; London: Kegan, 1971), 137–38.

3. Gerald O'Collins, *The Second Journey* (New York: Paulist Press, 1978), 81.

4. Ibid., 1.

5. Jung, *Psychological Reflections*, 137–38.

6. Kenneth Leech, *Experiencing God: Theology as Spirituality* (San Francisco: Harper & Row 1985), 127.

7. Teilhard de Chardin, *Divine Milieu*, 82.

8. Erik Erikson, Joan M. Erikson, and Helen Q. Kivnick, *Vital Involvement in Old Age* (New York: W. W. Norton, 1986), 36, 45.

9. Ibid., 38.

10. Mary Frances Lottes, SL. "Spiritual Guidance and the Elderly," unpublished paper, Shalem Institute, Washington, D.C., October, 1990, 3–4.

11. Margaret Guenther, *Toward Holy Ground: Spiritual Directions for the Second Half of Life* (Boston: Cowley Publications, 1995), 149.

12. Ibid., 5–8.

13. Ibid., 136–40.

14. Ibid., 135.

15. Ibid.

16. Ibid., 134.

17. Ibid.

18. Shaun McCarty, "On Entering Spiritual Direction." *Review for Religious* 35 (1976): 859.

19. Lottes, "Spiritual Guidance," 9.

20. Teilhard de Chardin, *Divine Milieu*, 89.

21. Jane M. Thibault, "The Spiritual Call of Later Life" *Weavings* (January–February 1991), 16–17.

22. Rea McDonnell, "Dying and Rising as a Way of Living," *Praying*, no. 10: 4.

23. Lottes, "Spiritual Guidance," 11.

24. Teilhard de Chardin, *Divine Milieu*, 89–90.

Companioning People with Dementia

Rita Hansen, John R. Mabry, and Robert B. Williams

G ood morning, I'm Arthur James. Wasn't the service enjoyable? I like coming to Holy Trinity." For the umpteenth time Arthur James introduces himself to other faithful worshipers at the service as though they had never before met. They all know Arthur, who is a spry, cheery, and pleasant eighty-year-old who accompanies his wife, Alice, to church every week. During the worship service, Arthur knows exactly what to do. He sings, recites prayers and psalms, stands, processes, kneels to reverently receive Communion, and is able to return unassisted to his place in the pew. From the view of any observer, Arthur's behavior during the service is really no different than anyone else's. It is Arthur's recurring introductions of himself and his need to be reacquainted with those who are with him every week that reveals something of the problems that he and his wife are coping with.

Occasionally, Arthur and Alice attend social activities at Holy Trinity. At a recent ham and bean supper, Arthur was unable to recognize Pastor Green, who was dressed in a flannel shirt and jeans. This was surprising because Arthur had always addressed Pastor Green quite enthusiastically when greeting him after services. Arthur was not able to recognize him because he was "out of uniform." Alice told us that Arthur does not recognize himself in recent photos. He can point himself out in photos taken when he was an adolescent and a young adult, but not beyond those years. Arthur has occasions when he doesn't even recognize Alice in photos, except in those taken when she was wearing her nurse's uniform.

Arthur is totally dependent on Alice for everything. He is unable to write, drive, shop, plan, carry out even simple household chores, adequately maintain his personal hygiene, select clothing appropriate for the occasion or season, find the bathroom, or recognize the voices of relatives or friends on the phone. He depends upon assistance and cues from others for normal life experiences he knew and lived before being afflicted with a loss of his "everyday memory." This loss has been noted by Arthur's physician as a likely symptom of dementia.

The Burdens of Dementia

Those afflicted with dementia have problems applying their thinking to ordinary tasks such as dressing, attending to personal hygiene, or remembering words or names. Over time, a person's ability to live a self-directed life is progressively reduced by problems with thinking and remembering. Such problems are symptoms of dementia, seen in persons with Alzheimer's disease; Lewy body disease; vascular dementia and dementia due to other medical conditions such as HIV; head trauma; Parkinson's disease; Huntington's disease; Pick's disease; or Creutzfeldt-Jacob disease. Symptoms of dementia are due to actual physical changes occurring in one or more parts of the brain. With the exception of Creutzfeldt-Jacob, most people afflicted with dementia experience a slow decline in thinking and remembering.[1]

Prior traits and behavior become exaggerated in people with Alzheimer's. No one really knows when Alzheimer's begins, and the symptoms or signs are different for every person. A positive diagnosis can only be made in autopsy. The key is to observe a progression of change in behavior, cognition, and emotion. Because of their uneven decline in thinking and remembering, persons with dementia often surprise family, pastors, and other caregivers by their responses. Arthur is a good example because he can participate fully in worship services but is limited in activities of daily living. Further, pastoral care personnel have observed responses that we have been taught are beyond the capabilities of a person with Alzheimer's. We do not really know enough about these people in general, and we must tailor our pastoral or spiritual offerings for individuals.

Early Stages: Recognizing Dementia in Directees

When Pamela showed up for her regular spiritual direction session, she was upset and shaken. "Let's take a minute of silence to center ourselves," suggested Leslie, her spiritual director. When she was calmer, Pamela explained that she seemed to be forgetting things more and more, and she was starting to panic. "I went to the supermarket because Jane and the kids were coming for supper. But when I got there, I forgot what I had come for, and for a few minutes, I couldn't figure out where I was. I was so scared I was shaking."

Leslie was tempted to say, "I forget what I went to the store for all the time!" But Pamela was crying now, and she realized this was more serious than simple forgetfulness. Memory loss in elderly people is normal and does not necessarily denote the onset of dementia. Pamela's experience may have been a simple case of age-associated memory impairment, but the red flag had been waved.

Leslie made a mental note of the experience and between sessions educated herself on the signs of dementia. When Pamela's experiences persisted, Leslie strongly recommended a medical consultation. Pamela was in strong denial for a while, but when another "episode" occurred while she was driving, she finally went to her doctor.

In this case, Leslie's attention paid off. A spiritual director should become attuned to signs of even slight behavior change in older persons being companioned. The disease usually progresses in a linear fashion and moves through seven stages.

Initially, there are no symptoms (Stage 1). A person does not notice as the disease begins its work. The impairment is no greater than occasional memory loss experienced by most people.

Gradually, a person will experience a very mild decline (Stage 2). A directee may complain about not being able to remember names of people they *know* they ought to know. They may misplace objects more and more frequently. This stage may be accompanied by frustration and self-recrimination for being "so forgetful." The directee will still be functional at work and will continue to be articulate in direction at this stage. Such complaints should prompt a director to pay attention but will not necessarily indicate that medical attention is necessary.

Eventually, however, the disease will manifest itself clearly (Stages 3 and 4). A directee may get lost when traveling to a familiar location, his or her work performance will begin to suffer, and family members will notice the person's increasing difficulty with names and proper articulation. A directee also may be frustrated with how little he or she retains when reading or have difficulty concentrating. A directee may be feeling shame because he or she has lost an item of great value. He or she may begin to experience increasing levels of anxiety and not a little bit of denial.

At this point a responsible director should recommend that the directee seek medical attention to discover the cause of his or her symptoms and to receive adequate medical care. The director should also turn attention to proper spiritual care for someone with progressive dementia, as spiritual direction in a typical setting and fashion may become increasingly difficult.

Spiritual Care as Condition Progresses

Each year the Gerontological Society of America brings out research about how religious or spiritual support positively mediates attitudes, coping, health, anxiety level, and life satisfaction in older people. There is, however, a lack of inquiry relating to religious and spiritual lives of elders who have serious cognitive impairment. According to Sandy Burgener, Rosemary Shimer, and Linda Murrell, "One explanation for the lack of attention to spiritual needs in demented elders may be an assumption on the part of the religious community, caregivers, and family members that spiritual support and practices may no longer be relevant or important for an elder with dementia."[2]

This assumption, of course, is not correct. As spiritual directors, we see in our daily experience that there is no part of life in which the Spirit is not at work. To assume that people with dementia do not have spiritual lives or that spiritual care is no longer relevant for such people is the twenty-first-century equivalent of such nineteenth century assertions as "Animals are machines that do not feel pain," or "Slaves are not human beings." These kinds of denials are ways that society has avoided collective responsibility, and there are many who would avoid the responsibility of treating people with dementia as real people. In certain circumstances, it may be tempting to any of us to want to avoid such responsibilities. But as spiritual directors, it is our responsibility to meet people where they are, to bear witness to the movement of the Divine in a person's life, regardless of their societal, ethical, or medical state.

When one becomes aware that a directee's condition is progressing, there are several ways that a spiritual director can be of assistance. In the early phase of dementia, it is helpful to assess how you should proceed with direction and include the directee in this assessment. Sometimes it's helpful to share what caregivers have learned about persons with Alzheimer's.

A director should also be prepared to assist the directee who is newly diagnosed with Alzheimer's disease with coping and grieving. Alzheimer's disease is a catastrophic chronic illness similar to cancer or stroke that carries with it a stigma and imposes the loss of one's role, which can result in a devastating identity crisis. Eventually the condition will require extraordinary adaptations by the person and loved ones.[3] The impact of being told that one has Alzheimer's is well demonstrated in David Snowdon's *Aging with Grace*.[4] He relates the story of a nun who was misdiagnosed as having Alzheimer's. Her greatest worry was that she would forget Jesus, but she became consoled by the thought that he would not forget her. All during the time that others around her believed that she had Alzheimer's, they would check on her to be sure she was not forgetting to turn off any equipment she used.

There are many effective and important things one can do in companioning someone as his or her condition progresses:

Provide a Safe Container for Feeling

Articulating feelings is difficult for the directee with dementia. This will also touch the feelings of the spiritual director. Feeling useless, low, angry, surprised, and taken unaware may be part of a long list of negative feelings that a person with dementia can display. Inhibitions are let loose, and he or she may say or do what could be inappropriate in a "normal" spiritual direction session. Directors can minister to directees with dementia by being present and listening as they describe their frustration and fears. The direction session may be the only safe space a directee has to process his or her feelings about what is happening, since family members may be in denial or may not want to talk about it.

Provide Comfort and Reassurance

Most people who suffer dementia are quite aware of what is happening to them, and fear and anxiety are common. People with dementia experience gradual loss of their internal landmarks, so anything that lessens the anxiety and distress caused by confusion and disorientation is a desirable goal for any caregiver. As every spiritual director knows, religious ritual and devotional activity go very deep. Attention given to this aspect of life may provide a mental "anchor" for people with dementia that can significantly increase their quality of life. A director may want to incorporate a ritual into the sessions that can be done outside the session, too, which may help the directee access the peace and comfort that the direction session affords between sessions as well. Simply reading aloud familiar scriptures such as Psalm 23 or the Lord's Prayer or reciting the rosary can bring comfort and grounding to a directee even in the midst of a very frustrating and frightening day.

A spiritual director may find it helpful to identify a souvenir or symbol (Bible, cross, rosary, icon, picture, prayer, hymn, etc.) from the past that the directee with dementia has used continuously. The symbol or souvenir can serve as a cue for the directee as to your continuing role. Directors can encourage directees to incorporate simple rituals into direction sessions and daily life, even if such rituals have not been particularly attractive to them in their earlier life.

Realize That Directees May Feel Very Alone

It is important for directors to remind directees that, like Daniel's fourth man in the fire, God is present in all the pain and confusion and is going through it all *with* them. The director is also with them and should remind them that he or she is not going to go away. Bringing to mind others who are committed to the directee will encourage relaxation and trust that the directee will be cared for and loved even when the condition worsens.

Determine Your Own Commitment

Directors at this stage should also ask themselves some very important questions: What is my commitment to my directees? Will I continue to accompany them even after they have gone into assisted living? Even after they can no longer pay for service? How much time can I commit to spending with my client as his or her disease progresses? Do I have sufficient emotional and spiritual support to continue companioning this person? Getting clear on these questions for themselves while their clients are still aware and articulate will help when comforting directees, as directors will know exactly what they can promise and their directees will not fear abandonment.

The most important thing at this stage is to provide directees with safe space to grieve the stage of life they are passing out of and to comfort them as they attempt to navigate the scary new world that is emerging. If there are hurts that are unhealed, apologies unsaid, or confessions unmade, directors can suggest that now is the time to make such connections, while they can still do so with care and attention.

Spiritual Care in Later Stages

Spiritual direction is ordinarily thought of as a quiet, uninterrupted hour. Since people with Alzheimer's have a very short attention span (or may be focused on memories), a standard one-on-one direction hour is usually impossible. Spiritual care in later stages of dementia is usually provided not by spiritual directors, or even by pastors or priests, but by people who are ostensibly performing other tasks, especially once a person has been admitted to a care facility.

As a nurse, I (Rita) found plenty of opportunities to minister to patients in the course of performing other duties. Directors who continue to companion former clients will find that there will be much opportunity to extend their attention to other residents while they are there. Even the average visitor to an Alzheimer's unit has ample opportunity to minister to many patients when going to see his or her own family members.

Ministry does not require a large amount of time to make a difference in a person's life. For instance, as a chaplain, I (John) regularly spent five to ten minutes with each patient as I made my rounds in the unit. More time might tax a person's ability to pay attention or focus. As conversation with people with dementia becomes more difficult, the simple ministry of presence becomes more and more important.

When spending time with people in later stages, one can do many things to help them:

Treat People with Respect

The greatest loss a person with dementia experiences is not the loss of memory (which is to be expected) but the loss of dignity. Family members can slide into behavior that infantilizes dementia sufferers, robbing them of their pride of place within a family and their sense of self-worth. Long-buried resentments may surface in children now forced into caregiving roles, and opportunities to "get even" for long-past events may unconsciously be at play. Loving families will want to be watchful of such dynamics, and spiritual directors can act as advocates for their clients even in an institutional environment.

As spiritual caregivers, we must also be careful to avoid the arrogance that suggests that God is no longer working in people with dementia—what do we know about the Spirit's intimacy with other people—*any* other people? The only appropriate assumption for a spiritual director is that Mystery is always unfolding in a person's life and that the Spirit is indeed at work in the inner world of people with dementia, however unfamiliar or peculiar such processes may seem to us.

Facilitate Reconnection with Memories

Responding to people with Alzheimer's or dementia from the perspective of their memories comforts and sustains them. Caregivers who can uncover past memories will discover that this can alleviate anxiety and help those they care for find a place of peace. Nursing home staffs have found they are able to stimulate memories via the paraphernalia of former occupations, reminiscence groups, music, religious services, and orientation to self when consistently addressed with their own names.[5]

I (Rita) knew Margaret only a month before she died at age seventy-six from asthma, which she had all her life. She was gentle and very friendly. Her rosary was always in her hand. The Blessed Mother was on her bed stand, the Sacred Heart and St. Joseph on the wall.

One night Margaret had an asthma attack, and the medication needed time to take effect. To distract her, I started to ask questions about another time in her life. "Where did you grow up?"

At first she resisted and couldn't remember. After gentle coaxing, she smiled as she recalled, "Brooklyn!"

I said, "I know where Brooklyn is." (Repeating a word is always good.) "Where did you go to high school?"

Margaret concentrated for a time. I was called out of the room, and a nursing assistant sat with her for ten minutes. When I returned, she smiled but couldn't remember "the long name of the high school with all different kinds of sisters . . . but my breathing is much better now. I feel comfortable."

"How about Bishop McDonnell?" I asked.

As she burst into an even bigger smile, Margaret added, "Oh, how could I forget the name of that place?"

Margaret and I graduated from the same high school, ten years apart. She shared stories, memories, prayer, and music. We sang together "Memorial, Memorial," our school song. Margaret went to her eternal reward thinking about being greeted by many old friends, religious sisters, and Bishop McDonnell himself. She had a great imagination about the party planned for her in heaven.

People are still people, even with Alzheimer's. We meet them where they are. We give them what they need, when they need it, and how they need it. In Margaret's case, songs and gentle promptings of her memory brought great comfort and increased the quality of her spiritual life.

Role-Playing and Confession

As Alzheimer's progresses, sufferers go more and more into early childhood regression and may become confused and irritated. Repetitive behaviors can also be troubling. Sufferers may mistake visitors for long-dead family members and relive important or mundane moments from their past. If you are present for such scenes, it is often best not to tell them you are not who they think you are. They will benefit from thinking you are someone else, and it is usually better to play along. Caregivers may discover much about the spiritual state of a person with dementia by careful observation of daily scenes acted out over and over again.

Sometimes scenes that dementia sufferers live out repeatedly are not pleasant ones. Their sins come back to haunt them, and they are forced to endure a living hell, as moments of great shame are replayed. While serving as chaplain, I (John) ministered to one person who insisted on confessing the same sin each time I saw him. Of course, he did not remember that he had confessed and received absolution for his transgression many times over. No matter. My hearing his confession and granting him absolution brought him comfort each time.

Continue to Be a Comforting Presence

Whatever decreases confusion and anxiety and brings comfort is of primary importance. Hearing one's name called often gives hope. A person's name may be her only connection to self and the world. Hope will lapse quickly in a person who doesn't hear her name, and it is very important to keep it refreshed. Without hope, flattened affect and withdrawal are likely to take over.

Maintain a Sense of Humor

Patience and common sense are necessary for the spiritual director working with victims of dementia. Take care of your own needs for rest, food, and recreation, and keep a good sense of humor. It is OK to laugh, and often it can defuse a tense situation. While chaplaining at an Alzheimer's unit in Pleasant Hill, California, I (John) ministered regularly to an elderly Irish woman named Mae. She suffered with Alzheimer's and frequently thought I was her son. One day when her daughter and son-in-law were present, she repeatedly asked me to help her with something. Her hands were waving in the air, and it was clear that whatever device she was manipulating existed only in her memories. She was frustrated that I was simply standing there and not assisting her. "Can't you see I can't make this work, Jerry? Help me!" she scolded me. I was taken aback because I didn't know what she was trying to do or how to help her. Finally, she dropped her hands in exasperation and sighed, "Ah, Jerry, you're not worth a damn, anyway." I might've taken offense, but her timing was so comic that the daughter, her husband, and I all burst out laughing. Mae joined in our mirth, though she did look a little bewildered. Whatever frustration or anger she was feeling dissipated quickly into giggles, and she marched off like a soldier to pronounce judgment on something else. Her daughter rolled her eyes and gave me a pat on the shoulder. "That's my mom," she said with a smile.

Ministering to the Families of People with Dementia

Ministering to the person with Alzheimer's means being present to the family as well. Mary had become extremely sweet and docile. The expression on her once-lively Italian face was flat. She was a brittle diabetic recovering from pneumonia. She did not remember being hospitalized two weeks earlier. Her nursing home room was switched because Medicare ran out. Mary's fifty-six-year-old daughter had taken an unpaid leave of absence from her job in New York because of all her mother's problems. The daughter didn't understand "how a good God could do this." She told me (Rita) she was "going to sue." She collected herself in the silent moments that followed. Mary told her daughter to "go see the priest." The woman didn't sue, after all, but the threat was a clear indication of the daughter's great distress and sense of divine abandonment.

Spiritual direction in such a situation may mean discerning God at work under all the dust of family conflict and conversation. This can be very delicately uncovered. Paul and Nelly were members of an Oakland, California, parish for many years. Paul had a terrible temper, often fueled by drinking bouts. Nelly habitually ran interference for Paul, but when she contracted Alzheimer's disease, her ability to do this effectively diminished quickly. Eventually she moved into a nursing facility, and Paul was, for the first time in many years, truly responsible for his own anger. When Paul's pastor, David, tried to companion him through this, he was repeatedly rebuffed, even to the point of verbal abuse. Finally, Paul told Pastor David to simply stop visiting. We are not always able to achieve a good outcome, yet God was using the difficult situation of Nelly's disease to call Paul to wholeness.

Caregivers can provide not only presence, but also education by recommending books that will help family members understand what is happening to their loved ones. In spite of its formidable title, one of the best is *The 36-Hour Day*—widely considered the bible of Alzheimer's caregiving.[6]

The Person with Alzheimer's and Liturgy

While assessing a group of residents diagnosed with probable Alzheimer's dementia at a nursing care facility, I (Robert) learned about their positive responses at weekly ecumenical worship services. These residents were ages sixty-three to eighty-nine years and very limited in their abilities to think or remember. Responses observed during liturgy included recitation of prayers, singing, receiving of Communion, weeping, and composure or quietness. These responses are noteworthy because some of these residents were unable to feed themselves, recognize family members, or respond to questions about who or where they were.

In spite of a decline in ability to think and remember, something triggered these people's memories and enabled them to respond to the liturgy as if unimpaired. This places some responsibility on us as caregivers to give attention to liturgy, and points to a need to work at thinking about how people with memory loss remember the world.[7]

When I (John) was serving as chaplain in an Alzheimer's unit, I would offer a weekly Communion service. Participation varied widely from person to person, according to the stage of dementia. At the end of the service, I went around distributing Communion and gave a host to all who would receive it. One woman was, to the casual observer, completely oblivious to all that was going on around her. She stared blankly into space, and her mouth gaped perpetually. I knelt by her, held her hand, and asked, "Do you want to receive Communion?"

She did not respond, yet I felt a response. Acting on intuition, I placed the host into her mouth. Just then a single tear rolled down her cheek. All appearances to the contrary, there was "someone home," and that one was still touched and fed by the body of Christ.

What do elderly Catholics and other liturgical Christians with severe cognitive impairment "know" as it relates to whether they are able to meaningfully receive Communion? In *Guidelines for the Celebration of the Sacraments with Persons with Disabilities*, the National Conference of [Roman] Catholic Bishops encourages clergy to consult with individuals knowledgeable about disabilities in deciding such questions. There is no reference to empirical studies relating to these issues. The most helpful approach is to use the same criteria applied to ordinary persons for those with Alzheimer's dementia. Worship and liturgy engage us from the beginning to the very end of our lives. Michael Mulvihill notes, "It is the liturgy that is the first school of prayer, and it is by participating in its celebrations regularly and frequently that we grow in communion with God."[8] This may explain how a lifelong history of attendance and participation in liturgy results in memories that allow persons with limited ability to think and remember to respond so well and meaningfully to worship when it is presented to them.

Selecting "old favorite" hymns is just one of many things that can be done to enhance the worship experience for persons with Alzheimer's. You might even choose hymns and music popular at the time when these people were young to reinforce the meaningfulness of liturgy and worship and increase the likelihood of response. Singing hymns such as "The Old Rugged Cross" or "Onward Christian Soldiers" with its sacrificial and militaristic theologies might make contemporary clergy cringe, but they are balm for the soul indeed for those who grew up with such hymns, and caregivers should remember that they are there to serve the needs of their people. Personal theological preferences need to be set aside in favor of what is going to provide the most effective comfort.

Repetition helps people connect and respond to liturgy. When I (John) led music with my guitar, we sang the same songs every week. No one ever complained, and the singing was often robust, as even moderately impaired people were able to participate.

With the growing need for ministry in this area, we authors wonder why there aren't worship kits for this audience, with examples of prayers, hymns, sermon topics, versions of scripture, and descriptions of favored clerical dress. The Social Welfare Committee of the Bishop's Conference of England and Wales notes: "Many of those with dementia are helped by stirring their long-term memories of the church with the use of familiar hymns, sights, and smells."[9] Come to think of it, maybe the kits should include pictures, incense, lace, recorded organ and choral music, and various vintage objects; anything that will help people with dementia to reconnect with worship experiences in their past.

To implement a meaningful program of spiritual care for persons diagnosed with dementia, knowing their religious history and practices (such as church attendance, preferred prayers, religious readings, and meaningful objects) is a good place to start.[10] This information can be obtained from family members or close friends. In some facilities, social workers include this as an essential part of patients' social history.

A Growing Need

All of these concerns take on special significance in the light of the prevalence of dementia among persons over sixty-five. Estimates (1989, 1992) of the incidence of dementia among persons over sixty-five range from 6.5 percent to 10.3 percent.[11] In this regard, the proportion of the US population over sixty-five years of age has gone from 4 percent (one of every twenty-five individuals) in 1900, to 12.5 percent (one of every twelve individuals) in 1990.[12] A leading geriatric specialist noted that "more than half of the people who have lived past the age of sixty-five since the beginning of recorded history are alive today."[13] By 2030, it is expected that one of every four persons (25 percent of the US population) will be over sixty-five![14]

Where are we likely to find older persons with dementia who can benefit from pastoral and spiritual care? Our first thoughts are of parish congregations, assisted living communities, nursing homes, and even homeless shelters. British researcher P. G. Coleman recently made the observation that we must consider "the pastoral care needs of the relatively large number of the present older British population who do not actively belong to faith communities and yet continue to maintain a measure of spiritual belief."[15] If estimates of the prevalence of dementia among persons over sixty-five noted above are correct, we can assume that many more people will be afflicted with dementia in the near future. Pastoral and spiritual caregivers across all denominations will find themselves working with individuals experiencing decline in their thinking and remembering, perhaps even including the caregivers themselves.

ROBERT B. WILLIAMS, PHD, CPSY, is a member of the Psychology Department at New Hampshire Hospital, Concord, New Hampshire, where he is assigned to the Elder Care Unit. He is also an adjunct assistant professor in the Department of Psychiatry of the Dartmouth Medical School.

RITA HANSEN is a member of the Third Order of St. Dominic. She is a registered nurse and holds a certificate in clinical pastoral education. She has a private practice in spiritual direction and is director of the bereavement ministry at St. Benedict's Parish in Crystal River, Florida.

THE REV. JOHN R. MABRY, PHD, is the co-pastor at Grace North Church, Berkeley, California, and director of the spiritual direction certificate program at the Chaplaincy Institute for Arts and Interfaith Ministry. His first priestly ministry was to an Alzheimer's unit in Pleasant Hill, California. He has served nursing facilities for more than ten years in both paid and volunteer capacities.

Notes

1. Cf. American Psychiatric Association, *Diagnostic and Statistical Manual of Mental Disorders*, 4th ed. (Washington, D.C.: Author, 1994), 139–43; American Psychiatric Association, *Practice Guideline for the Treatment of Patients with Alzheimer's Disease and Other Dementias of Late Life* (Washington, D.C.: Author, 1997).

2. Sandy Burgener, Rosemary Shimer, and Linda Murrell, "Expression of Individuality in Cognitively Impaired Elderly," *Journal of Gerontological Nursing* 19, no. 4 (1992): 17.

3. For more on this, see Victoria Cotrell and Richard Schulz, "The Perspective of the Patient with Alzheimer's Disease: A Neglected Dimension of Dementia Research," *The Gerontologist* 33 (1993): 205–11.

4. David Snowdon, *Aging with Grace: What the Nun Study Teaches Us about Leading Longer, Healthier, and More Meaningful Lives* (New York: Bantam, 2001).

5. Richard B. Ferrell and Robert B. Williams, "Exploring the Loss and Preservation of Abilities among Persons Diagnosed with Probable Dementia," in *Program and Abstract Book of the International Psychogeriatric Association European Regional Meeting, Geneva, Switzerland,* 1–4 (April 2003): 74 (abstract).

6. Nancy L. Mace and Peter V. Rabins. *The 36-Hour Day: A Family Guide to Caring for Persons with Alzheimer's Disease, Related Dementing Illnesses, and Memory Loss in Later Life* (Baltimore: John Hopkins University Press, 1999).

7. For more on this, see Cotrell and Schulz, "Perspective of the Patient with Alzheimer's Disease," 205–11.

8. Michael Mulvihill, *Liturgy, Worship and Prayer* (Birmingham, UK: Maryvale Institute, 1999), 17.

9. Social Welfare Committee of the Bishops' Conference of England and Wales, "Spiritual Needs of People with Dementia," press release, October 1999, www.tasc.ac.uk/cc/cn/00/000 306c.htm.

10. Cathy Young, "Spirituality and the Chronically Ill Christian Elderly," *Geriatric Nursing* 14 (1993): 298–303.

11. Lois Blume, Nancy Alfred Persily, and Jacobo Mintzer, "The Prevalence of Dementia: The Confusion of Numbers," *The American Journal of Alzheimer's Care and Related Disorders and Research* 7, no. 3 (1992): 3–11; Denis A. Evans, H. Harris Funkenstein, Marilyn S. Albert, Paul A. Scherr, Nancy R. Cook, Marilyn J. Chown, Liesi E. Hebert, Charles H. Hennekens, and James O. Taylor, "Prevalence of Alzheimer's Disease in a Community Population of Older Persons," *JAMA* 262 (1989): 2551–56.

12. Marilyn S. Albert, "General Issues in Geriatric Neuropsychology," in *Geriatric Neuropsychology,* ed. Marilyn S. Albert and Mark B. Moss (New York: Guilford, 1988), 3–10.

13. Albert, "General Issues in Geriatric Neuropsychology," 3.

14. Harold G. Koenig, "Trends in Geriatric Psychiatry Relevant to Pastoral Counselors," *Journal of Religion and Health,* 32 (1993): 131.

15. P. G. Coleman, "Spiritual Beliefs and Existential Meaning in Later Life: The Experience of Older Bereaved Spouses," *Proceedings of the British Psychological Society* 10, no. 2 (August 2002): 59.

Dreams and Spiritual Direction

Craig M. Mueller

A myth is a public dream, a dream is a private myth.
—Joseph Campbell

Throughout our lives we face transition, challenge, and change. Again and again we learn to let go of tight control and open ourselves to the healing, transforming love of God. Not until the final letting go of our death do we reach the total rest of peace and wholeness.

Yet each night we symbolically let go and in a sense die, by closing our eyes and resting. During this time we do not enter a place of nothingness but a rich, inner world of dreams. By seeking the wisdom of dreams, we acknowledge them as a gift of God for our health and salvation. While we may receive profound insight and strength from public rituals, sacred scriptures, and myths of our religious heritage, our own dreams provide a unique, personal application of divine wisdom.

Spiritual direction is a natural place where director and directee ponder, explore, and prayerfully consider God's grace, healing, transformation, and invitation. Our dreams can provide a deeper source of truth for our hearts to ponder when our conscious minds become weary of analyzing and strategizing. Dreams are a profound way to listen for the voice of the sacred speaking to us.

The spiritual awakening of the past several decades is rooted in human experience. Many people now seek a spirituality focused on their personal lives—their thoughts and feelings, their relationships, the events of daily life. Spiritual direction is gaining recognition today because it allows people to process and reflect upon the

145

spiritual stirrings within their own personal stories. Spiritual stirrings happen in dreams. Dreamwork is often taught in spiritual direction training programs both for students' own enrichment and to inform their practice of companioning with others.

Spiritual direction is not simply analyzing our lives using the "left brain" faculties, for this would make it an exercise in problem-solving. To embark on the spiritual journey and to enter a relationship of spiritual direction is to open ourselves up to mystery—to other ways of living, learning, reflecting, and being in the world. Spiritual direction teaches us to trust alternative ways of "knowing" ourselves and the sacred mystery within, about, and around us. Yet this is difficult for our rational, goal-oriented minds to grasp. When our cognitive side is caught napping, the mystery can begin to unfold.

Listening to our dreams is a very personal way of tapping into a source of rich inner wisdom. Dreams have been called "personal scriptures." The characters, events, and symbols in our dreams are uniquely ours. While some might dismiss dreams as simply rehashing the events of the day or revealing our deepest wishes and desires, many people have found in dreams a deep connection to the sacred in their lives. Dreams provide new information and insight; they reveal what our conscious mind doesn't already know. Dreams move us toward wholeness (*salvation*, to use religious language) and an awareness of deeper truths not always apparent in our conscious, waking state.

Dreams and Spirituality

Though working with dreams is seldom a part of religious curriculum in churches and synagogues, our Judeo-Christian sacred scriptures present a God who communicates through the symbolic language of dreams and visions (Jacob, Solomon, Samuel, Joseph, Nebuchadnezzar, etc.). Some would suggest that God no longer speaks to humankind in such a "direct" way, yet all of us dream. And those who have done inner work know dream content is not random or nonsensical. Rather, the dream is a gift from God, revealing or encouraging movements toward healing and wholeness.

Recently in my own dream life, two nonsensical figures appeared. They were two alluring brothers ages eight and fourteen. They were wealthy, sophisticated, and from another country. Who were these people, or what did they represent? Nothing about the dream resonated with me until later during a dreamwork session. I was reminded of my own particular vulnerability precisely between the ages of eight and fourteen. The brothers represented the wholeness and balance that I lacked at that age and that I seek on an ongoing basis.

The work of Carl Jung has been foundational for our contemporary understanding of dreams, particularly as related to our spiritual selves. In Jungian psychology the psyche refers to the personality as a whole. Our conscious mind is regulated by the ego, which is like a gatekeeper, deciding which psychic material is to reach the level of full awareness. The ego's awareness of self is limited and largely inaccurate. The unconscious mind is a vast sea of energies, even distinct personalities, living within us. According to Jung, our conscious ego is like a cork floating on the ocean of our unconscious. One part of the unconscious, the Self, is concerned with balancing various aspects of our personality and is a source of wholeness and meaning. Jung suggested that for Western Christians, the Self is the Christ within, humanity's highest aspiration. Individuation, the lifelong process of achieving wholeness, brings the conscious and unconscious into relationship. Through dreams, myth, ritual, and imagination, wholeness is nurtured and enhanced.

It might be helpful to think of the dream as revealing soul energy. Whether or not we understand the significance of a dream, it works independently to establish balance within our unconscious. We may not be aware of all this energy and its possibilities, but by unlocking the gift of the dream, we can tap into this wisdom. Without processing, the dream's raw material seems a jumble of symbols and scenes that make no sense. With the help of a companion, spiritual director, or dream group, we can be enabled to integrate insights of the dream more fully into our conscious lives.

> We acknowledge that God has given energy to our soul. In return, by doing dreamwork we consciously present to God the dream's gift of our life energy. We offer back to the Source ourselves transformed by the energy, or grace, coming to us through the dream. We are graced in receiving the dream, and our dreamwork returns the dream, now transformed, as an offering to God.[1]

It is both surprising and delightful to encounter a dream that starts out meaning nothing to us but after dreamwork offers profound wisdom and truth. The symbolic content of the dream tells us that we are not in the realm of absolutes, for there is never only one meaning to a dream. If symbols have many meanings, then the material in our dreams will have multiple levels of meaning and relevance.

I once had a powerful dream in which I chopped someone up with a spade and held his beating heart in my hand. My mother then inserted this heart into my chest in order to save my life. On one level, the dream seemed to be about my own unacknowledged angry, destructive feelings. But on another level, the dream caused me to look at my own heart. The mother figure, as my feminine side, pointed to the need for emotion, passion, and love to balance my strong analytical side.

There may be no such thing as totally unlocking the mystery of a dream once and for all. Like a good myth, it may speak to us differently at different times in our lives. Just as people return to certain scripture passages again and again, it is possible to return to a dream in the future and gain new insights about our inner truth. For those of us who like a more systematic approach to faith or our personalities, fluid and open interpretation of dreams is a humble reminder that life is ambiguous and sometimes contradictory. Paradoxes abound.

Our lives are seldom one extreme or another but rather a holding together of opposites. Such a spiritual stance continues to lead us to new awareness of both ourselves and the Divine; life is not static but continues to offer us fresh, surprising discoveries. The mystery of rebirth becomes a tangible, unfolding reality as God continues to transform us and our understandings of self, God, our lives, and the world.

In one dream, I met up with a professor-mentor from college as well as another character, a friend whose personality is opposite to mine in many ways. These two performed acrobatic stunts together. My friend was broken in pieces and put, unformed, into a container. As I walked away, an observer noticed some of the unformed material sticking to me. Here I was holding together opposites: myself, whom I liked to see as the orderly, proper, and controlled professor, and my friend, whose qualities of spontaneity and wit I admired. Hard work during my own midlife crisis has brought about rebirth and transformation as I let these two opposites do their stunts and let some of my friend "rub off" on me.

Receptivity to Dreams

Many people complain that they don't dream or that they don't remember their dreams. In reality, all people do dream. Studies have shown that certain stages of our sleep are marked with rapid eye movement (REM). Laboratory subjects awakened during REM sleep almost invariably report vivid dreams.

Honoring dreams and the unconscious takes some deliberate nurture and attention. If we value dreams and desire them in our waking life, such an attitude will be a signal to our unconscious that we want to remember our dreams. Usually this is exactly what happens. If one is awakened by a compelling dream in the middle of the night, most of the time it will be remembered in the morning. Those who are serious about dreamwork keep a pen or pencil, pad of paper, and flashlight or penlight on their nightstand. Upon awakening they immediately write, regardless of how strange or insignificant the dream or dream snippet seems. It is helpful to briefly review the dream while still semiconscious and to stay physically as still as possible. By writing down our dreams, we are inviting the unconscious to help us. We acknowledge that our ego's perspective is limited and that we seek the wisdom of an inner guide, even the Holy Spirit within us.

Before bedtime some people say a prayer, do a ritual, or in some way seek the sacred wisdom that will come in the form of a dream. A person desiring dreams may say a simple prayer before bed, such as, "Giver of dreams, reveal your wisdom to me this night." Seekers might place a symbolic object, such as a Native American dream catcher, near or above their heads. Periods of introspection and solitude, such as retreats, may make us more receptive to remembering dreams. Placing a dream notebook near at hand is a sign of expectation and intent.

Dreams in the Spiritual Direction Session

If dreams are honored as a deep source of wisdom for our spiritual lives, then it is natural that they be included in a spiritual direction relationship. The director may suggest integrating dreamwork into regular sessions. If the directee is receptive, some introductory information will be needed, since many people are not familiar with recording and discussing their dreams. A spiritual director who has used dreams in his or her personal work will be more comfortable incorporating them in a session with someone else. Some basic reading (see Recommended Reading at the end of this essay) will provide the spiritual director with concepts of dreams and the unconscious. However, a director should not attempt to work with someone else's dreams on the basis of reading alone.

Directees may occasionally bring a dream that troubles or fascinates them, or dreams may become a regular rhythm within the direction session. Directees sometimes express regret for having spent a whole session on dreamwork, but then they realize that nearly everything they had hoped to talk about in that session was brought up. In such a session, the dream is like an index of everything that is going on.

If the dream is recent, it is likely to contain emotional energy from the dreamer's current life situation. The dream may provide a new way of framing that life situation. The sacred is often revealed in ways contrary to what we might have first thought.

A directee told of a dream in which three babies were born in the nursing home where she works. A nursing home ordinarily seems to house people closer to death than to birth. The directee, usually proper and reserved, was experiencing the surfacing of a wild, rebellious side of her personality at that time. The dream, she acknowledged, pointed to that new birth. She was able to connect dream energy with God and her spiritual life, opening up a new dimension of the sacred by attending to a contrary paradoxical image.

A directee may seek specific direction or insight from dreamwork. While such guidance may come from material in the dream, it may be better to see the dream as raising questions rather than giving answers. The dream may invite us to reflect on aspects of our lives that we previously missed. We may see new possibilities for ourselves that we couldn't imagine before. The grace of the dream can propel us to a deeper faith and openness to life, ourselves, and the mystery of God.

Working with the Dream

A director may begin by asking the directee to read aloud the dream as recorded, in the first person (as if it were happening in the present). The directee may be encouraged to remember feelings associated with the events, people, or symbols in the dream. The dreamer can describe what associations each person or symbol in the dream has in his or her waking life. Most often each symbol is related to an energy within the dreamer. For example, if a directee dreams about his father's death, it is most likely suggesting not the literal death of his father but the death of a part of his father within the directee. The presence of death in dreams often suggests the death of an element in one's self in order that something new may be born. Thus, what could initially be troubling in the dream may be a hopeful and encouraging sign of change and growth.

A directee had a terrible dream about a young girl thrown from her seat on a Ferris wheel. The girl was totally destroyed when she hit the earth. At first the directee could think of nothing but her horror of the girl's death. In direction, she came to identify traumatic events in her childhood that destroyed her sense of wonder and excitement. By comparing her childhood to the present, she was able to see growth and spiritual movement and receive new energy, hope, and the gift of God's healing presence.

Some analysts suggest a dream could be read by adding the words "in me" after each symbol. Again, dreams use the language of metaphor and symbol and represent a certain energy in the dreamer. Puns or wordplays may also be evident. For example, the color blue may be used by the unconscious to suggest that someone has the "blues." Dreams about houses are often pictures of our personality or the self we live inside of. The house we grew up in links us with the past; a house in disrepair may suggest loose ends in our lives; a newly remodeled house may alert us to new energy and self-esteem. Going up and down stairs or elevators may reflect exploration of future and past, ethereal and spiritual, or earthy and foundational.

Since many of these connections may not occur to the dreamer, the spiritual director's role is to open up possibilities for interpretation. The director can act as an agent of free association, remaining, of course, nondirective.

By knowing the context of the dreamer's life, the director can suggest balance or perspective that the dream may be revealing. Often the dream speaks in extremes to get our attention and to compensate for our lack of conscious awareness. In Jungian terms, ego is conscious and accessible; shadow is unconscious and inaccessible. When the shadow enters our consciousness, it may reveal characteristics that we despise, find unacceptable, or refuse to acknowledge. These negative, embarrassing, or immoral parts may be repressed, but they may be just the positive source of energy our conscious life needs. A director can help look for the positive imbedded in the negative.

> Jung said about our collective shadow that he [the shadow] is 90 percent pure gold! Without a contact with our shadow we would become self-righteous, devoid of life, lacking in human understanding, sexually cold, unable to have living relationships with people, cut off from the earth, just plain dull, and subject to unconscious cruelties of a frightful proportion. When we look at some of the puritanic Christians who have tried to identify themselves with only righteousness, we can see this amply illustrated.[2]

We divide the world into dualities of good and bad, positive and negative, right and wrong. Yet this is also the source of much brokenness in our lives. Certain dreams may dramatize these opposites and encourage us to think about our lives in a more holistic way. Healing energy may be unleashed for us when we hear the voice of God speaking in ways contrary to our initial preconceptions. Peace and integrity may only come from embracing the seeming opposites in our personalities.

The spiritual director's role in dream interpretation may be as a gentle voice inviting the directee to see his or her life in fresh, creative ways. Dreams also provide our directees with a larger picture of life and show them what to focus upon. Amid fears and inner conflicts, dreams often ground directees in a position of strength. Dreams reveal emerging self-worth, which is the reality that all of us are created in the image of God and loved unconditionally.

One question a spiritual director can ask is, why did this particular dream come to you at this particular time? As a gift of wisdom from a Source beyond our and our directees' limited egos, dreamwork is approached with both gratitude and curiosity. A director may also suggest that the directee spend time in meditation with a scene or symbols from a dream if meanings are slow in coming.

A director, knowing a directee's communication skills, can suggest various forms of art, such as drawing, painting, or sculpting, to extend or draw out a dream. It is good to remind directees that the quality of art does not matter, but the process does.

A directee may be guided in active imagination, where he or she dialogues (either written or aloud) with a character or symbol in the dream. Dialogue may make the dream more "real" and help integrate it into the directee's life. Such dialogue is suggested in the example that follows.

A directee's dream had a large key as a primary symbol. The key is carried to a place significant to the dreamer. The directee (D) wrote a dialogue with the key (K), which opened up a deep place in his soul that could not be touched by rational analysis. It started like this:

D: O key, what are you? What is locked? What is closed?

K: You are not the self you used to be. Things are different. You can never go back.

D: Did I say I wanted to go back? What is the key for?

K: It isn't that simple. Only you know the key to inner peace.

D: That's what I'm seeking, asking you.

K: What were your feelings about the key?

D: It was terrible, like being stabbed. The pain was unbearable.

K: Is that what it was like to leave a place you deeply loved?

D: Yes, it was the greatest pain I've ever known.

K: Your loss and sacrifice are the key to all you are becoming. The key is your death, that you may be born anew. The key is your transformation. What is closed in you will bring forth something new.

All these suggestions can set in motion a flow of energy between the conscious and the unconscious. A spiritual director who works with dreams can assist directees to open up to the source of divine healing and wholeness beyond their rational minds. By following through and honoring the dream in some tangible way, such as with a ritual, directees can allow sacred wisdom to take root in their lives. Our dreams can be as rich as our own inner life and imagination and can paint a picture of the current landscape of our soul.

Thomas Merton and Dreams

Thomas Merton's spiritual journey is an excellent example of what Jung calls individuation, or the process of becoming a whole person—growing toward conscious awareness of one's true Self. For Christians, this would be a sense of Christ as the regulating center of the personality. Merton says, "The whole purpose of spiritual direction is to penetrate beneath the surface of a man's life, to get behind the facade of conventional gestures and attitudes which he presents to the world, and to bring out his inner spiritual freedom, his inmost truth, which is what we call the likeness of Christ in his soul."[3]

While Merton does not write directly about dreams within a spiritual direction session, he obviously values them as a part of his spiritual development and records many dreams in his journals. Several of these include female figures who represent his *anima*, which Jung defines as the unconscious, feminine side of a man's personality. The *animus* is the unconscious, masculine side of a woman's personality. In a dream recorded in February 1958, Merton was embraced by a young Jewish girl who said her name was Proverb. To honor the dream and its message, Merton dialogues with Proverb and thanks her for appearing: "How grateful I am to you for loving in me something which I thought I had entirely lost, and someone who, I thought, had long ago ceased to be. . . . Dearest Proverb, I love your name, its mystery, its simplicity and its secret, which even you yourself seem not to appreciate."[4]

Merton's further experience and reflection on the feminine element in his life led him to write the prose poem "Hagia Sophia." Later dreams include animal figures appearing as a Lady Latinist, a Chinese princess, and a black mother. Robert G. Waldron's book *Thomas Merton in Search of His Soul* includes possible interpretations of these figures in relation to Merton's life. Merton's recorded dreams invite the reader's interpretations, but we must remember that only the dreamer him- or herself can name and appropriate a dream's deep wisdom or truth.

If you were Merton's spiritual director, you might suggest possible ways of looking at his dreams to see whether they rang true for Merton himself. As director, you could commend Merton for his work with active imagination and poetry and encourage him to do more of the same. Since dreams raise questions rather than provide specific answers, you might encourage Merton to let the questions become a part of his prayer, journal writing, or other spiritual disciplines.

Conclusion

Whatever the stage of our life cycle, condition in life, or state of our soul, our dreams are filled with symbols, energy, and the movement of our spiritual life. Spiritual direction helps us become whole persons, and dreams are a unique way of touching our deepest realities. In seeing ourselves more clearly, we can also see the transcendent presence that is as close to us as our own breath. By sharing dreams and possible meanings, both director and directee behold the mystery of redemption as it unfolds in one of God's beloved children.

Recommended Reading

Berne, Patricia H., and Louis M. Savary. *Dream Symbol Work*. New York: Crossroad, 1989.

Johnson, Robert A. *Inner Work: Using Dreams and Active Imagination for Personal Growth*. San Francisco: HarperSanFrancisco, 1986.

———. *Owning Your Own Shadow: Understanding the Dark Side of the Psyche*. San Francisco: HarperSanFrancisco, 1991.

Jung, C. G. *Memories, Dreams, and Reflections*. New York: Vintage Books, 1965.

Kelsey, Morton. *Dreams: A Way to Listen to God*. New York: Paulist Press, 1978.

Mattoon, Mary Ann. *Understanding Dreams*. Dallas: Spring Publications, 1978.

Sanford, John. *Dreams and Healing: A Succinct and Lively Interpretation of Dreams*. New York: Paulist Press, 1978.

———. *Dreams: God's Forgotten Language*. Philadelphia: J. B. Lippincott, 1968.

Taylor, Jeremy. *Dream Work: Techniques for Discovering the Creative Power in Dreams*. New York: Paulist Press, 1983.

———. *Where People Fly and Water Runs Uphill: Using Dreams to Tap the Wisdom of the Unconscious*. New York: Warner Books, 1992.

Waldron, Robert G. *Thomas Merton in Search of His Soul: A Jungian Perspective*. Notre Dame, Ind.: Ave Maria Press, 1994.

CRAIG M. MUELLER is pastor of Holy Trinity Lutheran Church in Chicago. He is a graduate of the Shalem Institute for Spiritual Formation and does occasional freelance writing in the areas of liturgy, preaching, and spirituality.

Notes

1. Louis Savory et al., *Dreams and Spiritual Growth: A Christian Approach to Dreamwork* (New York: Paulist Press, 1984), 7.

2. John Sanford, *Dreams: God's Forgotten Language* (New York: Paulist Press, 1978), 185–86.

3. Thomas Merton, *Spiritual Direction and Meditation* (Collegeville, Minn.: Liturgical Press, 1960), 16.

4. Michael Mott, *The Seven Mountains of Thomas Merton* (Boston: Houghton Mifflin, 1985), 3.

Discernment of Spirits as an Act of Faith

William A. Barry, SJ

While directing retreats recently, I realized that discerning the spirits requires an act of faith. One of the retreatants had stated early and quite baldly that she hated retreats. I asked her why she kept making them if this was the case. She said, "Because we have to." She could pray in short periods, she said, but the idea of spending an hour at a time in prayer sent her into a tizzy. At the same time, she desired to experience the presence of God. Although the desire was strong enough to bring tears to her eyes as she spoke, she did not have much hope that it would be fulfilled. I asked her what she liked to do. "Listen to music, do puzzles, walk in the woods." So I suggested that she spend the day doing these things, with the desire that God's presence be felt. She was afraid of feeling guilty for spending retreat time this way; it did not seem like prayer. Over the next day or so, I prevailed on her to give enjoyment a try. On the evening of the third day, she said with a laugh, "I'm actually enjoying this retreat." She also had the sense that God might be enjoying it too.

But her guilt feelings did not disappear. She still thought that this should not be the way good retreats go. During a session we looked at the two different experiences—enjoyment of the retreat and guilt feelings. I then asked her, "Which of these experiences are you going to believe in?" She said she would like to believe that the enjoyable experience was from God. At that moment I had the insight that discernment of spirits is not complete until it ends with an act of faith. She could discern the difference between her experiences; now she needed to believe and to act on the belief. I thanked her for helping me to find this clarity. Here I want to explore my insight in an Ignatian context, in the hope of helping spiritual directors and others.

N. T. Wright develops a historical hypothesis about the nature of Jesus' vocation and self-consciousness. (It is a Christology from below, as it were, but arrives at a very high Christology.) To speak of Jesus' vocation, Wright notes, is not the same thing as to speak of Jesus' knowledge of his own divinity. "Jesus did not 'know that he was God' in the same way that one knows one is male or female, hungry or thirsty, or that one ate an orange an hour ago. His 'knowledge' was of a more risky, but perhaps more significant, sort: like knowing one is loved. One cannot 'prove' it except by living it."[1]

Jesus had to take the risk of faith that any human being takes when discerning a vocation from God. But Jesus' vocation, as he saw it, included actions that Israel's God had reserved for himself. Jesus, by entering Jerusalem on a donkey, symbolically enacted the return of Yahweh to Zion and took upon himself the role of Messianic shepherd, God's role. Jesus' discernment of his vocation required an act of faith in a unique relationship with God. He proved it by living it. Every discernment of spirits is like this— incomplete until we prove its truth by acting on it.

Ignatius of Loyola included rules for the discernment of spirits in *The Spiritual Exercises.* We know from his memoirs that he developed these rules on the basis of his own experiences at Loyola while recovering from battle wounds and at Manresa during months of prayer. At Loyola he engaged in two sets of daydreams. In one set he was a knight doing great deeds to win the favor of a great lady. In the other he was a follower of Christ after the manner of Saints Francis of Assisi and Dominic. Both sets of daydreams gave him great pleasure, but after the first set he found himself "dry and dissatisfied," while after the second set he remained "satisfied and joyful." He thought about the distinction between the two and "came to recognize the difference between the spirits that were stirring, one from the devil, the other from God."[2]

Here, for the first time, Ignatius discerned the movements of his heart. His discernment meant an act of faith that God was acting to inspire him to follow Jesus. Insight must be followed by action for the discernment to be complete, and the action is an act of faith in God's direction. Like Jesus, Ignatius proves that he is being called by acting on his insights.

The next instance makes the act of faith even clearer. After some time of consolation at Manresa, Ignatius began to be deeply troubled by uneasiness and scruples, even after detailed confessions.

> Although he was practically convinced that those scruples did him much harm and that it would be good to be rid of them, he could not break himself off. . . . Once when he was very distressed by them, he began to pray, and roused to fervor he shouted out loud to God, saying "Help me, Lord, for I find no remedy in men nor in any creature; yet if I thought I could find it, no labor would be too hard for me. Yourself, Lord, show me where I may find it."[3]

Things got so bad that Ignatius was tempted to commit suicide. He decided to embark on a total fast to beg God for relief, and did so for a week. At confession the next Sunday, his confessor ordered him to break the fast. With reluctance he did so and was without scruples for a couple of days, but then they returned with a vengeance. The story continues:

> But after these thoughts (of his sins), disgust for the life he led came over him with impulses to give it up. . . . He began to examine the means by which that spirit had come. He thus decided with great lucidity not to confess anything from the past any more; and so from that day forward he remained free of these scruples and held for certain that Our Lord had mercifully deigned to deliver him.[4]

Although Ignatius knew his qualms were doing him great harm, he did not, perhaps could not, act on this knowledge before. He was hanging on to a God who was an exacting taskmaster, almost a celestial accountant who was waiting to catch him out. He could not believe in a God who wanted his peace and act on this belief. Ignatius faced a choice. He may not have formulated it in terms of faith, but that is what it amounted to. Ultimately Ignatius had to decide what God he believed in. Here comes the breakthrough. When he chose not to confess his past sins, he had no guarantee that he was correct. He had to act in faith, hope, and love that God was not an ogre ready to pounce on mistakes and forgotten sins. This takes us to the first two "Rules for the Discernment of Spirits" suitable for the First Week of the Ignatian Exercises.

Rules for Discernment of Spirits

The First Rule

In the case of persons who are going from one mortal sin to another, the enemy ordinarily proposes apparent pleasures. He makes them imagine delights and pleasures of the senses, in order to hold them fast and plunge them deeper into their sins and vices.

But with persons of this type the good spirit uses a contrary procedure. Through their good judgment on problems of morality he stings their consciences with remorse.

The Second Rule

In the case of persons who are earnestly purging away their sins, and who are progressing from good to better in the service of God our Lord, the procedure used is the opposite of that described in the First Rule. For in this case it is characteristic of the evil spirit to cause gnawing anxiety, to sadden, and to set up obstacles. In this he unsettles these persons by false reasons aimed at preventing their progress.

> But with persons of this type it is characteristic of the good spirit to stir up courage and strength, consolation, tears, inspirations, and tranquility. He makes things easier and eliminates all obstacles, so that the person may move forward in doing good. (*Exercises*, p. 121)

From his experience (and perhaps from directing others who were painfully scrupulous) Ignatius came to believe that God acts differently with people depending on their orientation in life. For those who are trying to lead a good life (those of the Second Rule), troubling, anxious thoughts about sin are not from God but from the enemy of human nature, the evil one. Most people who want to carry out the Spiritual Exercises or who seek spiritual direction would surely be in this category. They are asked to make an act of faith that God is not the author of their anxiety, that God wants their peace and deep contentment. (A sign that these anxieties are not from God, by the way, is that they put the focus on the self, not on God and God's activity.)

My retreatant was faced with a similar faith choice, it seemed to me, and to her as well by the end of the retreat. There is no guarantee that God will act in a certain way toward someone trying to live a good life. One plants one's feet firmly in midair and marches on in faith, hope, and trust. The only verification we get is continued peace and joy on the journey. The "fruit of the Spirit is love, joy, peace, patience, kindness, generosity, faithfulness, gentleness, and self-control" (Gal 5:22–23).

Of course, events can disconfirm our discernment of how we are being led. Ignatius provides another example. At Manresa, he determined that his vocation was to go to Jerusalem to live and help souls there. Some commentators believe that this decision was, for Ignatius, made according to The First Time described in the Exercises:

> The First Time is an occasion when God our Lord moves and attracts the will in such a way that a devout person, without doubting or being able to doubt, carries out what was proposed. This is what St. Paul and St. Matthew did when they followed Christ our Lord.[5]

When Ignatius spoke to the provincial of the Franciscans who had charge of the holy places in Jerusalem about his desire to stay and help, he was told he could not remain because other pilgrims had been captured and enslaved and had had to be redeemed at great cost. Ignatius replied that he was firm in his purpose and resolved to carry it out. In spite of what the provincial said, Ignatius maintained that since there "was nothing binding him under sin, he would not abandon his intent out of any fear. The provincial replied that he had authority by the Holy See to excommunicate anyone who was unwilling to obey."[6]

We can see how determined Ignatius was that he was being led by God to remain in Jerusalem. But, threatened with excommunication, he concluded, "It was not Our Lord's will that he remain in those holy places."[7] Ignatius acted in faith that God was leading him to live and die in Jerusalem. Only by such an act of faith could he discover that he was in error with regard to discernment. Note, however, that it took another act of faith to change his direction. Ignatius believed that God was speaking through the provincial. In our own day many have discerned a vocation and been convinced that God inspired the decision, only to have events disconfirm it. For example, a young man discerns a vocation as a Jesuit priest but finds the Society of Jesus will not accept him. He had to act on faith to make his application, trusting that he would discover in the process that he was correct in his discernment. How he goes further with his life will be a sign of how openly he is seeking what God desires. If he goes through life angry and disgruntled because of this rejection, he shows too strong an attachment to his own will. If he can move beyond the disappointment, he can continue to seek God's guidance for his life direction.

Later Ignatius had other occasions to discern the "spirits," noting how the evil one cloaks himself as an angel of light for those who have advanced a bit in their journey into a deeper intimacy with God. On his return from Jerusalem, he decided that he needed more study in order to be able to help souls. Thinking about how exciting new insights about holy spiritual matters often distracted him from memorization, he said to himself, "Not even when I engage in prayer and am at Mass do such vivid insights come to me." Thus he realized that temptation was at hand. Ignatius went to his master's house, told all that went on in his soul, confessed his lack of progress, and promised to listen to him without fail. He made this promise with great determination and never again had those temptations.[8]

In this instance Ignatius had to decide in faith that such "spiritual favors" were not from God. Such experiences lie behind his Fourth Rule for discernment in the Second Week of the Exercises. The evil angel enters along the same way as the devout soul and then exits by his own way with success for himself. He brings good and holy thoughts attractive to upright souls and then strives little by little to get his own way.[9] Ignatius discovered that God is not the only source of pious thoughts and had to act in faith on his discovery.

Discernment of spirits rests on the belief that the human heart is a battleground where God and the evil one struggle for mastery. In the desert, Jesus of Nazareth was confronted and tempted by the evil one in the guise of an angel. If these were real temptations, then he, like us, had to discern what movements were inspired by God and what were inspired by the evil one. He, too, had to make an act of faith in who God really is based on his experience and knowledge of scripture. The Pharisees, and more than likely most Jews of the time, saw the real enemy of Israel, and therefore of God, as the pagans, especially the Roman occupiers. Over and over again Jesus warned his hearers that the real enemy of God was Satan, the prince of darkness. Satan had seduced the Israelites as well as the pagans. God's rule cannot come about by means proposed by Satan. Jesus, like any good Jew, believed that God was acting in history to bring about God's rule. (We might use the notion of "God's project" or "God's intention.") He also believed that God's enemy was doing everything in his power to thwart God's actions and intentions.

John Meier maintains that, for Jesus, human hearts are a battlefield of supernatural forces, God's and Satan's. "A human being might have a part in choosing which 'field of force' would dominate his or her life, i.e., which force he or she would choose to side with. But no human being was free to choose simply to be free of these supernatural forces . . . to pass *from* one was necessarily to pass *into* the control of the other. At least over the long term, one could not maintain a neutral stance vis-a-vis God and Satan."[10]

Faith is not just an intellectual affirmation of truths; faith is an action verb, a graced response to our self-revealing God. This goes for the faith of the church as well as for the faith of the individual who is trying to discern a path through life. According to John Macmurray, the world is one action ruled by one intention. He seems to say that if we believe that about the world, we are committed to a way of life.

> If we act as if the world, in its unity, is intentional; that is, if we believe in practice that the world is one action . . . we shall act differently from anyone who does not believe this. We shall act as though our own actions were our contributions to the one inclusive action which is the history of the world. If, on the other hand, we believe that the world is a mere process of events which happen as they happen, we shall act differently. Our conception of the unity of the world determines a way of life, and the satisfactoriness or unsatisfactoriness of that way of life is its verification.[11]

In *Persons in Relation*, Macmurray fleshes this insight out in more theistic terms. He states that when we think about our relation to the world, we think in terms of personal relationship. If the world is one action, then "its impersonal aspect is the negative aspect of this unity of action, contained in it, subordinated within it, and necessary to its constitution." The world conceived in this way is seen as the act of God, the Creator of the world, with ourselves as created agents. As such, we have "limited and dependent freedom to determine the future, which can be realized only on the condition that our intentions are in harmony with [God's] intention, and which must frustrate itself if they are not."[12]

Religious beliefs are always verified by action. "Religious beliefs" that do not issue in action in accordance with them are simply thoughts about the world, not beliefs. Someone may object, "But I am a sinner and often do not act according to my beliefs." True, but the very fact that you know you are a sinner who does not act according to your beliefs shows that you have beliefs that must be verified in action. If I say that I believe God is acting in this world and never try to discern how my own actions might be in tune with God's one action, then I show in practice that I do not really believe what I say I believe. A belief that God acts with purpose in this world must lead to attempts, however feeble, to discern how my own actions might be attuned to God's one action. These attempts to discern must lead to action; otherwise I will be acting with "bad faith" and will experience the malaise and stinging of conscience that Ignatius mentions in the First Rule.

God has not given us a list of truths to affirm but a task to carry out. We must try to discern in our time and place how God communicates with us and how God wants us to live our lives in this world in tune with God's Spirit, the one divine action at work in this universe. This is what the discernment of spirits is all about. Those of us who believe that God acts with purpose in this world and wants our friendship and cooperation are called to try to discern how God communicates with us and how we are being called to cooperate with this purpose. We then prove that we are believers by acting on our discernment.

I have not met my retreatant since that time a few years ago. I can only hope that she continues to believe that God wants her to enjoy God's company and puts the "treat" back in "retreat." I continue to be grateful for what I learned. Because of her, I feel, I now help those I direct to see discernment as a question about the reality of the God in whom they believe.

WILLIAM A. BARRY, SJ, is the author of more than fifteen books, including *With an Everlasting Love* (Paulist, 1999) and *Letting God Come Close* (Loyola Press, 2001, a revised edition of an earlier work on the Spiritual Exercises). He is one of the founders of the Center for Religious Development in Cambridge, Massachusetts. At present he is the co-director of the Jesuit Tertianship Program and gives spiritual direction and retreats. He is also the editor in chief of the quarterly *Human Development*.

Notes

1. N. T. Wright, *Jesus and the Victory of God* (Minneapolis: Fortress, 1996), 653.

2. Ignatius of Loyola, *A Pilgrim's Testament* (trans. Parmananda R. Divikar; St. Louis, Mo.: Institute of Jesuit Sources, 1995), 9–10.

3. Ibid., 34–36.

4. Ibid., 37–38.

5. Ignatius of Loyola, *The Spiritual Exercises* (trans. and commentary by George E. Ganss; St. Louis, Mo.: Institute of Jesuit Resources, 1992), 76.

6. Ignatius of Loyola, *Testament*, 60.

7. Ibid., 63.

8. Ibid., 79–80.

9. Ignatius of Loyola, *Exercises*, 126–27.

10. John Meier, *Mentor, Message, and Miracles*, vol. 2 of *A Marginal Jew: Rethinking the Historical Jesus* (New York: Doubleday, 1994), 415, italics in original.

11. John Macmurray, *The Self as Agent* (Atlantic Highlands, N.J.: Humanities Press, 1978), 221.

12. John Macmurray, *Persons in Relation* (Atlantic Highlands, N.J.: Humanities Press, 1979), 222–23.

Live Nearby, Visit Often: Focusing and the Spiritual Direction Process

Lucy Abbott-Tucker

The words were simple. "Do you have an image for how all of that feels inside?" The response came quickly. "It is a washing machine stuck on the agitated cycle." Then came the difficult question. "Would it be OK to just sit quietly for a minute and notice how that feels inside?" That was the moment I knew we were in trouble. Did my trusted spiritual director not understand? Agitated washing machines do not feel good inside, and I had no interest in going there. As our conversation continued, I learned she not only wanted me to see how it felt inside; she wanted me to honor the feeling. To accept it just as it was, without any attempts to change or manipulate how I was feeling into something better. That conversation, which took place more than twenty years ago, was my introduction to the focusing process.

Over the years I have come to a simple definition of spiritual direction. I describe it as an intentional conversation between two people who believe in the reality of God. Within this conversation, one person is primarily the listener, helping the other to hear and feel more clearly how God is present and active in daily life. The focusing process is one of the ways I believe we can be with another and "touch" the activity and graciousness of God within the day-to-day realities of life.

Eugene Gendlin, noted psychologist, author, and teacher at the University of Chicago, Illinois, first described the process in his 1982 book, *Focusing*. Gendlin was doing research on behavior changes in therapy clients. He was trying to discover why some people "get better" through the therapeutic process while others do not. The hypotheses he explored included the type of therapy being used, the skill of the therapist, and the length of the therapeutic relationship. Much to the surprise of Gendlin and his colleagues, none of those factors proved decisive. Rather, Gendlin began to notice that successful therapy clients had a particular relationship with the feelings connected to life events. This was more than simply naming the feelings, more than feeling the feelings; it was a relationship that listens to the wisdom of the feelings and cares reverently for what they have to say. When clients do this, an inner body wisdom that is life-centered and positive opens up, and changes that enhance life begin to happen. Instead of the repetition of painful stories and emotions, a shift occurs that teaches a healthier way of being and relating.

Gendlin noticed that some clients had this skill naturally, and he noticed positive life changes that could be documented through psychological testing. He said that some people gradually learn the skill in the therapeutic process and also make effective life changes. The clients who didn't know the skill and didn't learn it in the therapeutic process continued working hard to create effective life changes but were not successful.

Gendlin began to look more carefully at this skill, which he came to call focusing. He came to believe that everyone is born with the capacity to be in right relationship with their feelings, but for many people this was either not nourished or forgotten. When a person remembers or is taught how to listen and revere feelings, a natural, life-enhancing process is nurtured. This does not lead to magical life changes but is a slow movement into living with greater awareness and sensitivity to one's self and others. Again, some of the best news from Gendlin's work is that these skills can be learned and practiced by each one of us.

Katherine Hepburn once said her philosophy of marriage was "Live nearby and visit often." I think her advice could aptly be applied to the relationship we need to develop with the interior wisdom of our bodies. From a young age we learn to hide the emotions that displease others, so our angry, fearful, sad, guilty, jealous, sexual feelings all go underground. Often we even learn to minimize our happy, joyful, loving feelings. We distance ourselves from these feelings as though embracing them would be destructive to us or to others. We judge ourselves and others for how we are feeling and experience a sense of shame when others are aware of our feelings. We begin to learn how to control, manipulate, or force feelings to be other than they really are. Instead, focusing teaches us to live close to our feelings, to visit them often in a way that gives them a proper hearing and respect. As we do this, we are able to grow and evolve.

Edwin McMahon and Peter Campbell, founders of the Institute for Bio-spiritual Research, see the focusing process as deeply related to the concept of God's continued activity in the world. They see the Incarnation, God's becoming human, not just happening to Jesus but also happening to each one of us. The only vehicle in which this can happen is our bodies. It is therefore critical that we learn to carefully listen to and heed the wisdom of our bodies. When we live close to the interior responses we have to the circumstances in our lives, and visit them often with a sense of welcome and care, we are then able to move more graciously in life. While we may often be somewhat aware of the feelings associated with life events, the difference in focusing is in the way we listen and attend to the feelings. Rather than trying to strong-arm them into something different, forget them until access to their energy is lost, or offer them to God, in focusing we care for the feelings and listen carefully to their divine wisdom.

In his book *Reaching Out*, Henri Nouwen describes hospitality as the attitude of welcome that allows visitors to "sing their own songs, speak their own languages, [and] dance their own dances." When we can extend a hospitable welcome to the deeper feelings within our own experiences, allowing them to speak, sing, and dance, they carry the potential to help us transform from the "inside out." This is quite different from the many attempts we make to transform the "outsides" of ourselves that usually result in futile attempts, frustrations, and the perpetuation of unhealthy behaviors.

What does all of this look like when it is incorporated into the direction process? After the directee has spoken about what is happening in his or her life, we see if we notice a place of real energy. If it seems like focusing is appropriate, I invite the directee to sit for a few minutes of quiet in order to come to a centered place from which to begin the movement into the interior. This quieting time often happens naturally in the direction setting. I have noticed that some people take their time before they come to my office, while others ask for a few minutes of quiet to see where they might like to begin after they get settled. However, if we start out by catching up and chatting, I usually suggest a few minutes of quiet in order to see what needs to be talked about during our intentional conversation.

The next movement in the focusing process often occupies a substantial portion of the spiritual direction session. The person takes an inventory of those things that are taking up space in the interior. I often describe this as looking around inside and noticing what concerns and experiences are preoccupying his or her time and attention. Sometimes there are many; often there are just three or four. In this phase of the process, one is simply trying to name those things and get a little distance from them. In some ways, it reminds me of writing a grocery list. I look through the refrigerator and pantry shelves and write down those items I need to purchase. This activity does not get the shopping done, but it does clarify what I need to do once I get to the store. By making my shopping list, I free up my mind to attend to other things because I am not so busy remembering. So, too, when one takes inventory during the focusing process, he or she is not "taking care" of those experiences but simply acknowledging their presence. Naming them and then setting them aside for a few moments enables people to see what else is happening inside and creates a feeling of spaciousness within.

During a direction session, this movement happens as a directee talks about what has been happening in his or her life since the last direction session. There is usually much more material here than can be dealt with in one session. During this time, a director is mostly silent, listening to the stories being shared, trying to listen underneath the stories for the places of real energy, the ones that catch the thinking, relating, and feeling functions of the directee. At the end of this sharing, it is time to choose the number one issue.

What happens here is a sorting process, as the directee looks through all that has been named and chooses the one item that needs attention and care. There are many ways this step can happen within the direction setting. Sometimes it is easy to simply ask the directee to choose from all that has been named. Sometimes it is pretty clear from the amount of time and energy spent on one story that we have a beginning place for the focusing process. Occasionally it is the connection between stories that needs to be explored further.

What seems most important is that the director does not choose for the directee what is important but rather takes time to allow the directee to name the doorway into his or her own interior. Remember at this time that it really does not matter which doorway is used, since each person has only one interior. When working attentively within, with thoughts, relationships, and feelings in one arena of life, a person touches on all the arenas of life.

Once the doorway is chosen, it is important to have the directee ask his or her body if it is OK to spend some time with this material in a more intentional manner. When we ask and receive permission from our bodies to look more carefully at a particular life experience, we are beginning the gentle and gracious attitude that is necessary for truly being present to our interior. Even when a directee declines to be present to an issue, we can begin by being gentle and gracious toward the "no," recognizing that something precious within is being protected.

Once the doorway has been named and permission granted to enter, we begin the "heart" of the focusing process. Focusing is a body-centered experience. We want to notice and carefully attend to how the body is carrying the experiences of life, wherein we find real wisdom. The simplest focusing question, "How does all of that feel in your body?" is often the way to begin. Most people can respond to that question easily, often either naming a particular spot in the body along with its physical sensation or offering a metaphorical image. They might say, "It's tight in my stomach," or "It's like a plate across my throat," or "There's singing in my heart."

As often as I speak these next words, they never fail to touch me. "Can you just be with that in a gentle and caring way? Don't try to change the feeling, figure it out, or make it go away. Simply be present there." When a person attends to the feelings of life in this way, it is truly a sacred moment. If a person reverences whatever is real inside by simply allowing it to be, he or she gives an incredible gift of love to those feelings. The inner experience responds with receptivity and generosity. Often the feelings begin to tell their story. The more a person can simply welcome and gently love what is being said, the more will be revealed. In focusing, the director seeks to stay quietly and gently present to the inside story of the directee as it unfolds.

One of the joys of sitting with another in a focusing session is the privilege of witnessing the movement of grace inside another person. In addition, with a quiet, attentive presence, the director welcomes and celebrates what is happening in another. The director can be a mirror of the attitude the person is trying to muster. When I focus with another, I am encouraging growth that is truly transformative. With a few quiet questions the director can follow what is happening in the other. This is an interior process, and the director does not need to know or understand all that is going on for the directee. The gift being offered is presence to another while he or she is present to self in a loving way. What a director witnesses during those moments is the action of God's love within the other.

There usually comes a moment in the focusing time when the directee comes to a quiet resting place. The director can often observe this on the face, in the body posture, or in a kind of quietness that is very physical. At this time, a director will usually encourage the directee to rest there for however long is needed. When the directee is ready to talk again, he or she resumes the direction conversation. Directees are usually eager to share what happened when they were focusing and quite easily make the connections with the realities of life being discussed as the session began. Sometimes directees become aware of small changes they are being invited to make. Occasionally there is just gratitude that an interior feeling has been encountered in a caring manner. Sometimes a person sees the reason behind a repetitive life pattern more clearly. Other times it is difficult to understand what has happened, but there is a sense that something has changed and time is simply needed to live into the change.

At the end of a direction session in which focusing has been used, it is helpful to invite the directee to remember and perhaps name aloud what he or she desires to take away from the session and to thank the body for what it has revealed. Many directors find it helpful to thank the directee for what has been shared. The life stories directees have shared and the way they are striving to live in harmony with the love of God always enrich the director and invite the growth of both the directee and the director.

In the introduction to his book *new poems*, e.e. cummings writes that we are constantly being born when we are faithful to ourselves. The focusing process is one of the ways we can welcome and be faithful to the rebirths that are essential to our growth.

Recommended Reading

Gendlin, Eugene. *Focusing*. New York: Bantam Books, 1982.
————. *Focusing-Oriented Psychotherapy*. New York: Guilford Press, 1996.
Nouwen, Henri. *Reaching Out*. New York: Doubleday, 1975.

LUCY ABBOTT-TUCKER is a staff member at the Institute for Spiritual Leadership, Chicago, where she teaches and does spiritual direction. She also offers workshops relating to the ministry of spiritual direction both in the United States and abroad. She worked on the Guidelines for Ethical Conduct for Spiritual Directors International and has spoken on the Guidelines both in North America and Europe.

Steps of the Focusing Process

1. **Preparing.** Take a few minutes to allow the person to come to a quiet, centered place.

2. **Finding a space by taking an inventory.** Use a question such as, "What are the things that are taking up space inside of you now? Is there anything in your life that prevents you from feeling OK right now? Are there things you're looking forward to or excited about just now?" As things come up, ask the person if it is OK to put that aside for a little while. Continue this process until the person comes to a clear, centered place inside.

3. **Identifying the number one issue.** Invite the person to look over the things named and choose the one that most needs some attention or care at the time.

4. **Checking inside to see if it is OK to be with this issue.** Ask the person to take a minute to check in his or her body whether it is OK to spend some time with a particular issue. When the interior feeling is resistant or fearful, it is important to respect that response. It is OK to say no to dealing with a particular feeling at a particular time. The feelings and their wisdom will wait until the person is ready. When this happens the person can simply choose another issue or can decide to be present to the reluctance or fear he or she is currently experiencing.

5. **Being with the issue in a caring way.** Begin by asking the person, "How does all of this feel in your body?" When a person becomes aware of how it is inside, invite him or her to be present to the felt sense in a caring, attentive way. Gently remind the person not to try to change the feeling, figure it out, or make it go away, but simply to be gently present to it. As shifts or changes in the feelings occur, the person simply repeats steps 4 and 5 until the person comes to what feels like a stopping place for that time. Stopping does not mean everything is resolved; it simply means one has cared for one's feelings and listened to as much as possible just now.

6. **Concluding.** Invite the person to thank the body for what it has revealed. At times, a person may want to mark a particular place in memory in order to return to it at another time.

To Bring All Things Together:
Spiritual Direction as Action for Justice

James M. Keegan, SJ

Spiritual directors engage in a highly personal art in an intimate setting. "One-on-one" is a standard way of describing the encounter and sometimes even the work itself. The ministry is replete with intuitive feelers like me, who are often invited into the depths of the stranger in the next seat on the short flight from Boston to New York, but who could not recall whether he was bald or wore glasses or ordered a drink. For many of us, too, gazing out the airplane window can trigger an old, disquieting image of the spiritual director far removed from the mean streets below and enchanted by the beauty of the patterned lights. Hearing again that the promotion of justice is an integral part of the service of faith, first put so strikingly for American Catholics by their bishops in 1971, can make us want to get back on the next flight—wherever it may be heading.

We are religious people who take the gospel seriously, and we are usually informed people as well, aware of the violent, unequal society we always land in. Much of our training and work has focused on helping people to deepen their personal journeys. We have written, debated, and harangued for so long about the interface between spiritual direction and the work of justice that some have settled it for themselves by moving their work or residence into the midst of poor and oppressed people. Others have chosen to do well what they already do, maintaining, for instance, that "the poor" can be understood in a wide enough sense to encompass their clients. Still others have decided that they will limit their spiritual direction to men and women actively engaged in justice work or desirous of focusing their conscious energies in that area.

These are certainly legitimate ways of adapting the work of spiritual direction to the call to "action on behalf of justice." Successful or not, however, each of them results from a separate peace made with that call. What is still missing is a systematic understanding of what "action on behalf of justice" may look like within the ministry of spiritual direction per se. Perhaps the workaholism and fatigue of many spiritual directors are related to the unsettled shadowy figures of "the poor and the oppressed" who approach in the defenseless hours of the night. Seamus Murphy, who helped the Jesuits in Ireland reflect on the relationship of their ministries to the mission of faith and justice, discovered that while "people in social and youth ministries tended to experience consolation, people in education and spirituality often experienced desolation."[1] Our model for this action is social work or social activism, and that is not what spiritual directors do. The desolation may arise because we really cannot say what it is we do when we act for justice as spiritual directors.

When a spiritual director is engaged in action for justice *as a spiritual director*, what will it look like? I will develop four qualities that seem important in answering the question: it will be integral to the ministry itself; it will be action; it will be founded in a contemplative attitude toward life and reality; and it will be recognizably rooted in the gospel. These are not intended as an exhaustive response to the question but a development of some ground on which to stand in responding to it.

Action for Justice Is Integral to the Ministry of Spiritual Direction

Seamus Murphy argues that we do not have "an appropriate notion of what it means to do justice" in retreat work and spiritual direction. Instead, we assume "that justice being a dimension of all ministries means that doing justice in any ministry would be similar to doing justice in social ministry. The assumption appears to be false."[2] In other words, we assume that justice is about changing society and any of its structures that are hostile to gospel values. Since this work is so often focused on individuals, we may look for the ripple effect of a directee's spiritual development or expect that fidelity to God's grace will ultimately yield fruit for the poor and oppressed. These may be valid hopes, but they are external to the work of spiritual direction, whose goal is to help people notice the movement of God in their lives and choose to go with it. Directors who hope to see social action resulting from their work could be violating their contemplative stance should they try to steer their clients in the direction of those hopes rather than helping them to engage with the free action of God.

Murphy's work helps us to think more clearly about various ministries, their goals and means, and the relationship each has to the call to integrate justice with faith. He argues that since there are many valid and important ministries that serve the faith without any direct connection to social justice or service to the poor, then there must be various kinds of justice and various ethical theories, none of which are complete in themselves. The "promotion of justice" is integral to every ministry but means something different for different kinds of work. It is important, then, for people in various ministries to identify those particular notions of justice that are appropriate to what they do.

For example, the key question in a ministry such as migration and refugee services or work with homeless families may be, "In what way should human resources be deployed so as to have maximum effectiveness in bringing about a better world?"[3] Its goal would be to provide direct human services and to work toward a just social order; action for justice could be providing translation or housing services for refugees or advocating for the voiceless in city government. Only in an applied sense could this notion of justice be integral to numerous other ministries, such as Engaged Encounter, Marriage Encounter, or Family Enrichment. Their key question may be more, "How ought I behave in my relations to others?"[4] Action for justice may mean the respectful treatment of individuals as persons, and their action could be providing alternatives to abortion or encouraging dialogue between spouses or within parish councils. Here, it is human relationships that are to be made just.

So "justice" can show different faces in different ministries. Although the above questions and purposes may not be overlooked in the work of spiritual direction, they do not describe the operative notion of justice which, as Murphy says, is "easily and obviously connectable to the core elements in the work" of spiritual direction. Because spiritual direction is about helping people to recognize, engage with, and freely elect to move with the Spirit of God in their lives, action for justice will be concerned with the process of noticing, discerning, and choosing. The key question here may be, "What must be taken into account before one can accurately discern and choose to follow the Spirit of God?"

Action for Justice Is Action

If we make the mistake of applying only one notion of justice to all ministries, we arrive at an old familiar dead-end: since my work does not involve action for the poor or other activity that is more proper to social ministry, there is something deficient in it; something has to be added before spiritual direction can claim its status as a work of justice. So we may move our center into the inner city or invite the poor to our more rural settings. While these are highly laudable activities that may significantly influence the way we do our work, they are not constitutive of the ministry of spiritual direction itself.

At issue here is our notion of action. If "action" means only the activity appropriate to social ministries, for example, then spiritual directors really are inert! If what we mean by action, on the other hand, is intentional engagement in one or many arenas of human life, then people who bother to record or pray about their dreams or who open their secrets to a trusted professional are taking action. They are making choices that have consequences for themselves or for the multi-layered systems and structures in which they live. Responsible action means choosing and paying attention to the consequences of one's choices.

Spiritual directors are faced with action choices all the time: whether to continue to listen now or to speak, to focus on this or that aspect of what the directee is saying or omitting, to challenge an assertion or let it pass. They are acting as spiritual directors when they engage, inquire, give feedback or suggestions, and spend time afterward prayerfully reflecting and being supervised about their choices. Spiritual directors take action *as spiritual directors* in deciding how to respond to their directees, and such action can be responsible and just or capricious and self-serving, depending on whether or not its origins and consequences are considered. The action appropriate to this ministry does not look like the notion of activity proper to social ministry. It is what spiritual directors do. The next two sections will address the question, "What would make this action more or less just?"

Action for Justice Is Founded in a Contemplative Attitude toward All of Life

As our concept of action can be measured by a host of *Lethal Weapon* movies, our notion of contemplation may be found in the back pew of a darkened chapel with its eyes cast down. But contemplation is not necessarily quiet, passive, or inward any more than action is necessarily fast-paced. The first task of a spiritual director is to help a directee develop the nonjudgmental presence to his or her own life experience that we call a contemplative attitude. For spiritual directors this essential attitude is a human posture before the experience of living—a habit comprised of acts of listening to, attending to, and effectively engaging with the reality of another. In spiritual direction it is the activity of the whole person of the director involved with the whole person of the directee in such a way that the directee's experience of life can reveal intimations of God's activity and the invitations God may be making.

When one human being trusts another with the raw material of living, contemplation is an action science. Its object is the inner and outward events, experiences, and activities that constitute the life of this person. In the early 1990s, five of us worked together in the Roman Catholic archdiocese of Louisville, Kentucky, to develop practicum programs for spiritual directors. We began to clarify an understanding of contemplative action that broadened our knowledge and practice. We began to notice God's activity in four interrelated arenas of human life.

Steve Wirth, then the director of the spirituality office, was key not only in moving us to understand and incorporate work done by many others but in creating his own original synthesis of this material. Many of the ideas and references here are his. We are also indebted to those who developed the "Grid Arenas" and the "Experience Cycle" at the Center for Spirituality and Justice in New Rochelle, New York; Elinor Shea, who described their work in writing; Jack Mostyn, CFC, who dialogued with us extensively on this material; and writers like Peter M. Senge and Chris Argyris, who focus on developing teams and corporate bodies.

Arenas are places where choices are made that lead to the development or deterioration of relationship. In order to help directors engage with the whole reality of an individual, we have found it useful to be conscious of four such arenas that constitute the "frame" of a person's life: the Individual, Interpersonal, Structural, and Environmental. These are interconnected categories with porous lines between them, ways of expanding our noticing and understanding of human experience. It is my thesis that this Lifeframe makes it possible to understand how, in practice, we may "do justice" in spiritual direction by expanding our contemplative skills to encompass more of a directee's reality. It has also helped us to recognize that we have habitually acted unjustly toward our directees when our contemplative gaze has omitted significant areas of their life and experience.

The Individual Arena

Each of us has a relationship with ourselves, and this Individual Arena is where events in that relationship happen. Our therapeutic culture makes it relatively easy to notice happenings and influences here. I play "old tapes" to myself, messages from others that I have ingested and made my own: "Who do you think you are?" "You'd better not say anything about your feelings!" "You can do anything you want." I relate to myself in patterns of healthy and unhealthy ways. I may discover my "inner child" as dissociated from me or as increasingly one with me. I experience myself bodily: my foot hurts or I feel elated and tired after a run. When I pray I may become aware of my breathing, of my heart's rhythm, and of the inner noise around my quiet center. I act justly here when I can listen to and love myself, coming to know and include more and more of myself while maintaining secure and flexible boundaries.

Spiritual directors are often very helpful in this arena of a person's life. Sometimes, however, we narrowly interpret "holistic" spirituality as implying a oneness within the person, a coming-together of head, heart, gut, mind, spirit, and body, and may fail to notice that all of this activity occurs in only one arena of life. Body-awareness, quiet prayer, and inner healing are important and even essential elements of spiritual life. But "holistic" spiritual direction will recognize that these activities that occur in the Individual Arena are intimately connected with other arenas of spiritual development and activity.

The Interpersonal Arena

My individual makeup is partly a result of the interpersonal relationships that have most affected me, and it affects those relationships in turn. As we have said, the lines between these arenas are porous. In friendships, at home, in places where we sometimes least expect it, we find ourselves mutually aware of one another. We act interpersonally when we are more focused on "being with" one another and less focused on the roles or tasks that necessarily engage us much of the time. One evening, my friend Steve helped me put a wallpaper border around a couple of rooms. While we wanted to get the job done well, the evening wasn't as memorable for the work as for the spontaneous, interesting fun and conversation we had doing it. The next day, when he chaired our staff meeting, our relationship had shifted from an interpersonal to a structural way of being together, as we shall see below.

Justice demands that I recognize this interpersonal dimension in each human being but not always that I act interpersonally with others. In fact, there are times when such action is inappropriate, even offensive. The passenger in the next bus seat, who wants to know more about me than I want to reveal, may call for a gentle signal that we're fellow travelers but not friends, as does the anonymous salesperson who phones during dinner and calls me by my first name. Further, as we shall see below, there are situations when an interpersonal interpretation of reality can omit the possibility of justice. I do justice interpersonally when I treat other people as ends rather than means—for instance, when I reveal myself to and become interested in another who wants to be my friend.

For many years as a spiritual director, I panned for interpersonal experience of God as the real gold of spiritual direction, and I have developed fine tools to help a directee mine the lode. While such experience remains a touchstone for discernment, I have to admit some failure with people who did not unearth their riches here. I excused it by saying that spiritual direction is not for everyone, but I have discovered that, by keeping my focus on the Individual or Interpersonal Arenas, I may not have been helping some people to look in the place where God's activity was most accessible to them. I was not doing justice as fully as I could as a spiritual director.

The Structural Arena

We exist together in structures: families, jobs, parish communities, clubs, professional organizations. Because we tend to think of relationships as individual or interpersonal, we can miss the fact that much—even most—of our lives occurs in structures.

I spend at least eight hours a day at work. While I consider some of the people there to be my friends, I am only asking for trouble if I do not act consistently, while at work, within the structures provided for the accomplishment of our goals. Those roles and boundaries may be quite flexible, but they must underlay my activity at work. When I associate with the superior of my local religious community, we are often in structural positions: I am a member of the group for which he has some responsibility. Mothers and fathers have structural roles in relation to their families, and grandparents have different ones. A husband or wife who is awakened by the baby, gets the other children ready for school and then goes off to work, returns home in time to have supper, brings the children to Little League, and makes it to the parish council meeting may have almost no daily interpersonal or individual time beyond sleeping! The Structural Arena is where we actually live much of our lives.

Doing justice in this Structural Arena means paying attention to and caring for the roles, structures, and systems that comprise it. Parents are just when they act like parents in relation to the family structure, keeping a balance between those roles and their personal development. A religious superior is just when he or she acts for the good of the community rather than only to preserve good feelings. The structure or system for which they have some responsibility itself demands compassion and care. Failing that, the persons who comprise it, and their relationships, will suffer.

Let us look at a hypothetical situation. Alan, a young associate pastor in a large metropolitan parish, repeatedly complains to John, his spiritual director, that he is sick of the crises from all sides that get dumped on him in his work. The pastor is fond of his image as a humane and equitable administrator. Alan thinks otherwise. He sees the pastor as either withdrawing from conflict or entering it with authoritarian power. The pastor, of course, doesn't see that at all.

Alan is angry about being in the middle between him and members of the parish staff. When he finds a quiet space to pray, the anger pounces like a cat. Alan often imagines God as an old man who walks and talks with him, and he often feels that God hears and understands his anger and the fantasies it produces. As John explores this with him, his sense of God's presence deepens and solidifies, and he leaves with a stronger conviction that, whatever happens, God will be with him in it.

John has explored with Alan the interpersonal dimension of his experience and has probably helped him to deepen his friendship with God. They have explored his personal prayer. But the original experience occurred in the structure of his work, and that dimension has not been investigated. If God is nudging Alan to be just, it will most likely be in the arenas of his life where he is most engaged and committed. If direction stops here, John (and probably Alan) will miss the possibility that God may want to be noticed *in Alan's structure* as well as in their interpersonal relationship. In fact, in a gentle way, John may have "wrestled him back" from the Structural Arena to the Interpersonal, where both of them may be more comfortable.

What *could* happen here if John's contemplative attitude were wide enough to encompass the Structural Arena of Alan's life? John is quite clear that if Alan becomes aware of and at home with his real feelings about the situation, he will be more personally integrated. John also acts on the premise that as Alan reveals these reactions to God, their relationship becomes more mutual and whole. (He may be wrong about this, as we shall see in the next section.) What if John were not to stop here but to imagine that God also cares deeply about the transformation of social structures, concretely manifest here and now in the parish that employs this man at least five days a week? If John were to operate on the belief that God acts and invites us in our lives *as we are*, his desire to do justice would not lead his directee to some experience in the future or outside his present concerns. He would be interested in the liberating and oppressive realities already operating in the structures of his life. John's work with Alan could be doing justice not only personally and interpersonally but possibly on a structural level as well.

We are not saying here that John's aim is for Alan to transform the structures of his life but rather to help him explore more contemplatively what God may be doing there. The exploration might yield the following.

Alan has been aware of unspoken resentment brewing between the paid and volunteer parish staff. Volunteers feel they have no say over what goes on; the paid staff feels at the mercy of the volunteers. Volunteers feel they're asked to do too much and find it hard to say no; the others feel the same way but add that they're not paid adequately for all they do. Both groups find solace in criticizing the pastor. "The boss will find some way to say no to this!" Meanwhile, the pastor complains to Alan that he wants to be a "Vatican-Two-People-of-God" pastor but feels forced to make decisions because the buck stops at his desk. Everyone is stuck and no one can do any-thing about it.

As John helps him to investigate his feeling of powerlessness, Alan discovers that no one is comfortable with the situation as it is. He had not noticed before that they all appeared, from different angles, to be victims of some unseen force or value that kept them from saying the truth to one another. He also notices that the helpless vic-tim feelings tend to feed on themselves, getting more overpowering as they get more airtime. Alan recalls feeling depressed when thinking, in the midst of an informal staff gripe session, "They all love how they feel! If I had a solution to this mess, nobody would want to hear it right now." He asked himself why he was there to begin with; he had to admit that he, too, wanted to take sides against the pastor; he doesn't like that awareness. He wants to think and pray about what he has noticed.

Because John expects God's action can be noticed in this Structural Arena, he is aware that Alan's description of the group's powerlessness and his own complicity in it has the hallmarks of spiritual desolation or countermovement. He also suspects that Alan's realization that staff and pastor are in the same boat and his awareness of his own darker motives may harbor the seeds of consolation and the movement of God. It may be the crack through which God's Spirit is bringing light and transformation to the injustice in this system, which seems to have ensnared everyone in it and is felt per-sonally and interpersonally. If Alan's personal prayer radiates energy and mutuality with God, John will keep in mind that the same God will probably be evident in the play of consolation and desolation at work as well. Alan may resist hearing it, resting satisfied that he's handling his anger and that his prayer is rewarding. But John knows that if he sets the structural aside, he will be estranged from an important dimension of his life and will eventually feel it in his body and his interpersonal relationships. He will ask Alan about the parish if he doesn't bring it up.

If spiritual direction makes Alan aware of the presence of God in his work, the opportunities for justice there are as numerous as imagination can make them. He may simply be aware of the creative strength of his anger and no longer allow himself to be made a victim or to get triangulated, or he may confront the gripe sessions in ways appropriate to his position. He may help to unmask and devise a creative solution to the hidden agenda that seems undiscussible. Whatever the action, he can be helped by his spiritual director to recognize that its origins are in the same relationship with God that gives him personal comfort and that its implications are, however small, real steps toward justice that will shape the lives of many people.

There may even be more to the way God is acting here.

The Environmental Arena

One of the reasons that the just transformation of social structures seems so remote is that we easily confuse the Structural and the Environmental Arenas. Because racism, widespread violence, and the cycle of poverty seem invulnerable, we lose patience with the structures good people have created to diminish these cycles and despair of our personal power to address them in any constructive way. We may lose so much faith in them that all structures seem sinful or greedy. What we are really being moved by here, however, is not an unjust structure of a community but a wider cultural reality, a shared attitude in which the spirits of life and death can work as concretely as in one's personal prayer. What we feel helpless about much of the time is not the injustice of structures but the cultural assumptions that actually work in our daily lives. This may precipitate a real cultural or environmental desolation which, like the individual variety of the same, can easily convince us that action is useless—unless we become discerning persons.

The Environmental Arena is probably the most powerful and yet the most invisible of the four arenas. Recently I was in line at a busy supermarket when I discovered that I didn't have enough cash to cover what I had in my basket. The clerk said I could use a credit card in their new scanner. Well, it didn't work when I tried it. The clerk tried it, and it didn't work. We tried another card with the same results. The clerk got on the phone to the management. Meanwhile, I was very aware of the growing line and of the young couple right behind me. I began to make "Sorry, what can I do?" gestures. A few people changed lines before the manager arrived to straighten out the procedure. As I picked up my bag, I thanked the young couple for their patience. They both smiled easily and he said, "That's OK! We don't like to hurry. It's not bad to enjoy some time in line."

I had run right into an environmental event. I had lived in Kentucky for four years, after spending most of my life in Northeastern cities, where there are certain expectations about the ways Americans react to being in line: they don't like it; they see it as a waste of time; they want to get through it as quickly as possible. By holding up the check-out line, I was "sinning," in a way, against this construction of reality. My little "confession" ritual became a way of acting out my part in that social web of expectations that, while it was hidden from me, held me in its grip. The young couple suddenly made me aware that other people or groups of people construe this particular reality very differently, that there is more than "the" way to wait in line.

How might grace be operating here? I could have come away from the experience packing all my feeling into the Individual Arena, feeling like a fool for having been so apologetic, for not having known how to operate the scanner, for not being able to teach the clerk how to do it. Reflecting through the Lifeframe, however, I might notice that this couple had poked a hole in my unconscious adherence to a cultural expectation, that they had opened me up to the possibility of including another, more gracious way of seeing reality, that they had actually provided me the chance to escape from an oppressive mindset—a small change in the way I create my reality and treat others, but a real one.

What if my spiritual director were to catch this little incident and help me explore and pray further about it? She might notice that I tend to center on my feelings of foolishness and shame because, in fact, I can manage those feelings with a humor and self-deprecation that eventually dismisses them. What if she were to draw my attention to the couple and what they may have been offering to me? What if God were taking this opportunity to help me let go of some semiconscious stereotypes and prejudice? This was Kentucky, where things go more slowly. They were African-Americans, I a white middle-class priest, and we were all shopping in a run-down, poor-white-area store. My director may help me discover that an even more virulent layer of environmental smog could be lifted with the incident, the layer that has to do with my internalized cultural expectations of the "rednecks" who had stepped out of line.

God may have been inviting me to live in a more spacious environment. My spiritual director might do me an injustice should she not notice this but be satisfied that I had been helped to bring my personal feelings to prayer. Her action for justice here would be to encourage me to look contemplatively at the length and breadth as well as the depth of my experience.

If this seems far-fetched, consider that it is the same process through which, in the last forty years of civil rights work in the United States, the Spirit of God has changed the environment, the structures, the interpersonal relationships, and the way individuals act and think. Before Jackie Robinson, the first African-American ballplayer in major league baseball, was employed by the Dodgers in 1947, Branch Rickey, who hired him, told him privately to think about this: for three years Robinson was not to react in anger to any of the vicious racist treatment he was sure to get. Robinson thought about it, said he would do it, and then fulfilled his promise, even when the worst predictions came true. If he had personalized the insults and discrimination, if he had taken them as aimed at Jackie Robinson, he never would have punched the hole he left in the environment of racism in the United States, nor would the structure of professional sports have changed as it did. If I had been his spiritual director, would I have helped him to keep his eyes on and find hope in the environmental, cultural event that was going on as well as the personal, relational joys and costs involved? Holistic justice here means balanced care for more than just the individual and his or her intimate relationships.

The story of Alan, whom we considered in the previous section, could gain important perspective if John, his director, has vision wide enough to encompass events in the Environmental Arena. The clericalism that, in different ways, disempowers both clergy and laity may not have been expunged by renewal. The structures have changed in this parish, but the environment remains solid and seemingly impenetrable. Laity give advice, pastors make decisions, curates get stuck in the middle. John may be aware of the justice issues raised by the realities in Alan's life, even eager to help him involve God in the struggle. But if his vision is not wide enough, he may urge his directee into counterproductive prayer.

Aware of the environmental issue here, John might help Alan to ask whether his prayer is not a personalized replay of the staff's gripe sessions: he vents his feeling to God, feels accepted and relieved, and gets back to work. If he were willing to look at this, Alan might discover that his old man God has more to say but that Alan ends his prayer when he feels heard and relieved. His God may want to say, "Bring me to the parish with you tomorrow. Don't leave me at home. I would like to take a tour of that place with you and point out what I see." If Alan is stuck in a reactive-clerical environment, his prayerful tour with God might help him see there are other ways to think and act and live, ways that are more inclusive and more just.

Applying the Lifeframe to Our Practice of Spiritual Direction

The Lifeframe is a way of applying a contemplative attitude to the whole of a person's reality. A first task in spiritual direction is to help the directee become contemplative of his or her experience of life and of the God who is active in it. Directors most often teach this attitude by their own contemplative engagement with the person. It is my contention that spiritual directors act justly in direct proportion to the breadth of their vision. God cares deeply for each individual and the loves in our lives, but in scripture God seems even more concerned for communities, structures, and the culture-bound environments that create and maintain them. For years my spiritual direction has interpreted "holistic" in the Individual and Interpersonal Arenas as having to do with bringing mind, body, and spirit together. Now this interpretation seems a narrow definition unless I include the person's Structural and Environmental Arenas as well.

It has always been clear that genuine prayer transforms individuals, but it is difficult to conceive of the bridge to the transformation of structures and the environment because we have thought of them as distinct from the experience of the person sitting before us. But all of us encounter structural and environmental realities many times each day, and action for justice in spiritual direction can occur when the director expects God's movement in all the dimensions of life. When John invites Alan to talk about his work, to notice his helplessness there, to pray about the "we vs. they" antipathy it sets up, to listen to God in the Structural and Environmental Arenas, he is doing justice as a spiritual director.

What can we do, concretely, in response to this? First, I suggest that we ask our supervisors to help us notice the ways we habitually perceive and interpret reality. Does my actual practice of direction indicate that I value one or two of these arenas over the others? Does my working notion of "holistic" need to expand? A second suggestion is to begin to understand and develop skills needed to be contemplative in arenas where I am less naturally inclined. Some of the books listed can help us comprehend and become alert to events and dynamics in these various arenas.

The purpose of spiritual direction is to discern the Spirit of God from other influences and to achieve the freedom to choose life. The final part of this essay will ask how we can discern that the Spirit of God is behind one rather than another considered action.

Action for Justice Is Rooted in the Gospel

Beneath any system of Christian discernment is the assumption that one is coming to know the God revealed in Jesus Christ and to grow in likeness to this God. Without that foundation, "discernment" is an exercise in psycho-religious management skills and "justice" is determined by the currently governing legal system. Growing in companionship with God, on the other hand, a person can come to a very subtle awareness of the activity of the God of Jesus Christ in his or her ordinary life. What does that activity look like, and how can it be discerned from counterfeit?

At the risk of seeming to simplify the complexity of the good news, it is fair to say that what Jesus preached, insisted on, and was driven by was a vision of the "kingdom" or "reign" of God. It pervades all he says and does. He points to it wherever he sees it and creates its possibility where it does not exist. The vision is most comprehensively articulated in his constant banquets and feasts, where everyone is invited and no one excluded except by their own choice. The Eucharist, the banquet to be celebrated until he comes to establish the reign of God definitively, is the central image of God's desire and human hope. At the heart of God is a table set for everyone, and God is yearning to have them all home again. In its depths the human heart longs for this salvation: "Happy are we to be called to this feast!" The Christian image of justice is the banquet in God's house, where all are brothers and sisters.

This vision is constantly before Jesus. When he insists that forgiveness is the heart of ministry (John 20:22, 23; Luke 24:27) and of effective ritual (Matt 5:23–24), it is because forgiveness is the way God implements the divine desire to have everyone home again: "But I say to you, Love your enemies and pray for those who persecute you, so that you may be children of your Father in heaven" (Matt 5:44–45). Jesus acts out that vision of the Reign of God when he eats with Pharisees and tax collectors, heals people individually, and brings lepers back to their communities. He speaks of it in parables of inclusiveness and in words of forgiveness from the cross.

Scripture is clear about God's will. We know it because God has revealed "the mystery of his purpose," as Paul says in Ephesians 1:9–10 NJB: "that he would bring everything together under Christ, as head, everything in the heavens and everything on earth." Jesus' words and actions make this divine desire concrete in first-century Palestine. Spiritual directors act more or less justly when their engagement with directees makes this vision of communion incarnate in specific choices today. When spiritual directors act to help individuals bring mind, body, emotions, and spirit together, they are creating conditions for the reign of God within that person. When directees learn to bring the reality of their prayer to their loves and friendships, the intimacy that results is another instance of the inbreaking reign of God. God is active when individuals come to accept themselves, when they integrate their past with their present hopes, when they allow their gifts as well as their sinfulness into the banquet. God is present when couples fight or dialogue about what really matters, when friends forgive one another, when strangers treat each other like persons.

Following the Ignatian principle, "The more universal the good, the more it is divine," directors need to be aware of more than the Individual and Interpersonal Arenas. When Alan sees the "we vs. they" configuration of the parish staff as antithetical to the desires of God, he is free to choose among options that hinder or promote God's dream there in his workplace. When John helps him clarify and follow God's desire to "take a tour of the parish with you," or suggests that there may be other ways of seeing reality, he may be offering Alan the needed hope that God is indeed involved in these events, that things don't have to be this way forever.

Spiritual directors need to talk with one another about the ways God can be discerned in the Structural and Environmental Arenas of a person's life. From our understanding of God's reign, we notice God acting in our lives when "we vs. they" divisions are recognized and abated, when community or team members with personal visions share their assumptions about one another and try to understand before competing. The ways in which grace can be recognized in such structures may be best described in authors like Senge and Argyris, whose work with corporate structures moves beyond work seen as a means to an end, to what they call a "more sacred" view, one that has to do with "higher aspirations beyond food, shelter and belonging."[5]

Our everyday experience of the Environmental Arena, too, is full of grace and despair. When Nelson Mandela invited his jailers to his inauguration, he was putting a hole in the worldwide environment of racism as well as dismantling its structures of apartheid in South Africa. He did not eradicate racism, but he made it more possible for us all to hope in structures that give life to individuals, families, and friends. Likewise, the vision of God's reign is alive when Alan perceives that the very clericalism he hates has been his crutch, too, and other alternatives appear before him. Invited to another way of experiencing the world, he can be more compassionate with those still trapped, perhaps able to help them see more broadly too. This is the same coming together that marks Jesus' choices at every turn. A hallmark of God is the invitation to be wide of vision, to include all God's creation.

There is one further remark that must be made about inclusivity and the Lifeframe. We have said that the lines between the arenas are porous. They have to be, or we cannot do justice. If I attempt to help directees to become more whole but ignore (and help them to ignore) the relationship of that growth to the structures and environment that fill their lives, I am teaching them a limited contemplation that is not inclusive of their reality. That appears to be as unjust as it would be to help someone develop as a manager at work or a member of the community while ignoring the personal and interpersonal results of that development. The Lifeframe is an instrument for holistic contemplative work and, in that sense, is a tool for discernment of God's Spirit.

Conclusion

Churches insist that gospel values must include action for justice, echoing the long Judeo-Christian prophetic tradition. The heart of the call is God's desire to bring all of creation together. Action for justice in spiritual direction will not look like action for justice in another ministry but will converge with it if both advance the communion of spirit for which Jesus gave his life. Discerning the concrete particulars of that convergence, discriminating between the truths and the half-truths will be no less complex than discernment has ever been. In fact, it will be more difficult, since we have yet to delineate the dynamics of consolation and desolation in a broader way. There is a challenge before us, perhaps an invitation to widen our contemplative scope and to develop skills that will enable our directees to see the activity of God where they may not spontaneously look. Our hope is that the God who heals and transfigures individuals can be recognized and accompanied as the God who gives new life and transforming spirit to the communities in which they live.

Recommended Reading

Argyris, Chris. *Knowledge for Action*. San Francisco: Jossey-Bass, 1993.
————. *Overcoming Organizational Defenses: Facilitating Organizational Learning*. Boston: Allyn & Bacon, 1990.
Hall, Edward T. *The Silent Language*. Garden City, N.Y.: Doubleday, 1959.
————. *Beyond Culture*. Garden City, N.Y.: Anchor Press, 1976.
————. *The Dance of Life*. New York: Anchor/Doubleday, 1983.
Malone, Thomas P., and Patrick T. Malone. *The Art of Intimacy*. New York: Prentice Hall Press, 1987.

JAMES M. KEEGAN, a New England Jesuit, is the director of Eastern Point Retreat House in Gloucester, Massachusetts. He is a member of the Coordinating Council of Spiritual Directors International and was part of the editorial board that founded *Presence: An International Journal of Spiritual Direction*.

Notes

1. Seamus Murphy, SJ, "The Many Ways of Justice," *Studies in the Spirituality of Jesuits* (March 1994): 1.
2. Ibid., 5–6.
3. Ibid., 20.
4. Ibid., 22.
5. Peter M. Senge, *The Fifth Discipline: The Art and Practice of the Learning Organization* (New York: Doubleday/Currency, 1990), 5.